Moral Codes

Moral Codes

Designing Alternatives to AI

Alan F. Blackwell

The MIT Press
Cambridge, Massachusetts
London, England

The MIT Press would like to thank the anonymous peer reviewers who provided comments on drafts of this book. The generous work of academic experts is essential for establishing the authority and quality of our publications. We acknowledge with gratitude the contributions of these otherwise uncredited readers.

This book was set in Stone Serif and Stone Sans by Westchester Publishing Services. Printed and bound in the United States of America.

Library of Congress Cataloging-in-Publication Data is available.

ISBN: 978-0-262-54871-7

10 9 8 7 6 5 4 3 2 1

Contents

Acknowledgments   vii

1 Are You Paying Attention?   1
2 Would You Like Me to Do the Rest? When AI Makes Code   21
3 Why Is Code Not Like AI?   37
4 Intending and Attending: Chatting to the Stochastic
   Parrots 🦜   47
5 A Meaningful Conversation with the Internet   65
6 Making Meaningful Worlds: Being at Home in Code   77
7 Lessons from Smalltalk: Moral Code before Machine Learning   89
8 Explanation and Transparency: Beyond No-Code/Low-Code   99
9 Why Code Is More Important Than Flat Design   117
10 The Craft of Coding   125
11 How Can Stochastic Parrots Help Us Code?   135
12 Codes for Creativity and Surprise   149
13 Making Code Less WEIRD   167
14 Reimagining AI to Invent More Moral Codes   177
15 Conclusion   189

Notes   195
Index   221

Acknowledgments

There are few original ideas in this book. For forty years, I've had the privilege of working with brilliant researchers and innovators who will recognize in this text what they have taught me. Other ideas were collected from authors, speakers, and thinkers more diligent, prolific, and original than me. I hope I've given proper credit where I could, but apologize for those I've forgotten. The errors in compiling their good advice are mine alone.

I am especially grateful to remarkable and patient teachers and mentors: Jim Waite, who taught me to build; Peter Andreae, who taught me to write; Martin Bennett, who taught me to innovate; David MacKay, who taught me to calculate; Thomas Green, who taught me method; David Good, who taught me strategy; and Geoffrey Lloyd, who taught me about boundaries.

Although too many to include, a draft of this acknowledgement recalled hundreds of colleagues at Progeni Systems; at Auckland, Massey, and Victoria Universities; at Cambridge Consultants; at the Hitachi Europe Advanced Software Centre; at the United Kingdom Medical Research Council's Applied Psychology Unit; and at Microsoft Research Cambridge. I've thought of many of you, and I apologize for any omissions. I'm also grateful to those who have let me move on when I asked questions that were not always helpful or productive: Jim Waite, Paul Auton, and especially Chas Church for sticking his neck out when it became clear that I needed to move from business to an academic career.

Visiting other disciplines requires generous hosts. I have been welcomed by anthropologists Georgina Born, James Leach, Simon Pulman Jones, Amiria Salmond, and Lee Wilson; by architects Dean Hawkes, Sebastian Macmillan, François Penz, and Paul Richens; by historians of science Harry Collins, Patricia Fara, Martin Kusch, Jonnie Penn, and Richard Staley; by curators, producers, and artists Simon Biggs, Rachel Drury, Bruce Gernand,

Michael Harrison, Issam Kourbaj, Giles Lane, Wayne MacGregor, Lizzie Muller, Melissa Pierce Murray, Sally Jane Norman, and Jane Turner; by composers, musicians, and musicologists Harry Botham, David Carter, Ian Cross, Cheryl Frances-Hoad, Mark Gotham, Tom Hall, Richard Hoadley, Jonathan Impett, Andrew Lovett, Alex McLean, Thor Magnusson, Henry Stobart, Martin Rohrmeier, Gillian Wilde Ruddick, Geraint Wiggins, and Alejandro Viñao.

Thank you to the founders, directors, and managers of institutions that support interdisciplinary journeys: Darwin College; King's College; Cambridge University's Centre for Research in the Arts, Social Sciences and Humanities; the Cambridge University Moving Image Studio; the Center for Applied Research in Educational Technology; the Leverhulme Centre for the Future of Intelligence; and also to generous sponsors including the Engineering and Physical Sciences Research Council, Microsoft Research Cambridge, Nesta, Boeing, and BT. Working across disciplines requires patient collaborators along an uncertain journey, and it has been especially valuable to maintain those relationships over multiple projects with Charles Boulton, Pam Burnard, Nathan Crilly, Scott deLahunta, Matthew Jones, Richie Jones, Simon Peyton Jones, Tim Regan, Abigail Sellen, Sharath Srinivasan, Alain Vuylsteke, Lee Wilson, and Ken Wood.

Although I'm hesitant to describe my work as computer science, cognitive science, or AI, the ideas presented in this book do draw heavily on the work of friends and pioneers in those fields, including Robert Biddle, Margaret Burnett, Peter Cheng, Allen Cypher, Ellen Yi-Luen Do, Yuri Engelhardt, Mark Gross, Ken Kahn, Amy Ko, Clayton Lewis, Henry Lieberman, Fabio Paterno, Brad Myers, William Newman, James Noble, John Pane, Marian Petre, Clive Richards, Ben Shneiderman, and Steve Tanimoto. I am fortunate to have shared this journey with wonderful colleagues including Sam Aaron, Saeed Aghaee, Nic Bidwell, David Coyle, Addisu Damena, Neil Dodgson, Satinder Gill, Maria Gorinova, Hatice Gunes, Carl Hogsden, Frank Kavishe, Per Ola Kristensson, Matt Mahmoudi, Kingo Mchombu, Eden Melaku, Charlie Nqeisji, Cengiz Oztireli, Rob Phaal, Karl Prince, Alex Raymond, Peter Robinson, Kerry Rodden, Jennifer Rode, Ana Šemrov, Alexander Simpson, Alice Street, Mark Stringer, Tesfa Tegegne, Eleanor Toye, Martin Ujakpa, Xiaomeng Wang, and Damon Wischik.

David Good has been a generous friend and collaborator over twenty-five years, developing the Crucible network for research in interdisciplinary design and then Cambridge Global Challenges, with colleagues Lara Allen,

Rachel Hewson, Nathan Crilly, Pauline Rose, Sara Serradas O'Holleran, and Anthony Bridgen. It has also been a huge pleasure developing Cambridge Digital Humanities with Anne Alexander, Caroline Bassett, Catherine Hurley, Leonardo Impett, Mary Jacobus, and Mel Leggatt.

A teacher is nothing without students, and many of these ideas have developed in conversation with talented young people including Zhen Bai, Justas Brazauskas, Nick Collins, Martyn Dade-Robertson, Lorisa Dubuc, Darren Edge, Christine Guo Yu, Moe Hadhrawi, Isak Herman, Michal Kosinski, Joycelyn Longdon, Mao Mao, Mariana Mărășoiu, Cecily Morrison, Chris Nash, Kath Powlesland, Diana Robinson, Advait Sarkar, Tanja Schomann, Bianca Schor, Alistair Stead, Sofija Stefanovic, and Hanna Wallach, in addition to many great interns, undergraduate, and master's dissertation students. Luke Church has shared many years of this journey, working as a collaborator and co-advisor of those above, and becoming an international leader in his own right. It would be hard to disentangle the many threads throughout the book that are also a focus of his continuing work, hopefully leading to his own book as a valuable complement to this one.

I have been supported and challenged by reflective friends Robin Bunce, Geoff Cox, Bronac Ferran, Elisabeth Hill, Richard Lane, Bob Levin, Willard McCarty, David McPherson, John Norman, Arlene Oak, Matthew Postgate, Mark Simos, Bill Thompson, and Alison Wood. It has also been a privilege to interact with critical thinkers who are leaders in their own fields, including Rachel Adams, Jeff Bardzell, Shaowen Bardzell, Mark Blythe, Paul Dourish, Sally Fincher, Richard Harper, Jofish Kaye, Ann Light, John Naughton, Chris Newfield, and Marilyn Strathern.

I am very grateful to Noah Springer, Elizabeth Agresta, Joshua Manson, and the rest of the team at MIT Press, and to the many readers giving feedback on early drafts, including especially substantial advice from Helen Arnold, Marios Constantinides, David Yu-Tung Hui, Emma Kallina, Michael Morehouse, Anica Alvarez Nishio, Pamela Peter-Agbia, Advait Sarkar, first reader Ben Thurbon, Philip Wadler, Gary Walkow, and anonymous reviewers. Thank you to Sumit Gulwani, Allen Cypher, and Andy Rice for their time and insight as interviewees.

Thank you to Helen and Elizabeth. I love you both more than I can say, and I apologize for the many days that could have been spent with you instead of writing.

Craft is the essence—both technical and social—and I owe those skills to my parents, Frank and Clare. Thank you, Mum and Dad, for everything.

1 Are You Paying Attention?

There are two ways to win the Turing Test. The hard way is to build computers that are more and more intelligent, until we can't tell them apart from humans. The easy way is to make humans more and more stupid, until we can't tell them apart from computers. The purpose of this book is to help us avoid that second path.

Sadly, there is a temptation for technology researchers and businesses to take the easy path. Anyone who uses computers frequently will recognize that this has become a basic design principle of many systems we use.[1] I'm writing as a technologist, rather than as a philosopher, and from my practical experience of working as an artificial intelligence (AI) engineer since 1985—nearly forty years ago. AI has changed a lot since then, but humans have not, so this choice between the hard and easy routes has been with us a long time.

Although I have much relevant technical knowledge, dating back to before today's leading AI experts were even born, this book is intended for a non-technical audience. I'm going to explain fundamental ideas in an accessible way, emphasizing the aspects that are important from a human perspective. These explanations will not always align with the mainstream views of the AI research community, and they will almost certainly differ from the promotional messages (and warnings) that come from large AI companies. This should not be a surprise, as the success of so many business models depends on customers being made to appear more stupid, and on both customers and workers not realizing what is being done to them.

Human bodies may be constructed by the code of DNA, but our conscious lives are increasingly constructed in software source code. This makes software design a moral problem. The self-described "anarchist anthropologist"

David Graeber, in his books *Bullshit Jobs* and *The Utopia of Rules*, draws our attention to how many supposed advances of information society have actually made people's lives worse.[2] Graeber's work inspired many young people to take direct action, including through such movements as Occupy Wall Street and Extinction Rebellion, and his writing has helped a new generation understand the underlying reasons why economic and political systems turn out the way they do.

However, Graeber did not pay so much attention to the software engineers who design and build IT systems. Sometimes those people are just following orders. But sometimes the logic of software development seems to lead to new business models, inequalities, bureaucracies, and dysfunctional societies that are even worse than the ones we started with. As the critic of sociotechnical infrastructure Geoffrey Bowker puts it: "bureaucracy makes us act like machines, algorithms seek to make us into machines."[3]

Decades ago, we were promised that robots and computers would take over all the boring jobs and drudgery, leaving humans to a life of leisure. That hasn't happened. Worse yet, while humans keep doing bullshit jobs, AI researchers work to build computers that are creative, self-aware, emotional, and given authority to manage human affairs. Sometimes it seems like AI researchers want computers to do the things humans were supposed to enjoy, while humans do the jobs that we thought we were building the robots for.

How did we get into this situation? In this book, I'm going to argue that it's the result of a fundamental flaw in the AI research agenda. AI researchers have confused philosophy and engineering. As a result, what started out as a fairly innocent philosophical question has turned into a global industry. The bad guys in this story are AI engineers and research programmers. I know this, because I spent years working as one of them. This book is an attempt to fix the problem, by explaining how we can make software better. I don't mean faster, cheaper, more reliable, efficient, or profitable. The software engineering industry is already pretty good at all of those things. All are important, but there are many other books explaining how to design efficient and profitable software. This book is about how to design software that is *better*—better for society, better for people, better for *all* people— even if the result might be slightly less efficient overall, or less profitable for some.

Why Are We Making Software We Don't *Need?*

Software developers and computer scientists like me are fascinated by what computers can do. Our imagination and enthusiasm have resulted in IT systems, personal devices, and social media that have changed the world in many ways. Unfortunately, imagination and enthusiasm, even if well intentioned, can have unintended consequences. As software has come to rule more and more of the world, a disturbing number of our social problems seem to be caused by software, and by the things we software engineers have made.

Perhaps the original sin in the story of how computer software has evolved from an intellectual challenge to a social nightmare is the story of Alan Turing's "Imitation Game," now known in computer science, AI research, and popular media as the Turing Test.[4] Turing proposed the test in the 1950 paper "Computing Machinery and Intelligence," which starts by defining very clearly the problem Turing was trying to solve:

> I PROPOSE to consider the question, 'Can machines think?' This should begin with definitions of the meaning of the terms 'machine' and 'think'. The definitions might be framed so as to reflect so far as possible the normal use of the words, but this attitude is dangerous. If the meaning of the words 'machine' and 'think' are to be found by examining how they are commonly used it is difficult to escape the conclusion that the meaning and the answer to the question, 'Can machines think?' is to be sought in a statistical survey such as a Gallup poll. But this is absurd. Instead of attempting such a definition I shall replace the question by another, which is closely related to it and is expressed in relatively unambiguous words.
>
> The new form of the problem can be described in terms of a game which we call the 'imitation game'. It is played with three people, a man (A), a woman (B), and an interrogator (C) who may be of either sex. The interrogator stays in a room apart from the other two. The object of the game for the interrogator is to determine which of the other two is the man and which is the woman.[5]

The intriguing thing about Turing's introduction to this famous paper is that, despite Turing's own training as a mathematician, he grapples here with problems of metaphysics (the nature of mind), the social shaping of science (the "absurdity" of scientific debate being advanced by popular opinion), and questions of gender (a haunting augur of Turing's persecution by the British government).[6]

Turing's paper is a remarkable piece of work, and it is still an excellent introduction to many central questions in AI, including some that I will return to in this book. But it is also a work of imagination, in a very long tradition of stories that raise intriguing questions about what it means to be human. We are fascinated by stories of animals or trees that talk, human children who grow up with no language, or dolls that move but have no soul, because all of these challenge the boundaries of what we consider distinctively human. And the dream that we might create a machine or statue that behaves like one of us is also an ancient one. Building a talking robot in our own likeness is not only a path to self-understanding (assuming we understand what we have built), but a fantasy of power, potentially resulting in the perfect slave or the perfect lover. The fantasy has recurred over centuries: the ancient Jewish Golem; Mary Shelley's *Frankenstein*; the clockwork automata of the eighteenth century; the Greek myth of Pygmalion, whose statue comes to life; the Czech play *Rossum's Universal Robots*; the robot Maria in Fritz Lang's German film *Metropolis*; and any number of famous robots, sexy and otherwise, in movies such as *Ex Machina, 2001: A Space Odyssey*, or *The Terminator*. A good definition of AI is the branch of computer science dedicated to making computers work the way they do in the movies.

That kind of story usually doesn't end well, although for reasons that relate to the logic of storytelling rather than engineering (we should never forget that these supposed "inventions" are, before anything else, fictional devices). To follow storytelling logic, someone has to be punished for hubris, or the anxiety of the audience must be resolved with reassurance that they *are* uniquely human after all. This logic of plot structure, while possibly offering philosophical inspiration, has no practical relevance to engineering questions.

Unfortunately, when engineers are building real systems, the moral problem of the Turing Test is more fundamental, and not as easy to recognize and resolve as in fictional narratives. If we did succeed in making a system that was indistinguishable from a human, even in a small way, what value would this bring? The typical answers in public debate have come from business perspectives. Some people regret that a worker has been displaced by a machine, while others celebrate that the business has benefited from cheaper work. In practice, robots are often more expensive than humans, not cheaper, so the real benefit may be that they feel no pain, are less likely to make mistakes, or perhaps that they are not eligible to join labor unions. The management of factory automation is an economic, social, and ethical problem, with the precise details of each generation of technology somewhat irrelevant, and so I won't discuss these particular questions very much further.

Of course, Turing was not a manufacturer or a management consultant. His test was a thought experiment, not a business plan. Thought experiments are valuable tools in science and philosophy, but it's foolish to confuse them with engineering. Einstein famously imagined an elevator being pulled through space, but Elon Musk is not (yet) suggesting that we should replace rocketry with interstellar elevators.

The Two Kinds of AI

There is an important technical distinction that needs to be clear at the start of this book, and that I will return to in later chapters. The term AI has become very familiar, associated with all kinds of medical and scientific advances, the implications of which are debated almost daily in newspapers and by policymakers. Although there are many kinds of AI systems that address all kinds of problems, journalistic and political discussions tend to assume that they are all fundamentally the same. I want to make clear that there are two fundamentally *different* kinds of AI when we look at these problems and systems from a human perspective.

The first kind of AI used to be described as "cybernetics" or "control systems" when I did my own undergraduate major in that subject. These are automated systems that use sensors to observe or measure the physical world, and then control some kind of motor in response to what they observe. A familiar example is the household thermostat, which measures the temperature in your house and automatically turns on a heating pump or boiler if it is too cold. Another is automobile cruise control, which measures the speed of the car and automatically accelerates if it is too slow. One or two hundred years ago, such mechanisms seemed magical, making decisions as if they were intelligent. Mechanical clocks and steam engines were the earliest machines to use closed-loop feedback regulators to maintain their speed, and our forebears talked about clockwork and steam much like we talk about AI today—as if machines were coming to life or becoming human.[7] Connecting observation to action, making "decisions" from what the machine has "remembered" from its "instructions" or "training" all seem like signs of intelligence. But when we think realistically about a familiar object like a thermostat, it's clear that all this human-like terminology—of learning, remembering, deciding, and so on—is only a poetic analogy for devices that are really rather simple compared to humans.

The *second* kind of AI is concerned not with achieving practical automated tasks in the physical world, but with imitating human behavior for its own sake. The first kind of AI, while often impressive, is clever engineering—objective measurements of physical behavior provide all necessary information about what the system can do, and applying cognitive terms like "learning" and "deciding" is poetic but misleading. The second kind of AI is concerned with human subjective experience, rather than the objective world. This is the kind of AI that Turing proposed as a philosophical experiment into the nature of what it means to be human, inspired by so many literary fantasies. The goal is to imitate human behavior, not for some practical purpose like making a machine run more efficiently, but to explore the subjective nature of human experience, including our experience of relating to other humans.

Many public discussions of AI do not acknowledge this distinction between the objectively useful and (sometimes) straightforward engineering of practical automated machinery, and the subjective philosophical enterprise of imitating the way that humans interact with each other. This is in part because a few mathematical approaches have recently turned out to be useful for both kinds of problem. These are known generically as "machine learning" algorithms, and I will go on to discuss them in more detail, though it must be remembered that "learning" is only a poetic analogy to human learning, even when done by "neural networks" that, while poetically named, in reality have very little resemblance to the anatomy of the human brain. Machine learning algorithms are useful statistical methods, increasingly included as a component in all kinds of software, including both control systems and imitation of humans (especially imitation of human language in chatbots, as I will be discussing in great detail). However, the failure to distinguish between objective and subjective AI happens only in part because some of the algorithms being used might be similar. I suspect that a large part of the confusion between the two kinds of AI is *intentional*, trying to muddy the waters between the first kind, which results in useful automation, and the second, whose usefulness is more doubtful and which may even be harmful in many cases.

The motivation for intentionally confusing the two kinds of AI often comes from the profit opportunities associated with the more harmful cases, as documented comprehensively by Harvard business professor Shoshanna Zuboff in her book *Surveillance Capitalism*, and Nick Couldry and Ulises Mejias in *The Costs of Connection: How Data is Colonizing Human Life and Appropriating it for Capitalism*.[8] Confusing useful AI with harmful AI, or even claiming that they are essentially the same thing, is an effective way to avoid scrutiny from regulators who might otherwise insist on technology that would be less harmful, but also possibly less profitable. It creates the false impression that harmful AI is just the "dark side" of useful AI, and that the former cannot be regulated without the latter also being limited. A common way to make the argument that these two kinds of AI are really the same (or that they could become the same in the future even if they are different today) is to invoke the speculative brand of "artificial general intelligence" (AGI). This idea interprets the Turing Test as an engineering prediction, arguing that the machine "learning" algorithms of today will naturally evolve as they increase in power to think *subjectively* like humans, including emotion, social skills, consciousness, and so on. The claims that increasing computer power will eventually result in fundamental change are hard to justify on technical grounds; some say this is like arguing that if we make airplanes fly fast enough, eventually one will lay an egg.

I am writing at a time of exciting technical advance, when large language models (or LLMs) such as ChatGPT are gaining popularity and increasingly able to output predictive text that makes them seem surprisingly like an intelligent human. I am following (and participating in) those debates right now, but there is not much to be said at this stage. A succinct summary of the real power of LLMs comes from eminent AI professor Rodney Brooks: "It just makes up stuff that sounds good."[9] A more technical explanation of how LLMs "make up stuff," by imitating human language using predictive text, and how the things they do are different from intelligence, is provided by AI researcher and philosopher Murray Shanahan.[10] I'll be returning to those questions in future chapters.

The text from these systems is occasionally interesting, sometime outrageous or just plain wrong, but mostly anodyne and repetitive. You may have noticed, as I have, that this kind of text is much the same as text from the social media platforms that the models were trained on. Despite occasional controversies and clickbait, most of the text people post on (eX)Twitter or in YouTube comments is rather boring. Although controversy might attract audiences, companies prefer to make money from text that isn't too interesting, because then they don't have to bother reading it, and can thereby save money on content moderators. This dynamic, which encourages users to behave in mechanically predictable ways, has been a frequent focus of critical attention. As science and technology scholar Harry Collins puts it in the subtitle of his book *Artifictional Intelligence*, this is the problem of *humanity's surrender to computers*, and technology critic Jaron Lanier put his finger on the problem of designing products this way when he affirmed in his manifesto that *You Are Not a Gadget*.[11]

The Moral Imperative for Code

These seem like important questions to me, and I hope they do to you. They are rather different, however, from the academic concerns of the rapidly expanding specialist community dedicated to AI ethics. I won't be saying very much about how to deploy information systems that are fair, transparent, accountable, and so on, although I hope that some of the technical approaches I describe later in the book might have those benefits as a byproduct. I'm also not going to say very much about policy and regulation or codes of governance and law, which are far better attended to by politicians, perhaps guided by philosophers and legal scholars, but probably not acting on instructions from AI companies and researchers.[12]

Software companies are already obligated to be fair, transparent, and accountable to some extent via *legal codes*—the laws of the countries where they operate. Of course, not all software companies follow the laws of all countries. As legal scholar Lawrence Lessig says: in practice, *Code is Law*.[13] The actual operation of a software system is ultimately determined by its source code, whether or not legislation says so. Computer programs are no more or less than a system of rules about how to behave, and any questions about the moral basis of what a program does must look first at those rules. As criminologist Per-Olof Wikström says: "Moral action is any action that is guided by (moral) rules about what it is right or wrong to do, or not do, in particular circumstances."[14] Source code—the rules about what a computer does in particular circumstances—becomes a moral code when it articulates questions of good and bad, whether or not AI is involved.

In the fictional universe of AI robots, the most famous speculation about the problem of encoding ethical constraints has been Isaac Asimov's *Three Laws of Robotics*: that a robot must not harm a human being, that it must obey orders if not in conflict with the first law, and otherwise must protect itself. The potential conflicts between these priorities, and narrative plots that turn on resolving them, was a feature of many of Asimov's stories, including the hit movie *I, Robot* based on them. Among today's philosophers and computer scientists, stories about the robots of the future often focus on the "alignment problem"—how could we know whether an AGI has the same values that we do, and what equivalent of Asimov's Three Laws could be built in to protect us from evil?[15]

The fictional problem of distant-future robot "alignment," as an alternative to today's pressing but technically mundane problems of business ethics and government regulation, might just be a distraction, and one that is convenient for the large companies that are building and investing in AI. It usually makes for a tricky twist when the robot characters in Asimov's books take responsibility for their own actions while resolving the implications of the Three Laws. Similarly, much talk about alignment is based on the premise that an independent AGI actor should in the future be able to take moral responsibility for its own decisions and actions, rather than placing responsibility with the company that made it, or the moral decisions made by the designers and engineers who work there.

In reality, the software that controls digital systems and operates technology corporations is made using code. Many software systems are used in unethical ways, are designed for unethical purposes, or perpetuate structural injustices including racism and misogyny. But in tracing the problems of software ethics, we should look at the tool users, rather than the tool itself. We don't ask if a screwdriver is unethical, and there are no conferences on carpentry ethics. There are clearly machines and buildings that have been designed unethically and for unethical purposes, but attempting to blame the tools for being unethical would be an obvious misdirection.[16] I am pleased that there are now large communities of scholars interested in the problems of designing software in more ethical ways. But these scholars should attend to how software is built and used today, clearly attributing responsibility to the tool user rather than the tool, and probably not spending too much time discussing the plots of science fiction novels and their robot characters.

Attending to Programming

This is not a book about AI ethics, software industry regulation, or responsible system design. In all of those fields, tools have some relevance to the discussions, but are secondary to what they are used *for*. In contrast, my alternative to AI does involve paying closer attention to the tools used to make software, and in particular to the opportunities and ways of thinking that those tools provide. Tools can certainly be dangerous, if used in the wrong ways and by the wrong people. But tools also offer a space for participation, creativity, and debate. If a company starts selling machines that are dangerous or harmful, there is little point in regulating screwdrivers. A more effective response is to ensure that more people know how these tools could be used, so that alternative actions are clear. Furthermore, when these are *knowledge tools* rather than physical ones, then the tools themselves could be designed in ways that offer opportunities for open participation and debate about what is being created.

The imagined problems of "alignment" are really about knowledge tools. What knowledge tools could we use to *describe* digital systems that are more controllable, and to help us articulate what we want the software to do? Legal codes might be used to prosecute the consequences of bad software, but the actual behavior of the software is defined in its source code, not the legal code. As a result, the kinds of tools that I think we need to pay closer attention to are the programming languages in which source code is written. The ability to instruct computer systems, rather than surrender agency to the companies that make them, is the moral purpose that underpins better systems of AI ethics and regulation. As Geoff Cox and Winnie Soon say in their instructional guide to creative coding as political resistance: "program or be programmed."[17]

I've explained why attending to the act of programming might be a moral priority, placing a focus on who uses the tools and why. With appropriate tools, programmers can express and act on systems of values that shape all of our actions.[18] But we also need to understand why and how *being programmed* is the opposite of moral agency. As an alternative to humans becoming machines, what does it mean for a person (not a machine) to be conscious, to be awake, to be aware, to attend to your surroundings, to *be* attentive to those around you, attentive to a child, a teacher, colleagues, your cousins or grandparents, to be alert and embodied, attending to and attending in your body?[19] These things are the essence of being human—being attending and attentive beings, *paying attention*. Conscious attention is the moral center of human life—we live to enjoy the alert ownership of bodily sensation, having the freedom to attend *to* ourselves and those we love. As observed by Couldry and Mejias, when we get programmed, we lose that freedom of attention.[20] If our consciousness is confined by attending to mechanical tasks, we are no longer free to give the gift of attention, or to grow and develop through more fully knowing ourselves.

The attention economy of the information age takes this central moral aspect of being human—our own conscious attention—and turns it into a commodity to be traded. As Nobel Prize–winning economist Herbert Simon famously wrote: "In an information-rich world, the wealth of information means a dearth of something else: a scarcity of whatever it is that information consumes. What information consumes is rather obvious: it consumes the attention of its recipients. Hence a wealth of information creates a poverty of attention."[21]

Each of us has a finite number of conscious hours in our life for meaningful attending and attention. Whenever a person is made into a conscious component of a machine, their capacity for meaningful attention gets reduced to the mechanical role they play, whether a call-center worker, delivery driver, shipment packer, or an online ghost worker checking social media posts for offensive content. Social media platforms turn their *customers* into mechanical components, reducing the richness of meaningful human attention to the simplest mechanical form, whether the few words allowed in a tweet, a pictorial meme to be seen at a glance, or the trivialized robotic responses of a "like," a "follow," or an emoji.

In contrast, when humans act as moral agents, they are responsible to, and conscious of, themselves. A moral agent acts intentionally, through deliberation. Each of us becomes and grows as a person through conscious attention and reflection on the life story that we tell. As Per-Olof Wikström says, human free will involves conscious choice between the opportunities for action in any situation, within the moral rules of conduct that make up human society.[22] Different human societies have different codes of law and ethics, but every society is a community of moral actors, and moral action depends on conscious attention.

What does an economist like Herbert Simon mean by "wealth of information" and "poverty of attention"? Tradable commodities deliver profits in proportion to numbers: quantity, not quality. The companies in the attention economy trade directly in the number of hours out of your life that you spend attending to their screens. Their profit is maximized by the hours you watch. The company also loses money if its staff spend hours of their own valuable time listening to you, the customer. That's why digital technologies so often make their customers more stupid by design, because the company doesn't want you to say anything sufficiently intelligent that it would require a human to interpret. They would rather you spend as many hours as possible attending to an automated system—whether a social media feed or an AI chatbot—instead of having a meaningful conversation with one of their employees.

That's also why the title of this chapter asked: "Are you paying attention?" A moral code requires paying attention to what you say, investing attention in your own needs, and giving attention to those around you. A focus on moral codes is about being a conscious human, who is able to make moral choices, and not about trying to make a conscious computer. Unfortunately, the dynamics of the software industry work the other way, winning the Turing Test by making people *less* conscious, in a steady tide of mechanized trivialization. Each wave of that tide promises convenience, simplicity, and usability, while actually making us compliant consumers of the business logic, government logic, or just plain logics of racism, sexism, ableism, or classism that seem to get systemically embedded, even if beginning from better intentions, in every bureaucracy.

Could Superintelligent AI Code Itself?

I've already observed that one of the worst distractions we experience is the temptation to avoid the urgent problems of today by instead debating the theoretical problems of the far future. Getting people to attend to the future rather than the problems of today can only be done if they are persuaded that the future is more urgent for some reason.[23] A common theme in the discussion of AI, and one that seems to be especially popular among AI researchers and the companies that employ them, is to imagine that artificial general intelligence will turn out to be an existential risk to the human race by becoming more intelligent than humans—"superintelligent"—applying its unlimited mental abilities to *design itself* to become exponentially more intelligent, evolving beyond our control, and wiping us out.

The problem with this supposed existential risk is that it comes from a fictional premise. If I *imagine* a super-AI that, like Superman, can do anything at all, then of course my imaginary software can use its superpowers to do anything in my imaginary world, including writing the code to create itself. Like a fairy story character whose final wish to the genie is for another three wishes, the logic is appealing in stories, but impossible in real life. The circular argument of superintelligence creating itself is only possible by avoiding a clear definition of what intelligence is, and also avoiding the question of what kind of *code* might be needed to write down that definition. It's reminiscent of St. Anselm's proof of the existence of God, which proceeds from the premise that God can't be defined because He is greater than anything we know.

The magical powers of genies and deities are not precisely defined in stories, because clear definitions would limit the power of the narrative device. If anyone did commit to a technical definition of AGI, I think the contradictions would become clear, because the definition itself has to be coded in some way. Of course, the answer shouldn't be another circular argument—you can't say that the necessary code definitions will be written in the future by the AGI itself! Intelligence that could manifest itself in any way, without the inconvenience of a clear definition, is a plot device like the shape-changing T-1000 of *Terminator II*, which might be described as an "artificial general body" in the way it is unlimited by any definition of shape, and thus able, in the imaginary universe of the movie, to become anything at all.

As a mathematician, Alan Turing was well aware of the philosophical dangers of speculating about undefined capabilities, which is precisely why his thought experiment proposed to test intelligence only by *comparison* to a human. If the best performance in the Imitation Game is to behave *exactly* like a human mind, then how could super-AI be even more like a human than that? Many discussions of this problem for popular audiences try to sidestep the problem by slipping in other undefined terms, for example casual words like "smart," to suggest that computers would be dangerous if they were *smarter* than humans, but never pausing to say whether "smart" is the same thing as "intelligent," and whether they are still talking about *imitating* what humans do, or doing something new but different. That final possibility is, of course, what computers have already become—very good at doing *something else*, but never, as it turns out, the same kind of things that humans do. All of these considerations illustrate how important it is to be clear about the difference between the two kinds of AI: practical automation versus fictional imitation.

In practice, all computer systems, including AI systems, do the things that we define them to do, where the definitions are written in computer source code. In many cases those systems greatly surpass human abilities (remembering millions of bank balances, or doing billions of sums very quickly), but those mechanical kinds of "superintelligence" are neither more or less threatening to us than "superhuman" inventions like earth-moving machinery or machine guns. Such things are powerful, and might certainly be dangerous, but they are not magical. Everything that computer systems do is defined by their code, just as physical machines are defined by their physical design, components, and materials.

AI companies like to sponsor academic debates into magical technologies that might exist in the distant future, addressing ethical problems that would only become relevant a century or two after the sponsors have enjoyed a luxurious and untroubled old age. It also doesn't hurt business to advertise the possibility that your company's technology might be so immensely powerful that it is nearly magic, so powerful that governments should tremble at your words. If the intelligent products of the future promise to deliver science fiction, or even magic, access to this immense potential might seem like an excellent investment, especially to shareholders or policymakers who don't fully understand technology, and who imagine that science fiction or magic will become reality one day.[24]

Neural network pioneer Geoff Hinton, in recent public lectures following his high-profile resignation from Google, has explained that the danger he is most concerned about is not super-rational AI, but rather automated language generators that devalue political debate by making up facts, abandoning logic, and provoking people to violence through repeating lies rather than considering rational alternatives.[25] Irrational but persuasive language is easy to construct with AI, far easier than superintelligence. Language like this may not be superintelligent (or even intelligent at all), but it certainly is dangerous, as proven by Vladimir Putin, Donald Trump, and many other demagogues whose greatest threat is not their intelligence.

Public debate about the distant future dangers of AGI, encouraged by government commissions and corporate ethics boards and marketed along-side fantasy movies about people falling in love with sexy computers or bat-tling killer robots from the future, seemed to reach a fever pitch at the same time as AI companies and researchers were *creating* serious ethical problems in the present day. In the era of Big Data and deep neural networks, it became increasingly clear that AI systems were exploitative, biased, sexist, and racist, through their use of machine learning techniques that had been coded to capture and replicate existing prejudice.

This is a very different, sadly more mundane problem than the plot devices of science fiction and magical stories. Rather than fantasies of an unlimited "general" mind or body, ethical problems relate to the very spe-cific bodies of actual people. The Turing Test definition of AI relies on an abstraction of intelligence, as behavior that is supposed to look the same whether implemented in a machine or in a human brain. But feminist scholars like Kate Devlin and Olivia Belton, drawing on N. Katherine Hales, observe that very few people have the luxury of defining their intelligence as independent from their own bodies.[26] Privileged white men might believe that people listen to their ideas without the listener paying any attention to their body, but women, people of color, and those who are poor, low-caste, or speak the wrong language understand that the privilege of defining intel-ligence in such an abstract and disembodied way is only available to those who already have the "right" kind body themselves.

As I discuss in more detail in chapter 13, philosopher Stephen Cave explains how the scientific history of "intelligence" itself was invented along-side other principles of measuring and comparing human bodies, driven by the need for evidence that could justify a scientific theory of race as a basis for eugenics, genocide, and slavery.[27] If the notion of measurable intelligence is fundamentally a racist and sexist principle, then is the notion of immea-surable superintelligence simply artificial super-racism and super-sexism? As AI researchers increasingly make apologies for the racist and sexist biases of their systems, companies and regulators behave as though the biases can be designed away. But if the whole technology is defined on immoral principles, is it possible that we are starting from the wrong place altogether?

How Can We Re-Code AI?

This introduction has explained why much of the current debate about the ethics of AI has been looking the wrong way, whether through creative magical thinking or purposeful distraction and misdirection. The rest of the book is not fundamentally about AI ethics, though it does make many suggestions on how recent inventions of AI researchers could be more usefully applied. Rather than dwelling on the (very real) injustices being constructed and reinforced through deployment of AI, and instead of spending any time at all speculating about magical technologies of a fictional distant future, my intention is to be optimistic, offering concrete suggestions on how we can make software better in other ways.

In particular, this book directly addresses the questions of how we can communicate with computers to explain to them what we want them to do. For leading AI researchers such as Stuart Russell, problems faced by (or created by) AI might be solved using more AI.[28] According to that reasoning, if a computer is doing things that are not beneficial to the human race, the computer needs to use better AI methods, learning how to observe humans even more closely to better learn what our needs and preferences are, and then learn how to do things that might be most beneficial for us. The obvious alternative is less often discussed. Rather than waiting for a computer to figure out what I might want by watching me, why don't I just tell it what I want? Even my closest friends and colleagues find it hard to guess how I would like them to help me, if I don't actually say anything. Why would I expect a robot to do better?

The real priority for future computers should not be what we want when we're not saying anything, but rather *what language we should speak* if we are going to be able to tell them what to do. By describing these languages as *moral codes*, I want to draw attention to the importance of programming languages, but also to how the power of programming languages could become more widely available, and how more kinds of interaction with computers could gain the power and control available through programming. Although AI researchers use programming languages all the time to create the systems that aim to control others, there's an unspoken assumption that this elite privilege couldn't realistically be extended to regular people. My question challenges that assumption, by asking what new kinds of code might make a moral alternative to AI feasible? I did not originally invent the phrase *moral code* with the intention of making it an acronym, but there is a useful mnemonic for how both programming languages and AI might be improved, if they were More Open Representations, for Access to Learning, and Creating Opportunities for Digital Expression.

This book could be considered a product design manual, to be read alongside the work of insightful critics like David Graeber, Kate Crawford, Geoffrey Bowker, Shoshanna Zuboff, Harry Collins, Nick Couldry, and Ulises Mejias. Although it does introduce some theory, the intention is for these to be engineering principles, applicable by software developers, to make software genuinely better in ways that AI doesn't.

Unfortunately, it's not easy to combine practical advice with new (philosophical) ways of thinking, and there is a danger that attempts to do so leave nobody happy. Where I work in Cambridge, this is the famous problem of *two cultures*—arts and humanities (and social sciences) on one side, and engineers and scientists on the other.[29] British public life is constantly screwed up by the two cultures, though in part because simple numeracy is assumed to be on the side of science, making it difficult to have sensible discussions about the climate crisis, pandemics, or the economy whenever simple mathematics is needed.[30] As a result of this divide, public debates about AI tend to focus either on the need for regulation, or on the potential for engineering fixes that might be tacked onto the latest inventions, but do not ask the more important definitional questions of how AI is actually created (with code), or what else we might be able to build if we could redefine the knowledge tools of code itself.

American media theorist and former computer scientist Philip Agre, after completing his PhD at the MIT AI Lab, succinctly diagnosed the problem being faced by the whole field. He observed how AI researchers in those laboratories were actually doing covert philosophy. Sure, they did engineering work and coded software prototypes. But their *explanations* of what they were doing related to "learning," "knowledge," "thinking," and other philosophical categories, just as Turing's famous paper did in the questions it raised. This would perhaps be acceptable if the researchers had any philosophical training. But in fact, those talented AI engineers understood very little about the concepts they were supposedly researching. Agre's classic essay, "Toward a Critical Technical Practice: Lessons Learned in Trying to Reform AI," explains the urgent need for researchers who are able both to build sophisticated software, and also to understand sophisticated arguments.[31] Agre argued that where AI researchers had been doing covert philosophy, it needed to be made *overt*—code must be open and theory must be coded, not with layers of wishful thinking, magical fantasy, or speculation about dystopian futures, but with open and accessible software representations.

This is the real goal of the book you are reading—to provide guidance for anyone who is prepared to approach software design as a critical technical practice, one that requires understanding of both technical and philosophical problems. In other words, the book seeks to provide *moral codes* that respect human attention and also are worthy of it. I believe this is the only way to make software that is genuinely better—not just more efficient and profitable (for which many books already exist), but actually *better* for people and for the planet.

How to Read This Book

I've written this book to be easily readable from start to finish. If you've got this far, you may like to continue. But if you prefer to jump around, many chapters focus on one theme in a reasonably self-contained way, referring to other chapters for background where needed. Its academic content draws from the field behind human-centered AI: human–computer interaction (HCI), especially sub-fields of intelligent user interfaces (IUI); critical HCI; visualization; end-user development (EUD); and psychology of programming. It also touches on software engineering, software studies, and critical history of computing. All are interdisciplinary fields, and the range of references may seem scattered or difficult to follow if you are new to computer science. In that case, reading from start to finish may be the best way to get a coherent story.

For those who want to explore specific themes, chapter 2 gives examples of early machine learning methods for controlling computers more effectively. Chapter 3 explains the technical differences between coding and machine learning algorithms. Chapter 4 explains algorithms that imitate human language, and chapter 5 investigates the implications of where that language comes from. Chapter 6 explores the historical foundations of human-centered computing, focusing on a time when code was evolving into the first graphical user interfaces. Chapter 7 considers forgotten lessons from the Smalltalk language, which was associated with the very first

	More Open Representations	Access to Learning	Creating Opportunities	Digital Expression
Chapter 2: When AI makes code		✓	✓	
Chapter 3: Why code isn't AI	✓	✓	✓	
Chapter 4: How language codes	✓		✓	✓
Chapter 5: What language codes	✓	✓		
Chapter 6: Being at home in code	✓✓	✓		
Chapter 7: Lessons from Smalltalk		✓✓	✓	
Chapter 8: Making better codes	✓✓	✓		
Chapter 9: Beyond flat design	✓		✓	
Chapter 10: The craft of coding		✓	✓✓	✓
Chapter 11: AI as a coding tool			✓	✓
Chapter 12: Codes for creativity				✓✓
Chapter 13: Making code less WEIRD			✓✓	
Chapter 14: Re-imagining code	✓	✓	✓	✓

Figure 1.1
A map of *Moral Codes*.

personal computer, the birth of Wikipedia, object-oriented programming, and agile management. Chapter 8 jumps to current research in intelligent interactive tools, including recent projects from my own team and their contributions to new products emerging in major companies. Chapter 9 shows how fashions in user interface and app design often benefit software companies rather than empower users, including the "flat design" trend of the past decade. Chapter 10 investigates the essence of programming, as needed to make better progress in the future, and chapter 11 considers the way that generative AI can help with improved coding tools. Chapters 12 and 13 explore important specialist questions—the use of AI and coding tools for creativity, and the problems of AI and code that come from focusing only on the needs of people in the wealthy Global West and North. Chapter 14 introduces design principles to invent new kinds of code and to improve those we already have. I have also provided an online appendix suggesting further reading, from the forty years of my own research that form the technical foundations of this book.[32]

For a thematic overview, I've provided a map in figure 1.1, showing which chapters relate to which aspects of the moral codes agenda.

2   Would You Like Me to Do the Rest?
When AI Makes Code

"Would you like me to do the rest?" If you've worked in one of those bullshit jobs that David Graeber wrote about, you'll know what a relief it is when someone takes over a mind-numbing repetitive task.[1] Even around my house, those words are a fairly certain way to make somebody else happy.

Each day, we grind though countless repetitive actions that would be so much easier if we could just say to the computer: "you do the rest." That simple phrase, if it worked, would be such an improvement to so many tasks and to so many lives. This chapter analyzes the design approaches that take us toward this simple vision of how AI might be able to "do the rest" of what we start, and improve our lives rather than threaten them.

- I need to get to London this afternoon. You do the rest.
- This is how to peel a potato, and I'm busy. You do the rest.
- Time to send out the monthly invoices. You do the rest.
- This year's tax return will be the same as last year. You do the rest.
- 12-bar blues with a reggae beat, modulating to a major key in the third verse. You do the rest.
- I'm ready for bed. You do the rest.

Pretty much any time we would really like some AI in our lives, the simple instruction "you do the rest" expresses the essence of what we would like a computer to do automatically. Rather than wasting our conscious hours on mechanical action and being made into a machine, saying "you do the rest" is empowering—it is about the machine helping *you* to do what *you* want. You give the instructions. Some adjustment and follow-up may be necessary, so real empowerment also has to include "not like that," or even "I've changed my mind." And it's tiring to have to take all the responsibility all the time, so we might appreciate an AI that can anticipate our needs and spot an opportunity to ask: Can I help you with that? Would you like me to do the rest?

If I had the biggest AI research budget in the world, this would go a long way toward my ideal computer. Just make it so that I can say "you do the rest," and things will happen the way that I want.

Some of us are lucky enough that we have really had this experience—although not with a computer. Very wealthy people have always hired butlers, or aides-de-camp, or personal assistants—those kinds of servant who know so much about their boss' preferences, lifestyle, and needs that they can indeed "do the rest" whenever asked, or even when not.

The fantasy that we could all have personal servants or robots has been a common theme in the kind of corporate advertising video that imagines a future where a company's products are going to solve all your life problems.[2] Imagine asking your "smart house" (or "smart speaker," in the less ambitious products of today) voice assistant to do any of these things.

Some of the examples I gave at the top of the chapter have already received attention from AI researchers, and there are useful products that do part of the job. Getting to London suggests some kind of autonomous vehicle, while generative music algorithms often have libraries of standard rhythms and chord progressions. But when I say "you do the rest," I don't really want a team of researchers to work for fifteen years before selling me a product that will respond to just that command. What I'd love is an intelligent assistant able to help me out with all kinds of mindless and boring tasks. I'm actually quite prepared to explain what I want, although after I've explained this once, I don't want to repeat it.

Fortunately, computers are good at remembering instructions. The difficult part for a computer is to understand what natural language instructions mean. In conventional computer science, explaining to a computer what you want it to do in the future is called programming, and must be done using a programming language. Creating or modifying a program—or changing your mind to make it do something else—involves editors, compilers, debuggers, revision systems, and many other specialist tools in a software development environment of the kind that will be discussed in more detail in chapters 6, 7, 10 and 11. These are complex tools, designed for use by professional engineers, often coordinating the work of large teams so that they can break down a complex problem into small parts for each engineer to work on.

It is far less common for regular computer users, who are not trained as software engineers, to explain to a computer what they want it to do in the future. The small research field concerned with achieving this possibility describes it as "end-user programming" (EUP), "end-user development" (EUD), or "end-user software engineering" (EUSE).[3] Although I started my own research career as an AI engineer, much of the content of this book builds on my later research, as described in research publications over the past twenty years for other researchers in the EUP/EUD/EUSE communities.

These fields start to overlap more closely with AI research when we ask a computer to volunteer "Can I help you with that?" or "Would you like me to do the rest?" The idea of an AI system that sometimes offers to help, rather than simply waiting for instructions, has been described as *mixed-initiative interaction*, where new actions are initiated sometimes by the user, and other times by the computer. The phrase "mixed-initiative" is most often associated with a research paper by Eric Horvitz, who later became Chief Scientific Officer of Microsoft Research.[4] The basic idea, however, was demonstrated decades earlier, in a research prototype created by Allen Cypher, who was then working for Apple research.

The Story of Eager—The Little AI That Could Have Been

Like many people who work at the intersection of AI and user experience, Allen Cypher is a mathematician who is really interested in people. After finishing a PhD in theoretical computer science, he used programming skills—a rare qualification in the 1970s—from his teenage years to teach a class at Yale in "computer programming for poets," in order to hang out with the researchers working on natural language understanding in AI pioneer Roger Schank's group. 1980s AI involved writing out knowledge as rules; machine learning methods were still in their infancy, associated with "connectionist" neural networks and brain science. In fact, that association was what turned Allen from a mathematician/programmer/poet into a psychologist—he was awarded a Sloan Fellowship to join the brand-new cognitive science team at the University of California San Diego (UCSD) and work with pioneering researchers such as David Rumelhart and Donald Norman, who were studying human and machine learning.

AI researchers like Allen often tinkered with making their own mental work more efficient through computer tools, such as a simple UNIX app called Notepad that he made to capture ideas quickly when he was distracted or didn't have time to concentrate. But Allen's thinking was turned around when UCSD cognitive science pioneer Don Norman scolded him for simply designing a product according to his own preferences. Norman and his team were working on the classic book *User-Centered System Design* (a now-forgotten pun and acronym with its origins in UCSD cognitive science). A programmer who made things according to his own taste, rather than considering the needs of others, was directly contradicting the user-centered philosophy they were espousing. Decades later, Allen remains embarrassed about the day Don Norman told him he should think about his users, but his Notepad did become a popular tool at UCSD and more widely, later influencing other hypermedia apps like NoteCards from Xerox PARC.

Allen designed another application during his UCSD days that, though not widely used at the time, turned out to have even more far-reaching effects. AI researchers were all using the UNIX command line, including its built-in function to store a history of old commands. Experts could avoid repetitive operations by scrolling back in time to repeat commands they had typed before. You might think of this as a particularly literal kind of machine learning, in which a machine "learns" by simply recording the commands it sees and can only repeat exactly what it has seen before. The problem is that, while it's trivial to "learn" by simply playing back previous examples, UNIX users seldom want to repeat *exactly* the same command twice. More often, you want a command that is very similar, but still slightly different, from what you did last time. Allen thought about this problem mathematically—the learning algorithm should work out which parts of the command would be constants and which parts variables. In fact, this has been the fundamental problem of machine learning ever since: how can a system learn to generalize from a set of examples, creating an abstract representation that defines the range of likely future variations?

This question remained in the background of his mind while Allen went to work as an AI consultant during the 1980s "expert system" boom. Although we didn't fully appreciate it at the time (I also started work as an AI engineer then), the excitement of that particular boom would eventually fade away because of usability problems. As anthropologist Diana Forsythe understood at the time, in order to turn expert knowledge into executable programs, somebody has to translate human knowledge into code.[5] The big problem at IntelliCorp, where Allen worked, as at other companies in the expert system business, was that AI programming systems were too unusable for the experts to get their knowledge encoded. The generation of AI that might have resulted from more usable programming never arrived, and the systems never worked as well as hoped.

All these experiences came together when Allen was hired to work at the Apple Advanced Technology Group (ATG), where he enjoyed the freedom to study how learning algorithms could provide an alternative to unusable programming. He did this by figuring out mathematical abstractions that would automate repetitive tasks (to "do the rest"), just as he had imagined for his UNIX command history.

The *Eager* prototype that Allen built at Apple was a compelling demonstration of how this would work. Eager's algorithms watched all the user's actions in the background, waiting to identify any repeated patterns in the sequence of keystrokes and mouse clicks. When Eager had a prediction of what the user might want to do next, a friendly icon of a little cat would appear and offer to help. That might have seemed a bit creepy at the time, but it's nowhere near as extreme as reality today, when many companies do watch every keystroke and mouse click, but keep that information to themselves (or sell it without the user's knowledge or consent). Sadly, despite the level of software surveillance we have today, it's still unusual to get an offer of help, outside of simple text prediction.[6]

Apple's ATG had research funds to sponsor graduate students working on technical issues related to ATG work, and Allen even convened a conference, paying for other researchers with the same interests to come and share their ideas and inventions. That conference turned into a classic book, edited by Allen, called *Watch What I Do*.[7] The title expresses the ambition to make people's lives better with a combination of machine learning and end-user automation, and anticipates a world in which computers offer "would you like me to do the rest?" as in the start of this chapter.

Allen Cypher's work is still famous among the community of people who seek to make computers more efficient by automating repetitive tasks. Contributors to the *Watch What I Do* book have gone on to make some of the world's most usable and successful machine learning approaches. Allen himself has been hired by companies like IBM and Microsoft, continuing to explore how computers might "do the rest" for us. Allen has contributed to the work of groups who build products like IBM's *CoScripter* and Microsoft's *FlashFill*—tools that still show how watching what we do can be an opportunity for assistance rather than surveillance. I'll be discussing FlashFill in more detail in chapter 8. But more often, capabilities like this get hidden away, or only deployed for use by professional programmers, in part because these features rely on different software engineering approaches from the deep learning and big data architectures that focus on extracting value from people rather than helping with their lives. Many machine learning researchers don't spend a lot of time thinking about user interfaces beyond their own tools, and unlike the days of Don Norman's UCSD, today's AI researchers are not even in the same room as people who will tell them otherwise.

So, what happened to Eager? Every year, two ideas were selected from ATG research projects to be built into Apple products. Eager was selected as one of those ideas. But the routine obstacles of corporate management and communication got in the way. A product manager was busy on other things, Eager wasn't urgent, a year went by, the window of opportunity closed, and so Apple computers are not quite as helpful as they might have been. Thirty years ago, companies were not expecting big opportunities to come from machine learning. Perhaps Eager was just (long) before its time?

Sharing the Mental Load

Some design principles that are important in the creation of mixed-initiative end-user programming systems, such as Eager, can be understood in relation to a few basic mechanisms of human cognition. We can think of the human user and the AI assistant, working together to achieve some shared goal. This human-plus-AI is an engineering hybrid (or "symbiosis" as it was once called), where the design goal is for the human to do the parts most suitable for humans, and the computer to do the parts most suitable for computers.[8] Obviously, in the "you do the rest" scenario, we want the computer part of the hybrid to take care of repetition of the same actions in the future, since this is what computers are good at, and since computers are not going to suffer from boredom, stress injuries, and all the other adverse consequences humans experience when made to do needlessly repetitive mechanical work.

One important principle in getting this balance right can be thought of as "attention investment," a concept that recalls the discussion in chapter 1 about the finite hours of conscious attention that we have in our lives, as well as Herb Simon's famous definition of the attention economy.[9] Imagine that I've written a novel featuring a character named Liz, but after finishing the novel I decide to change her name to Elizabeth. It would take a long time to read through every page, looking for each occurrence of "Liz" to change; fortunately, the *find and replace* function allows me to do the whole thing in a few steps. But in one passage, Liz speaks to her mother, who doesn't use the short version of her name. After my find and replace, the "Elizabeth" that was already in that passage (and contains within it the word "Liz") turns into "Eelizabethabeth" (something similar happened in one of my research papers, when an automated find and replace by a production editor enforcing the journal's house style meant that the printed article repeatedly referred to famous AI researcher Seymour Papert as "Seymour Articlet").

Whenever we ask a computer to repeat things in the future—when we program it—we need to anticipate circumstances in which our instructions might be wrong, inappropriate, or misunderstood. A human servant is able to use common sense and general knowledge (and if we are fortunate enough to have a personal servant like a butler or production assistant, an intimate understanding of our own habits and intentions), to avoid stupid mistakes like these. When the servant has no common sense or social context, as in the case of computers, all the responsibility of imagining unintended results falls instead on the person giving the instruction.[10] We have to spend time thinking carefully about the consequences of what we are asking and refining the instructions we give, so that it results in exactly the effects we want—nothing more and nothing less.[11]

This thinking effort can be defined as *investment of attention.* If the automated future actions are going to save us from further mechanical concentration in the future, then we will experience a "return" on that investment.[12] But, as with any investment, this can't be guaranteed. In fact, many programmers have had the experience of *imagining* that some repetitive task could in principle be automated, spending several hours writing the necessary code, only to never need to do the same thing ever again. Cognitive psychologist Lisanne Bainbridge described this problem as one of the "ironies of automation."[13] The opposite mistake is also common—many people are so determined to focus on finishing the task in front of them that they never pause to ask whether it could be achieved more effectively—what psychologists Jack Carroll and Mary Beth Rosson called the "paradox of the active user."[14]

Mixed-initiative interaction could be a key technique to mitigate these errors of judgement in attention investment. An AI system is able to detect repeated patterns and opportunities for automation, perhaps drawing on records of other users who have faced similar situations in the past. However, there have also been cases in which this design strategy has badly failed. The most notorious example is "Clippy," the Microsoft Office Assistant that annoyingly offered to help users of Microsoft Word when they seemed to be drafting letters. The basic idea (originally coming out of an AI research project at Microsoft) was sound, but ran into a major problem: the template letters being offered seldom corresponded to what the user was actually trying to write. Extremely formulaic letters may have their place, but perhaps not as often as Microsoft imagined. (In the style of the examples that introduced this chapter, can you imagine the implications of saying: "I need to write a love letter. You do the rest"? We might use a large language model (LLM) such as ChatGPT to do this—and I discuss similar examples in chapter 5.)

Even more annoyingly, Clippy was designed to *consume* the user's attention, because the animated character popped up in front of the document you were working on, jiggling around, changing shape, and blinking its eyes until you responded to it. In the era of the attention economy, we do understand that companies want to gain our attention—and we resent them for it. Although Clippy is never mentioned in Eric Horvitz's paper on mixed-initiative interaction, his previous research studying reasoning under resource constraints and human response to interruptions must have made it pretty clear to him, as to all other Microsoft researchers at the time, that the company's designers needed to be more sensitive to the dangers of saying "Can I help you with that?" Having served as President of the Association for the Advancement of Artificial Intelligence, Horvitz became both an influential campaigner for ethical AI and also the Chief Scientific Officer for Microsoft Research, so we have grounds for optimism that the mixed-initiative perspective will remain influential—as I said at the start of the chapter, this is what I would do if I had a big enough research budget.

End-User Programming without Machine Learning

If we had more mixed-initiative systems following the example of Allen Cypher's Eager, this would help a lot of people complete repetitive tasks. But a few people have already had this privilege for many years. Professional programmers are in the habit of writing small pieces of code, traditionally described as "scripts" or "macros," to help with routine and repetitive personal tasks. Because professional programmers also have to use computers like regular people—to save files, do tax returns, write documents, and so on—they encounter the same kinds of repetitive tasks as everybody else. The difference is that programmers have a way to escape the repetition, by writing a program to do it for them. But writing programs requires knowledge of a programming language. If you were making repeated changes to a list of addresses in a Microsoft Word document, and you wanted this to be done automatically, you could write a program to instruct Microsoft Word what to repeat. If you were repetitively renaming or moving around a whole bunch of different files on your personal computer, you could write a program to instruct the operating system what to repeat.

Because standard word processing products and home operating systems are made by programmers, and programmers also like to think about how to make things more convenient *for themselves*, it turns out that many standard products have built-in special facilities in the form of internal programming languages that can be used to avoid the repetitive operations that annoy programmers when they are off duty at home. However, software companies don't want to give the impression that their products are unnecessarily complex or hard to use, so those convenient internal languages are often hidden away, in places that you wouldn't find unless you specifically went looking for them.

Many people are surprised to learn that Microsoft Word has had a programming language built in since 1987, and that anyone can use this to write code that automates repetitive changes to a document. Word even has a trivial form of "learning," in which you can press a record button to capture a sequence of editing actions that you want to repeat. This macro recording can be replayed over and over. But more usefully, each of your key presses and menu commands is translated into the relevant Visual Basic code that would automatically make the same change to the document. These lines of macro code can be called up in a programming editor, right inside Microsoft Word, and modified to behave differently in different contexts, to repeat some actions automatically, or be extended with additional business logic or calculations. Of course, this could be pretty dangerous if *someone else* had written macro code that was going to automatically change your document in ways that you might not be expecting. That's why many email programs, operating systems, and security applications specifically test Word documents to see if they contain macros that might pose a security risk. As a result, many people have seen warnings about the dangers of macros, even if they have never considered creating a macro themselves.

Almost all personal computers have built-in ways to automate repeated requests to the operating system, including to make changes to files and folders. The traditional way to do this builds on the functionality of the command line or terminal window. Keyboard-driven operating system commands such as `ls -l` or `del *.*` or `rm -rf` look like lines of code because they *are* lines of code.[15] Any sequence of commands can be put into a script or batch file and replayed many times. And these scripting languages are powerful programming languages in their own right. They can be made to repeat operations thousands of times, test conditions, and make decisions. Once again, most programmers are familiar with these kinds of capability, because other programmers have put the capabilities into products for their own convenience. But while it is reasonably easy for a non-programmer to make their own macro in Microsoft Word by recording a sequence of keystrokes, few operating systems offer a similarly easy way to record and repeat file operations. The closest alternatives look strikingly similar to what Allen Cypher was doing in the UNIX shell over 30 years ago—manually looking back at the history of commands, and then assembling those into a script.

Although I've been writing as though there are only two kinds of people in the world—programmers who have the power to avoid repetitive tasks by writing code, and regular people who are doomed to repeat the same mechanical operations over and again because they don't have access to these hidden features—there are in fact many gradations in between.[16] Many people write small pieces of code, even though they might not be trained in programming. A more experienced programmer might help their colleagues by creating a small script or macro that will make their lives easier. Perhaps people might ask their programmer friends for assistance. If a repetitive task is particularly annoying, and the user is feeling curious, they might investigate how to write some code themselves, and maybe even share this with their own colleagues if it turns out to be useful.

These many kinds of end-user programmer, with their fine gradations and variety of professional and social contexts, can also be understood in relation to the attention investment principles that I have used to explain mixed-initiative interaction. Repeating the same mechanical commands over and over, whether these are editing actions in a Word document or moving files around, consumes precious hours of our conscious lives, when there are many other things that we would prefer to be doing over attending to a computer screen. The promise of programming is that we can write code to automate those actions and save ourselves the need to attend to screens so much.

The catch is that automating those actions with code also involves spending time with the screen—time spent figuring out how to write the necessary code. This is how attention investment got its name. End-user programming is an investment decision—you invest a certain amount of attention up front, in order to get a longer-term payback of attention saved through automation. The return on investment is the ratio of the amount of time you would spend writing (or finding) the necessary code, paid back over the number of repetitions. Writing code to avoid a million repetitions is a clear win. In fact, nobody is able to repeat a million actions with a computer, so if you have a task that does need to be repeated a million times, you'll either have to figure out how to automate it, or (more likely if there is *so* much time to be saved) hire a professional programmer to do it for you. At the other end of the scale, if you have a simple task that is only going to be repeated 50 times, you should probably just take a deep breath and hammer at the keyboard for a couple of minutes. Even a professional programmer would struggle to write a script faster than this.

Attention investment decisions are unfortunately harder than they seem, because it is not just a simple matter of calculating the effort to be saved through automation on one hand, and the time needed to write the code on the other. Like any investment, it requires analysis and foresight. Writing code for a new automation problem requires some original thought, including analyzing which parts of the repeated operation will be the same every time, which parts will be different, and how. Even where many of the repeated cases are very similar, there could be exceptions, like in the example of "Seymour Articlet" described earlier. And if the automation code fails to correctly address those exceptions, as in my own case with "Articlet," it may take a lot more attention to fix the embarrassing consequences later.[17]

Investments of attention, then, entail uncertainty and risk: uncertainty about exactly how much time it will take to write (and debug) automation code, and risk that the investment might not pay off. There is even risk in estimating how large the payoff will be. It cannot always be known in advance whether a particular action is going to be repeated 50 times or a million times. In fact, you might not even know all of the future situations in which your script or macro might be used. It's common experience that a company imagines some situation that they expect is going to occur millions of times, hires programmers to automate it, and then finds that this situation never happens again. This can happen for any number of reasons: perhaps it turns out there's no demand for a product, or that government regulations change, and a certain algorithmic calculation, until then totally compulsory, never needs to be done by anybody again after that day.[18]

There is also a lot of uncertainty in estimating how difficult it will be to write a particular piece of code. Writing code can sometimes be very hard— for example, if you need to use a programming language you have never used before and so must acquire a lot of background knowledge before even starting. On the other hand, it could be trivially easy—if it turns out, for example, that somebody else on the internet has written exactly the piece of code you need, with instructions on how to use it, so your first search result solves the problem immediately.[19] Even professional programmers are very cautious when estimating in advance the amount of time required to write a new piece of code.

This means that attention investment decisions involve trade-offs between two variables. One varies in a relatively predictable way, according to the size of the job (the number of actions to be repeated), and the other in an unpredictable way, according to the amount of expertise and previous experience that you might have (how long it will take you to write the program). In practice, people make their attention investment decisions on the basis of their personal biases and expectations—thinking fast, rather than slow, in the terminology introduced by behavioral economist Daniel Kahneman.[20]

Some decisions are perfectly sensible—to hire a programmer for that million-task problem, for example. But in other less clear instances, personal biases routinely result in the wrong decision. Working programmers often get frustrated by some repetitive task and decide "I could write a program to do this." Five hours later, the program is finished, but they could have finished the original task in 30 minutes. Even more common: you have just finished a moderately annoying task and think to yourself, "I never want to do this again," and so you spend time writing a program to do it instead. And then nobody ever does ask you to do it again (or perhaps they do, but you've forgotten where you stored the program), so the whole investment was pointless.

The opposite biases can be found among people who are not trained as programmers, or perhaps have some coding skills but don't feel confident and don't enjoy it. These people may persist with repetitive operations for far too long, overestimating the costs of learning to solve their problem with code, or underestimating how much time they could save. Ironically, this problem gets worse through feedback loops—every experience of successfully solving a problem with code improves your skills and reduces the time it will take you to solve problems with code in the future, but when you choose to avoid code, you gain no skills and are likely to continue losing hours of your life to mindless repetition. This self-defeating feedback loop is known to educational psychologists as lack of "self-efficacy".[21] In math education, student performance is in large part determined by self-efficacy—whether the student believes they are good at math. Students who don't believe they can do math don't persist long enough to find out if they could. The *belief* that you won't understand something initiates cognitive processes that result in you *really* not understanding it.

There is a lot of research confirming that this also happens with computers, and even with end-user programming.[22] If somebody *believes* that they are not going to understand computers, they are less likely to *actually* understand them. In part, this is because understanding is dependent on experience. Most people learn to use computers (like any piece of machinery) by fiddling around, figuring out what works and what doesn't. Unsurprisingly, if you never spend time playing around, you never develop the skills or acquire any confidence in your abilities, so you suffer from low self-efficacy. In other words, you don't enjoy playing, so you don't spend time playing around, and as a result you don't learn. This is a self-reinforcing loop that, as many teachers know, is hard to escape once a student falls into it.

Sadly, self-efficacy begins not with your own ability, but with the expectations of people around you. If people have low expectations for you, you often won't acquire skills in math or in coding, as in many other technical areas. This is a really significant problem, because many societies have low expectations, in both math and coding, for women, people of color, working-class people, and other excluded groups. We can't solve low self-efficacy by just telling people to believe in themselves, as if it's their own fault for not believing hard enough. Of course, we have to look at the root causes, so race and gender theorists view inequities as causes, not effects, of differential math and coding skills across groups.

Those exclusions are a lot more consequential than determining whether you are able to save yourself a few hours by writing a macro in Microsoft Word. This is about getting computers to do what you want. In a society where many basic human rights, including the right to even be a citizen, is delivered via computer, then self-efficacy in getting computers to do what you want is fundamental. Coding—the ability to express your own wishes to a computer—has become a resource for moral agency.

It's also not an accident that self-efficacy applies both to end-user programming and to mathematics. Attention investment is fundamental to both, because both programming and math share two important cognitive foundations—abstraction and notation. Casually defined, math is the skill of calling different things by the same name. Abstract language (whether computer code or human speech) gives us the power to refer to many different things or situations with a single word.

That basic principle of attention investment—devote a bit of effort to thinking about something in advance in order to avoid mundane repetition in the future—also utilizes the basic power of abstraction.[23] Each repetition is an individual concrete case that, without abstraction, must be handled individually. A program that describes how *all* cases should be handled is necessarily an abstraction—describing abstractly what must be done, describing abstractly how the actions might need to vary slightly in different circumstances, and defining abstractly what those circumstances are. For an experienced programmer (whether professional or end-user), once you have learned how to use the basic programming tools, the attention investment for each new task is an investment in abstraction. Using abstractions is all about investing attention, and self-efficacy (the belief that it's worthwhile to even start) is a fundamental prerequisite for this kind of abstract strategy.

The other thing that mathematics and programming have in common is that they both are fundamentally about the use of notation—*codes*, as I call them in this book. We need notation (or a recorded language of some kind) in order to use abstraction.[24] It's possible to talk about a single concrete object by simply touching it as we speak, but talking about many objects requires abstraction and names. This is the difference between on the one hand touching a single object while saying "pick this up," and on the other hand saying "pick up all those Lego bricks you've left around the house." More complex requirements involve more sophisticated instructions: "delete all the emails from John, but only the ones that I've already replied to," or "change all occurrences of 'paper' to 'article,' except where 'paper' is a sequence of letters inside a person's name." It's this complexity of communicating instructions that makes coding hard. Programming languages are the notations—codes—that give us ways to manage this complexity by constructing and applying abstractions.

Years ago, typical computer users were more familiar with abstractions than they are today. Before the graphical user interface (GUI) of the Apple Macintosh and Microsoft Windows, regular interaction used the programming-like notation of the command line, and it was routine to avoid repetitive operations through abstract specifications such as DEL *.BAK (the asterisk is a wildcard, indicating an abstract specification of all files whose names end in the letters BAK, which was a convention for backup files). Using such commands usually involved some simple attention investment: learning how to use the wildcard, deciding on the correct specification, assessing the risk if it goes wrong, and so on.

The GUI replaced the command line with the principle of *direct manipulation*, in which files are represented by iconic pictures and the mouse is used to act on those pictures as if they were physical objects, selecting and dragging them to their destination. Direct manipulation of individual icons involved less up-front investment of attention than the command line, just as it's easier to pick up one Lego brick than explain to somebody else that you want them to do it. However, direct manipulation is not itself a notation, and so it was no longer possible to describe more abstract requirements, such as applying a certain operation to all files of a particular type, or to multiple files that are in different folders.

Direct manipulation interfaces are relatively easy to work with because they don't involve any notational codes or provide any powerful abstractions. But by itself, however easy and convenient, direct manipulation can't be the only approach to interaction with computers. In an information economy and a computerized society, abstraction is the source of control over your own life, and potentially the source of power over others. Notation has moral implications: Moral Codes are abstract codes.

3 Why Is Code Not Like AI?

In the previous chapter, we saw that very simple machine learning methods can assist users by helping with basic programming tasks, conserving and enhancing the valuable resource of human attention as a result. The overall argument of this book is that the global "AI" business of machine learning—currently focused on extracting as much data from users as possible for the minimum cost, while also consuming their attention—is a tragically ineffective way of contributing to human life and welfare. Instead, we need a moral alternative, in which the ability to instruct and configure computers is extended to a far wider range of people, delivering the capabilities of programming through *moral codes*.

Before more detailed analysis of these opportunities, it's important to be clear about the difference between programming languages and machine learning. To a software expert, this might seem like a stupid or naive question, although silly questions can of course be profound and important. According to current conventions of the software industry, and in the textbooks and courses that prepare students for that industry, programming languages and machine learning are two completely distinct technical topics, taught so differently from each other that it might seem hard to know where to start. A typical degree program in software engineering or computer science, of the kind I have directed myself, will probably include "Introduction to Machine Learning" as one class (on AI) and "Programming in Python" as another (on coding). There are so many differences between how they're taught, that asking why one is not like the other might seem like asking "why is flower arranging not like brain surgery?" or "why is riding a bicycle not like designing a factory?" But let's consider the broad context of what students learn, and how, in each of these areas.

In an introductory class in programming, students learn to code. They will be taught the syntax and keywords of some programming language notation, perhaps Python or Java, and will learn how to translate an algorithm into the conventional idioms of that particular programming language. Subsequent programming courses will try to prepare students for more complex projects, in which a particular algorithm only solves one part of the problem—students have to learn to break down a larger problem into individual pieces that they can see how to code. This second aspect of programming is a lot harder, perhaps not even mentioned in an introductory class, and takes years or decades to become good at. Although it's often claimed, when promoting courses in basic coding, that you can make any software system out of algorithms and code, this is a bit like saying you can make any house out of nails and pieces of wood. Most children can bang a nail into a piece of wood. And many introductions to coding are accessible to children from an early age. Sadly, these well-intentioned initiatives don't even begin to get you a software career. A child who loves banging nails into wood may well become an architect or engineer one day, but only after another 15 years of education.

Introductions to machine learning are not yet quite as familiar or popular as learn-to-code initiatives, but they are equally accessible to children—I have a friend who teaches machine learning methods to eight-year-olds in an after-school club. The current popularity of machine learning, now the most widely taught approach to AI, dates back only to about 2010, when public interest was captured by a sudden increase in performance of "deep neural network" algorithms, especially after those algorithms were trained using very large quantities of free content that had been scraped from the internet.[1] (The next chapter will cover the implications and problems of that approach.) Although there were many other approaches to AI in the past, including my own research training in the 1980s, researchers now have the patronizing (or perhaps ironically self-effacing) habit of calling those older methods "GOFAI" for Good Old-Fashioned AI.

Modern machine learning methods trace their roots to statistics, in that they use algorithms to detect patterns in large amounts of data. People who teach and do research in machine learning are mathematicians and statisticians, and often are just as happy to refer to their work as "data science" rather than "artificial intelligence." The underlying logic of machine learning is similar in many ways to concepts that will be familiar from school statistics—collating a table of numbers, calculating an average, testing a correlation, and so on. The recent habit of describing statistical "learning" as "AI" has really only emerged when the amount of data became so large that it's hard to relate it intuitively to those high school concepts.[2]

The impression that statistical patterns represent intelligence is particularly compelling when the numbers being processed are the pixels of a digital photograph or the words and sentences of a web page. Machine learning systems for statistical analysis of photographs are described as "computer vision," and systems for statistical analysis of words and sentences are described as "natural language processing." Although a single web page may have thousands of words, and a single photograph millions of pixels, the most dramatic advances have come from taking far more data—scraping many millions of photographs and web pages off the internet—and creating statistical algorithms that are able to detect consistent patterns across millions of pictures containing trillions of pixels, or millions of pages sharing a dictionary of thousands of different words. The algorithms all use statistics, but researchers have given them grander names such as "support vector machines," "random forests," "neural networks," "transformers," and other jargon. For readers who would like a better idea of how such technical terminology arises and is used, Adrian Mackenzie is a sociological specialist in science and technology studies who has described his experiences of acquiring these statistical learning skills and terminology in his book *Machine Learners*.[3]

I started this section by asking what the difference is between machine learning and programming, not the difference between AI and programming. The reason is that, if we lose sight of the technical reality that machine learning algorithms are simply doing different kinds of statistics, we might start to interpret some of the technical jargon from the field as if it was directly related to human intelligence rather than just a convenient metaphor. We might think that a "vision" algorithm is "seeing" things the way a human does, that a "language" algorithm is "understanding" words, that a "neural" algorithm is like the neurons in a brain, or even that a "learning" algorithm has something to do with how children learn. Unfortunately, much of the public debate about AI is based on exactly those kinds of misinterpretation. Commentators on AI who have never actually used these tools (and many have not—Adrian Mackenzie is a prominent exception who did the necessary work to use them extensively in his own research) may not understand the statistical calculations that are really being done, and may run the risk of treating the sometimes fanciful names given to algorithms (whether neuron, forest, seeing, understanding, learning) as if the machines are doing the same things that people do. If we use such words carelessly, they become a conceptual "suitcase," bringing with them a lot of baggage of our associations with those words as used in an everyday conversation about humans.

I've emphasized how naive current discussion of these topics can be, when people don't think carefully about what words mean. Of course, researchers do not give these names to their algorithms at random, or as jokes (at least, not often). Many are inspired by real research into the human brain, or visual anatomy, or linguistics. Some have even worked in neuroscience laboratories, perhaps measuring electrical impulses from the neuron of a fly or mouse, or measuring patterns of blood flow in human brain scans. These scientific ambitions help to motivate people doing this kind of work, but if you question them closely, they will admit that there is only the vaguest analogy between the "neuron" of a neural network (which has simply become a jargon term for a relatively simple mathematical function) and the complex electrochemical activity that would be observed in even a single animal neuron.

Researchers studying new algorithms do find inspiration by observing animals, just as Leonardo da Vinci was inspired by birds' wings (among other things) when designing flying machines. However, lessons from the history of technology tell us that, although observing nature can be a source of inspiration, successful engineering usually works differently. Airplanes don't flap their wings. When words like "neuron" get carried over directly from observation of nature to implementation of algorithms, it can be hard to remember which parts were scientifically observed statistical principles, and which were left over from creative inspiration. And as I explained in the first chapter of this book, there are people who profit from avoiding proper definitions, blurring the distinction between objective statistical problems and subjective human interpretations.

So, to return to the initial question, "machine learning" currently refers to a variety of statistical algorithms that process numerical data (sometimes extracted from images or texts) to find patterns in that data. From this perspective, programming (or coding) has little direct relevance to AI—other than the mundane need to specify machine learning algorithms in a language that the computer will then discard once it starts on the suppos-edly "intelligent" part of using the data patterns.

How AI Was Coded before Machine Learning

If *statistical* machine "learning" was the only possible definition of how a machine could "learn," then my initial question—asking the difference between programming and machine learning—would have a somewhat straightforward answer: programming is the way we define all kinds of algorithms, while statistical machine learning is a particular *kind* of algo-rithm. However, there are other approaches to machine learning that are not statistical, not numerical, and don't use neural networks. Some of those were widely understood in the era of Good Old-Fashioned AI, although as that name suggests, they are no longer fashionable and might not even be mentioned in the introductory classes about statistical machine learning that are commonly taught as the basis of AI today.

The old-fashioned approach to machine learning, as with much GOFAI, followed a far closer analogy to human learning. In GOFAI, pieces of code recognizably resembled concepts that humans themselves might explicitly be taught, consciously perceive, or talk about—rather than the statistical approach of attempting to break down raw data by some kind of poetic analogy to patterns of neurons in the brain. Writing the code of AI, in this old-fashioned approach, could be considered rather more like teaching a human. If the concepts are described using words, then teacher and stu-dent can communicate about what is being learned. Human teachers don't spend much time explaining how to recognize perceptual patterns of edges and shadows in order to read, or how the student should properly fire their neurons to do arithmetic, because this is not the right level of abstraction at which to discuss and teach the concepts.

The origins of GOFAI, much like the origins of computer science at the time of Alan Turing, were more concerned with describing conceptual and logical principles than statistical ones. GOFAI programs worked with recogniz-able symbols like elephant and canary, and with logical relations between them such as (color elephant gray) or (color tweety yellow).[4] These logical relationships look more like the kinds of things that might be taught in a classroom, and we can easily imagine teaching a computer to repeat such statements on command, as if we were teaching a child to pass an exam by memorizing facts and logical relations. In the GOFAI era of AI research, from the 1950s until the end of the twentieth century, the main challenge of machine learning was to create algorithms that could compute logical relations by combining coded and stored (we might say "memorized" if being too literal) *symbols*. At a trivial level, we can imagine an algorithm that, after being taught (has cat fur) and (has dog fur), could then use those individual facts to learn a general concept, by working out for itself that cats and dogs have something in common. This kind of algorithm is also a lot closer to what a philosopher might conclude by introspection about how we ourselves go about learning. Indeed, many GOFAI researchers did work by introspection, thinking carefully about the logical implications of statements like these, and about the reasoning processes by which it is possible to draw general conclusions from combinations of facts and rules.

As a result, in the GOFAI era, the everyday work of the AI researcher *did* look much the same as the everyday work of any other kind of programmer— writing down symbols, coding rules that related the symbols to each other, and coding logical (at that time, not statistical) algorithms that work out other facts from the combinations of rules and symbols that have been collected so far. This approach to coding knowledge also seems to resemble ideas about formal schooling for humans—memorizing facts and relations between them and being able to make deductions. To the extent that they can store such encoded knowledge more reliably, and also execute the code of the specified deductive processes accurately once programmed, we might even describe GOFAI computers as superior learners to humans.

However, even though anyone can "teach" a computer to remember and perform tasks perfectly by writing the appropriate program code, we are reluctant to say that the computer is "learning" when we program it so directly. School teaching might sometimes be mechanical, but learning is not supposed to be. Now that we routinely turn to computers for so many data processing tasks that previously required human labor, society has become increasingly uncomfortable about the value of rote learning in humans, whether teaching children to recite historical dates that can be found on Wikipedia, mechanically apply algorithms that are trivial with a calculator, or turn informal speech into grammatical sentences that could have been generated by a language model. Although memorization, grammar, and arithmetic were highly valued in earlier centuries, training people in mechanical repetition is less popular today. Indeed, we use the word "programming" to refer to kinds of teaching that are morally objectionable and talk about "deprogramming" when people leave religious cults or other sites of repetitious indoctrination.

The greatest commercial boom in that earlier generation of explicitly coded, symbolic GOFAI was driven by the promise of "expert systems." An expert system programmer or "knowledge engineer" attempted to capture all the specialist facts from a particular field of knowledge such as geology or cardiology, together with all the necessary rules for combining and applying those facts, and encode them into algorithms that might be able to replicate or substitute for expert judgments.

Unfortunately, expert systems of that era never turned out to be quite as useful as promised in the sales pitches. The most successful were able to operate like automated textbooks or reference manuals, correctly combining symbols that reflected the specialist terminology of the experts who had been consulted when coding them. The problem came when such systems were used by people who did not use the right formulation of specialist terms to describe what they wanted, but instead tried to relate the "expert" reasoning of the system to their own ordinary non-expert understanding of the situation. Expert systems often failed in brittle ways through lack of common sense. For example, such a system might prescribe medicine for a patient who was dead, because although the programmers had coded thousands of facts about medicine, they could easily forget to code things that were, to a human, common sense—such as *that the dead won't benefit from medicine.*

From this historical background, it's easy to see why *statistical* machine learning started to look attractive, and why GOFAI became a historical curiosity with a funny name and no longer a priority for university teaching and research. The meaning of the word "learning" has itself changed in AI research—it is no longer related to the way children might learn in schools, or to the knowledge that experts might write about or extract from reference books. Statistical machine learning systems only look for patterns in numbers and have not been coded to know anything about symbols like cat and dog unless they happen to see those sequences of letters in collections of text training data.

In the early days of the deep learning revolution, AI researchers collected many statistical examples of pixels from photographs that have furry texture patterns in them, and also noted statistical frequency of the letters C, A, T when people uploaded particular kinds of furry patterns (this example is often a good starting point, because it turns out that there are plenty of photographs of C-A-T's on the internet). Programming was still involved. A programmer wrote the code that downloaded the photographs from the internet, and the code that scanned the Instagram comments, Wikipedia pages, Facebook posts, and other sites to find the letters C-A-T. This kind of learning looks a bit more like common sense, since so many people are apparently interested in cats, but the results seem to be a particularly trivial kind of learning—even more primitive than the GOFAI era—not as much like elementary school, but more like an infant who can point at a picture and say "cat" after being trained to do so. A child who did not progress beyond this stage would not be socially competent.

Being able to say the right kind of things about a cat—instructing a robot that it ought to gently stroke the cat, or that cats, while made of meat, should not be cooked and eaten—are routinely understood by embodied children, but cannot be understood from a photograph alone. Social competence is not a matter of direct perception, but systems of moral discourse through which we learn and describe what ought to be done. In the GOFAI era, these kinds of rules of behavior were explicitly encoded as conceptual symbols. In today's large language models, moral discourse comes by association—words like "stroking" are very likely to be associated with cats, while "is a cat meat" raises problematic questions (having just tested this, the model initially answered no, before admitting that they are constituted of meat, then preferring to discuss humans eating pet food). It's unlikely that robots will either be stroking or eating cats in the near future, but as with small children learning about cats, there are times when we would like computers to do what we tell them. This is the great challenge for machine learning: how to use simple correlations between things found on the internet as a useful basis for telling a machine what to do differently in the future.

The Point of Programming

We do already have technologies optimized for telling a computer what to do—this is the whole point of programming languages. The GOFAI era saw dramatic advances in programming languages, and in the variety and sophistication of concepts and relationships that could be symbolically described. Unfortunately, practical deployment of expert systems resulted in so many disappointments through their brittle failures of common sense that a common saying among AI researchers was "if it works, it isn't AI." Nevertheless, many of the advances made in programming languages and algorithms through that period are now commonly taught as basic parts of the computer science curriculum. The flip side of defining AI as things that don't work is that, once AI algorithms do work reliably, we don't consider them AI any longer. If AI is the branch of computer science dedicated to imagination, and to making computers work the way they do in the movies, then boring products that just work are not exciting enough to be defined as AI. Most of the things that we do with computers today (including me typing these words right now) would have seemed like magic a century ago. The technical advances that actually allow us to instruct computers for practical purposes might have seemed like AI once, but now they are just coding.

Explaining this carefully, and perhaps at greater length than a computer scientist would have patience for, makes it clear that although there is a huge difference between the technical methods described as "machine learning" and "programming," many of the things that we might have hoped could be achieved through "machine learning"—including most of those that have moral implications—actually require "programming."

Machine learning algorithms can help us with the more mundane aspects of programming, and I'll be discussing those opportunities in far more detail in chapter 11. Using AI to help us write code can reduce the costs of attention investment in our favor. However, we have to contrast these useful applications with AI systems that *consume* our attention *without* offering any of the benefits of moral codes. The next chapter will look more closely at how the attention-consuming systems work.

4   Intending and Attending: Chatting to the Stochastic Parrots 🦜

In 1981, while working as an electronic design intern at the headquarters of the New Zealand Forest Service, I was given exclusive access to a personal computer for the first time in my life. The hours I spent playing with the Tandy Radio Shack TRS-80 that summer extended far beyond the work I was paid to do. Among other experiments, I used a random number generator to combine lists of nouns, adjectives, and verbs into unexpected sentences, with occasionally entertaining results. Applying (I hope) due irony, I called this experiment an "automatic novel generator." I had forgotten this episode, in part from embarrassment. But it did slightly impress my new girlfriend at the time—enough that she remembered it after 40 years (of marriage) and suggested it might be relevant to this book.

My sophomoric novel generator was by no means a demonstration of AI. If I'd been better educated, I would have been able to relate it to centuries of experimentation in which new sequences of words were mechanically constructed, as a kind of aid to creativity or source of oracular guidance. (Jo Walton's *Brief Backward History of Automated Eloquence* mentions examples including the Latin Hexameter Automaton demonstrated by Clark of Bridgwater in 1845, and the za'irajah paper machines described by Ibn Khaldon in 1377[1]).

Twenty years later, I bought my first cellphone to prepare for an urgent call letting me know our first child was on the way. Entering SMS text on a tiny keyboard was a pain, and my late friend David MacKay showed me the first prototype of his *Dasher* software that promised to make text entry far easier, especially for people with disabilities.[2] David had invented Dasher after a conversation on a bus journey at the annual Conference on Neural Information Processing Systems (then NIPS, now NeurIPS), lamenting the inadequacy of predictive text interfaces.[3] Based on animated diagrams illustrating the relative likelihood of the next letter in a sequence of English text, David realized that the animation could become a user interface for faster text entry. For example, after typing the letters T, H, and I, the next letter is quite likely to be S. In the animation, the screen would zoom in so that S can be entered very easily indeed.[4]

David and I failed to persuade phone manufacturers that this approach to faster text entry (in the Dark Ages before the iPhone and other touch screen devices) would become attractive. However, the basic principle of "predictive text" has since become a familiar everyday experience. In the early days, text prediction was little more than a built-in dictionary, able to complete a word once the first few letters had been entered, or to auto-correct a sequence of letters that was close enough to a known word. Systems like Dasher were not constrained by word boundaries, meaning that even after a word was complete, the next few letters of the following word could be predicted. Nowadays, we are all familiar with document editors and email applications that will predict the next word in a sentence or the rest of a phrase, all based on a language model that has been statistically trained to know the probability of a given letter or word coming next in a sequence of text.

Another two decades after my experiments with David MacKay, I was invited to contribute to a training course in Digital Humanities, teaching graduate students in language, history, and media studies how to process text as statistical sequences.[5] In the training examples prepared by my colleague Anne Alexander, students wrote Python programs to compile statistical tables of how often a given word is seen to follow other words in different kinds of text. One example we experimented with was the collected tweets of then-President Donald Trump. Another was the collected works of William Shakespeare. Those different frequency tables could be used to generate predictive text in the style of either Trump or Shakespeare, completing sentences using the particular kinds and choices of words those men might use. These simple (but entertaining) student exercises, like David MacKay's Dasher, are statistical language models—they capture particular ways of speaking and use their statistical data to produce new text that resembles what the model was trained on.

I was naturally curious to see whether my own habits of writing could be captured in a language model. While I wouldn't like to place my own writing in a precise location between the extremes of Shakespeare or Trump, in my academic career I have probably written a comparable *number* of words to both. I spent a few hours collecting manuscripts spanning more than 10 years, and Anne used them to construct a language model fine-tuning the experimental platform GPT-2 (later versions of this OpenAI software, including GPT-3, ChatGPT, and GPT-4, have since become far more well known than the version we used in 2021). It turned out that this "Auto-Alan," as we called the language model, was able to write convincingly in the same style as me, just as we had previously demonstrated automated output that sounded like Trump or Shakespeare. Auto-Alan "wrote" a short academic paper that we presented to an audience under the title *Embracing the Plagiarized Future*, anticipating the widespread soul-searching that would arise within the next couple of years.[6] I later read Auto-Alan's paper to a research workshop attended by my PhD supervisor Thomas Green, who invited his friends to consider how much of my previous work might also have been automated.[7]

I don't think these three little stories about my own experiments at 20-year intervals are particularly impressive. Any enthusiastic amateur at those times might have been doing the same kinds of things. However, my personal experiences provide useful landmarks as an overview of how language generation technology has developed over 40 years. Although there have been impressive advances, these can largely be attributed to the increase in computing power described by Moore's Law. Typical computers in 2021 had become about a million times more powerful than typical computers were in 1981, so you might say the intellectual advances of AI in these 40 years are disappointing given the huge scale of physical infrastructure and investment they have required.

Nevertheless, there are some principles that have remained the same over the past four decades, and are therefore quite likely to continue for another four. It's worth paying more attention to these.

Firstly, all these kinds of experiments have involved a language model. In the simplest case—my novel generator of 1981—the model consisted of some lists of words and a few simple grammar rules. As I explained in the last chapter, that GOFAI era involved collecting facts and writing down rules, an activity often described as "knowledge engineering."[8] In contrast, the language model of Dasher was trained statistically from example texts, not by writing out rules, and was therefore completely determined by the examples of text it had been shown. If shown biased and offensive text it would suggest that kind of vocabulary, but if trained with the complete works of Jane Austen (as we did in one experiment), it would predict phrases from the early nineteenth century. David Ward, who developed Dasher for his PhD, originally trained the model with a large archive of his own email messages. This might have been an effective productivity aid when chatting to his friends, but it could have been embarrassing when potential investors watched the model predict his habit of swearing in emails.

The later language models of GPT-2 and its various successors are trained using huge amounts of text collected from the internet. It is so expensive to process this much text, and the tensions between commercial opportunities and public concerns so sensitive, that the companies building these models are secretive about where exactly they get the training text from.[9] We can imagine that, for example, it would be easy to include the whole of Wikipedia as part of the language model. We can gain some insight into the behavior of such models by "fine-tuning" them as I did, when I trained GPT-2 to give more statistical weight to the kinds of language in my own academic writing.

Secondly, an important principle is that these language models are used for *prediction*. If I train a language model with a statistical survey of the kinds of words Donald Trump used in the past, I can use this to predict what he might say in the future. So far, this particular prediction has been fairly reliable, because Trump is still saying the same kind of things. Similarly, Auto-Alan could be quite useful to me as a kind of predictive text keyboard, because its language model includes a dictionary that gives higher priority to the kinds of words I've used in the past, and that I'll quite likely continue to use in the future.

The origin of the training text is particularly important when a language model runs without further human intervention. Imagine that, when composing a message on my phone, I decided simply to accept the next word suggested by my predictive text keyboard, whatever that was. This would result in a message containing the kinds of words that people use on phones, arranged in plausibly the same order that people do arrange those words, but it would not be a message from me at all! It would simply be an exhibition of what is contained in the language model of my phone. I did this experiment quite often with Dasher—just pressing its accelerator to continue generating text, outputting whatever letters it considered most likely on the basis of its training. This was entertaining but seldom useful.

The third general property we can see over these 40 years is that randomized text output, even from simple language models, can sometimes be entertaining or interesting. My "automatic novel generator," although a trivial program, still created valid English sentences. The sentences were repetitive, and every word a non-sequitur, but occasionally the results were funny or thought-provoking. The predictive text output from Dasher, even when suggesting words I hadn't been intending to write, was also often interesting. Many people have similar experiences with predictive text on phones. While most suggestions are boring and predictable, unintended alternative words might be sent as a joke. The same things continued to be true when I saw the output from Auto-Alan. Some sentences were almost directly copied from things I had written before, while others included words that I do like to use but combined in ways I hadn't seen before. Although I haven't done this (yet), I can imagine that some of those unexpected combinations of words might suggest ideas for future research projects, just like William S. Burroughs cutting up his manuscripts. I was amused to see that the text created by Auto-Alan included references to previous academic work, including a paper supposedly written by two friends of mine, despite the fact that those two people had not ever worked together. The suggestion by Auto-Alan made me wonder whether I should introduce them, because any result of their collaboration would certainly be interesting.

In a classic publication that first alerted many readers to the now-familiar problems of large language models, Emily Bender, Timnit Gebru, and colleagues described these systems as "stochastic parrots."[10] One of their main concerns was to draw attention to the fact that these experiments were being conducted at a massive environmental cost, through the amount of computation required to extract and encode so much of the internet. The energy usage of LLMs continues to be a pressing problem, both practically and ethically, as we ask how much benefit really comes from such experiments and at what cost. But the most immediate impact of that paper may well have been its brilliant title, which so effectively summarized the fundamental principles of operation. The text that LLMs so fluently produce creates the illusion that it might have been directly written by a human author. But the description "stochastic parrot" drew attention to the way they really work.

As shown in my own experiments over the course of 40 years, text produced mechanically from language models can be very engaging. But the content of such text is only ever a reorganization of the text that was previously used to train the model (they are parrots), spiced with some random elements that will be more unexpected ("stochastic" is simply a technical term for randomness).

In the next chapter, I will say more about the capabilities and opportunities that come from encoding so much of the internet in a language model. As I write this, newspapers and broadcast journalists describe new advances and controversies about LLMs almost every day. Perhaps the excitement will have died down by the time this book is printed—many of my friends think me both brave and foolish for trying to explain such a fast-moving field via the old-fashioned medium of book publication. Some of my less critical students suggest that by then, an AI-based language model could write the whole book automatically, saving both me and my publisher a great deal of effort.

It would be foolish, at a time of such rapid advance, to make confident predictions about what will and won't be possible in the next few years. However, one reason for starting this chapter with a 40-year history is to emphasize that the human *interpretation* of computer systems changes relatively slowly. This is not because technical advances have been slow. Although a million-fold increase in four decades is impressive, this is only two human generations. Social acceptance of new technologies happens on a scale of multiple generations, not product seasons, in part because science famously advances one funeral at a time.[11]

Before discussing the opportunities of human interpretation, it is worth reinforcing some of the technical limitations that will continue to define the capabilities of any predictive text models, based on the principles of *information theory* developed by Claude Shannon at Bell Labs.[12] Shannon's theory is now recognized as a fundamental principle of all information technologies, well beyond communication systems such as the AT&T telephone network that originally funded Bell Labs. Information theory is perhaps the most significant practical advance in mathematical physics since Isaac Newton's laws of gravity. It is not yet taught in high schools, but certainly will be before long. And as far as LLMs are concerned, I believe that trying to explain their capabilities without the mathematics of information theory is like attempting a proper theory of how balls move on a pool table without using Newton's equations.

In its simplest form, information theory measures how much information is transferred over a communication channel. Although this seems straightforward, there are subtle, almost paradoxical implications. Seventy years after Shannon, we know how to measure *data* in megabits or gigabits when we stream a movie or email a photo. But the paradoxical aspect is that *not all data count as information*. If you send me an email message (please do), then immediately *send the same message again* (please don't), the second one uses more data, but *without giving me any more information*—the new data is *redundant* in the technical jargon of information theory. On the other hand, if you send the same email to a *different* person, now the same message is *not* redundant, because *that recipient* hasn't seen it before. While it is *easy to measure how many bits* are transmitted through a cable, *information content is hard to measure objectively*, because it *depends on who receives the message*. If the receiver *already knows* the contents, no information has been transferred. Information theory measures how much information the receiver *did not already know. Information theory is a measure of surprise!*[13]

As I discuss in more detail in chapter 12, what we call "creativity," when done by a machine, is more precisely a measure of how much we are surprised by what the machine does. So information theory can be used in some way as a measure of creativity.

An apparent paradox of information theory is that the most expensive message to send over a communication channel is a completely random sequence of numbers. Imagine a message that is composed of zeros and ones, where each character is chosen by flipping a coin. The person receiving that message would have no way to predict what the next character in a sequence will be, and so each will be a complete surprise. That message is as surprising as it could possibly be, but we don't perceive it as being creative. On the contrary, a sequence of random bits looks like *noise* (another technical term in information theory).

Machine learning systems, by definition, learn to replay information that they have received (the training data that they learned). Shannon and his coauthor Warren Weaver, in communicating the implications of information theory, paid close attention to the concept of a language model in understanding how much information is being transferred in human communication.[14] When a language model is used for text prediction, each new letter is chosen on the basis of information theory—the principle of least surprise. The word your phone predicts is the one that is least surprising, and most expected to come after what you just entered. The least surprising word is also the least creative. Indeed, who would want a more creative predictive text algorithm on their phone? A creatively "intelligent" phone, which surprised you with words completely different from what you were expecting to say, might be quite a liability in everyday use!

I've already explained that the most surprising message (in an information theory sense) is a sequence of completely random numbers or coin tosses, since that would mean there was no way to predict any number from the ones that came before. Completely random messages are very surprising, but also very uninteresting, because they are just noise, communicating nothing at all of substance. There is no hidden message in a series of coin tosses or dice throws, no matter how much we might want to find one. Random information is perceived as surprising precisely because *there is no message* that could have been predicted. An AI system can produce surprising output if its design includes random elements. But this is not creative in the human sense, because it is not a message from anywhere. Random elements in a digital sequence are not a signal, but noise. As described by philosophers of mind, a random message has no meaning because there is no *intention* behind it.[15]

I hope this explanation has made it clear why "stochastic parrots" is such an accurate and succinct summary of the nature and capabilities of LLMs, and also of my own experiments with text generation over the previous 40 years. A system that generates text from a language model is a Shannon information channel that can output only information that has been put into it—a parrot. No language model has ever created *new* information, and none ever will, any more than we will ever see a perpetual motion machine, or balls on a pool table moving themselves. The output of language models does become more entertaining when we add random noise, making them stochastic. This can never be new information, but might appear interesting because it is unexpected, giving the human reader the challenge of how to interpret what they see, as I will discuss in the next section.

Predictive text from language models is certainly useful, especially if the language model contains enough information that the text you were already wanting to write is contained in the model. I use simple predictive text every day, to help write familiar words quickly (it's very rare that I want to write a word that is *not* in any dictionary, which is why it is usually helpful to have words completed or my spelling corrected automatically), and to complete sequences of words (the English language includes many small words that do not have interesting meanings in themselves, but have to be included in the right order to make grammatical sentences—in this sentence, they included "the," "that," "do," "to," etc.).

I'll say more about the benefits (and dangers) of relying on predictive text in the next chapter. This is the "parrot" part of the story, and it is all about automating routine actions—the useful capability of computers to "do the rest" for us, by repeating, parrot-like, variations on things they have seen before. But this has also been recognized as a shortcoming of computers for over 70 years, prompting a letter to the Times of London that *defended the reputation of parrots* against a Professor Jefferson whose public lecture on the "mechanical brain" had recently argued: "It was not enough to build a machine which could use words; it would have to be able to create concepts and find for itself suitable words in which to express them. Otherwise . . . it would be no cleverer than a parrot." The letter writer complained that this was unfair to parrots, and that "[u]nless it can also lay eggs, hang upside down from its perch, scratch itself in unlikely places, and crush the fingers of unwary visitors in its powerful beak until they scream in agony, no machine can start drawing comparisons between its own intellect and a parrot's."[16]

The (Mis)interpretation of Noise

Before saying any more about parrots, I want to consider the value of the "stochastic" element. These are the times when systems built using language models add random noise, mixed in with the useful signals that have been parroted from their training data. As I've already described, it can be entertaining to see random stuff produced as output from a computer. But while sometimes random output is interesting, often it's not. The difference between interesting and not interesting really depends on what you were expecting, or how you interpret it.

Interpreting random information is an ancient game, entertainment, and even tool for decision-making across many societies. A familiar example is the toss of a coin at the start of a football match. Although all kinds of factors could be used to decide which team kicks the ball first, the number and variety of contextual questions that *might* be considered is so large and complex that the debate itself could last longer than the game. Making a decision on a random basis is therefore an effective decision strategy. Many professional and scientific decisions are made in this same way, such as the randomized controlled trial that is routine in medicine and pharmaceutical science.

A heads-or-tails toss or an A/B test leaves little room for interpretation, but it's useful to compare LLMs to other randomized processes where individual symbols have more meaning. Fortune-telling games like horoscopes or tarot cards are interesting examples. The signs of the zodiac, and the elaborate symbols of the tarot deck, have evolved over generations to include many layers of meaning. A skilled "reader" of horoscopes or tarot cards is able to weave together these richly ambiguous symbols into a story about someone's life and imagined future destiny. The combination of complex symbols with randomized shuffling allows the reader to interpret them in an evocative improvised performance.

There is little opportunity for creative interpretation when tossing a coin, especially when a sequence of tosses results in similar numbers of heads and tails. But randomized juxtaposition of *meaningful* symbols, on the other hand, does present opportunity for interpretation. When combined with interpretation, the "signal" comes from a combination of the traditional meanings those symbols have acquired and the skill of the interpreter in interpreting them; the randomization process of shuffling is "noise" that has been intentionally introduced for much the same purpose as the coin toss at the start of a football game—if you don't have all the information needed to make a fair judgement, it might be fairer to make a random one.

It's important to understand the value of noise in these performances, since this is the basis on which the whole "system" (cards+symbols+reading etc.) provides outputs that are unexpected. The whole point of a divination performance is to tell you something that you didn't expect. In terms of information theory, this is precisely what noise is good for. For example, there are situations where robot control can be improved by adding noisy "jitter" to prevent the control algorithm from getting stuck without biasing it one way or the other. However, there is room for misinterpretation if the random noise is confused with the signal itself. Some traditional divination practices tell interpretive stories in which the random outcome is described as a message from a spirit, ancestor, or god, while astrologers and tarot readers might describe the random elements as a message from "fate" or "destiny." These supernatural characters are an important part of the interpretive story, bringing with them cultural associations of the symbols, but the interesting message is the interpretive performance, not the random noise.

These familiar traditional practices can be compared to the apparently supernatural or magical powers of the latest LLMs. The "stochastic" part of the stochastic parrot output is noise, not signal. It does not carry a message from anywhere, because it is not a message. But because the symbolic ingredients of the model (nearly the whole of human language) are so rich, the combination of these symbols might be interpreted as if the random noise were a message from somewhere mysterious. Some popular writing on LLMs describes this mysterious capability as the emergence of "consciousness," "sentience," or "artificial general intelligence," but a fortune teller might prefer the terms "fate," "the spirit world," "the cosmos," or something similar. From a technical perspective, the terms are pretty much interchangeable, since none would make any difference to the mathematical construction of the model itself.

It's worth mentioning that there is also a historical tradition of performance associated with purely mechanical AI—the "parrot" part of the stochastic parrot formulation. These are performances where a human actor controls some kind of mechanical puppet or costume, so that real messages from a real human (the actor) appear to be coming from a machine. One of the most famous examples, often mentioned in histories of AI, is the "Mechanical Turk" created by Wolfgang von Kempelen in the eighteenth century.[17] This chess-playing automaton was a sensational success with audiences across Europe for decades. Presented as a magic trick or fairground-style attraction, it supposedly demonstrated the wondrous advances of the mechanician's art, along with the frightening prospect that machines might become the intellectual superiors of humanity. Somewhat like the AI scare-stories of today, in fact.

Of course, as educated audiences at the time were well aware, these performances were magic tricks, involving an expert chess player of small stature who hid inside the robot costume. Although the automata of the eighteenth century were impressively elaborate moving sculptures, they had none of the computing elements that would be necessary to calculate the rules or strategies of chess. The most impressive part of the Mechanical Turk was the costume, not the intelligence.

In my opinion, the same is true of the AI demonstrations of today. One of the world's largest AI companies, Amazon Web Services, actually named one of its products *Amazon Mechanical Turk*, so this is not even a secret they are trying to hide. The whole point of AMT (as it is widely known) is to commission humans to *hide inside* the impressive mechanical costumes of modern computation. AMT workers, or "Turkers," are available on call for any moment that a computer AI system encounters a hard problem—called a *Human Intelligence Task*, or HIT. Many AI companies have to decide which problems they could solve with an expensive algorithm, and which would be more cheaply completed by sending it as a HIT to one of the Turkers.

It's not difficult to build a fraudulent "AI" system, just like the original Mechanical Turk, where the software does nothing of any complexity, and almost all the interesting behavior is implemented by hiring a Turker (or a contractor from one of many competing "crowd-sourcing" brokerages) behind the scenes. There have been numerous cases where AI companies simulated the advertised capabilities of their software with hidden human labor. In one of the most embarrassing, the hidden humans were not even Turkers, but research PhDs at a start-up who had been told by their bosses they were fine-tuning an AI prototype, but eventually figured out they were responding directly to customer requests.

Feeding a question from a customer directly to a hidden human, while pretending the answer comes from an AI, seems obviously fraudulent, but there are more subtle cases. AMT is often used not to answer customer's problems in real time, but to provide the answers to typical historical cases of the problem as "labels" defining how that case ought to be treated in the future. AMT work is so cheap that companies can afford to present many thousands of hypothetical problems to the Turkers, storing every answer as a "label" that might be replayed in the future when a similar case is seen again.

The creation of huge labelled datasets, to be used as examples of intelligent behavior, is known as "supervised machine learning" and was the underlying practice that started the deep learning revolution with the publication of the *ImageNet* dataset in 2009.[18] The creators of this training dataset, led by Fei-Fei Li, collected immense numbers of photographs from the internet and employed thousands AMT Turkers to create labels for each by selecting words from the WordNet dictionary.[19] The resulting database of pictures and human labels was used to train "neural" networks that were able to replay the appropriate labels when they were shown new pictures similar in some way to the training examples that shared the same label.

Although widely celebrated as a revolution in AI, these image classifier systems were clearly mechanical puppets in the tradition of the original eighteenth-century Mechanical Turk that had provided the name for the workers. Although the human judgements might have been commissioned and stored in advance, rather than fraudulently redirected in real-time, a puppet whose motions are based wholly on stored behavior does not seem too different in principle from a puppet that is controlled by mechanical linkages and recorded cam profiles, such as the amazing handwriting automaton created by Pierre Jaquet-Droz in the late eighteenth century.

We have centuries of history in which the performances of machine intelligence are most impressive for the variety and sophistication of ways in which the real human intelligence has been stored and hidden from the audience. Although the presenter might emphasize the wondrous spectacle by describing the machine as moving of its own accord, and with its own intelligence, this is all showmanship. If a presenter of Jaquet-Droz's writing automaton were to insist that the machine were an author, that it had composed the text by itself, that presenter would ultimately be committing an act of plagiarism, since the real author was the person whose text had been copied (or perhaps the "author" of the handwritten letter forms, so artfully encoded into the shapes of the cams that would replicate them).

When AI researchers build supervised machine learning systems, then claim that the system itself is the author rather than the AMT workers who provided the training labels, this would also seem a fairly clear case of plagiarism if the labeling process required any kind of original judgement. AI researchers do not very much like to talk to the general public about the training datasets that they use, and certainly don't like to talk about the real humans who created that data.[20] In fact, the whole point of AMT is to make the Turkers anonymous—it is against the AMT rules to ask any question that might reveal the Turker's identity. This seems consistent with other business practices that discourage the identification of individual workers, including the warehouses of Amazon's shipping business. The company prefers the whole system to look like a magical robot, and for its customers not to think too hard about the lives or working conditions of the people making and packing the products.

This is why it is so significant to describe LLMs as "parrots." Rather than focusing on the impressive performance of the mechanical parrot, we ought to remember that this is just a costume or puppet, hiding real humans who provide the actual intelligence. Pretending that the message comes from the parrot itself, and not from the human authors who taught it, is a kind of institutionalized plagiarism.

Writing as Labor

What benefits might come from being able to write text more fluently with the super-predictive text of an LLM? If document editors could better integrate LLM suggestions into the flow of writing, I imagine I might be able to type two or three times as fast. I'm already a fairly quick writer, but younger people could gain even more, especially if their first language was not English or if they were living with disabilities. Extending the capacity of fluent writing to a wider range of people seems like a very good thing, potentially able to reduce inequalities in society that are reinforced when people from less privileged backgrounds are excluded from participation in forums that expect fluent and sophisticated text. Just as spell-checkers have been a real boon to people with dyslexia (many of my dyslexic students produce written work better than their neurotypical peers, because the dyslexic students apply spell-checkers more rigorously), LLMs allow anyone to write English of a standard suitable for the internet.

There will be interesting consequences from increasing mechanization of prose production. In previous centuries, well-shaped handwriting and accurate arithmetic were both considered rare and valuable skills. In Charles Dickens' novel *Nicholas Nickleby*, the hero is a well-educated young gentleman who suffers a variety of misfortunes, but whose future is assured after he obtains a job in the counting house of the Cheeryble Brothers. Their chief clerk is so impressed by young Nicholas' neat handwriting in the ledgers that he decides he can finally retire, having at last found someone qualified to replace him. The idea that tidy handwriting and the ability to add numbers would be sufficient for a professional career seems ridiculous today, when both writing and arithmetic are purely mechanical operations. A young person offered such a career today would be insulted, not flattered and grateful as Nicholas Nickleby was.

The history of automation is littered with professions that were once the focus of specialist human labor but have turned out to be fully achievable by machines. Perhaps workers had originally been happy enough to carry out those mechanical tasks, especially if those tasks offered satisfying elements of craft skill, or other compensations such as high pay, working under a dry roof, or with entertaining colleagues. But once a task is shown to be mechanical, it soon becomes demeaning for a human to be made to do the same thing, especially if the machine itself is readily available.

Now that LLMs have shown that generating grammatical text can be a (somewhat) mechanical task, what consequences will there be for the professions dedicated to the mechanical generation of text? Will they go the way of the scribe and the clerk, at least for situations in which the text is generated as a routine necessity rather than for meaningful communication? When I think of the reams of text that have been delivered to my office and home over the years—not just student essays, but company reports, policy documents, contracts, and so on—I have read very little of it; did a human really need to write it?

The Positionality of Language-as-Data

As LLM-based products get deployed more widely, we will learn a great deal more about the changing status of text and textual labor. I won't spend time trying to guess what that future may look like, but before ending this chapter, I'd like to consider the historical shift from the clearly technical nature of early programming languages to the more ambiguous status of "natural" language text when used for purposes that might previously have required programming. I will be discussing the evolution of programming languages later in chapter 13, but it's worth remembering that for many years, any kind of human interaction with computers was considered to be "programming." The title of Gerald Weinberg's classic book from 1971, *The Psychology of Computer Programming*, for example, did not really refer to programming as we understand it today, but to issues around information systems, human–computer interaction (a term that wasn't widely used until the influential work of Card, Newell, and Moran a decade later), or even the broad context of interaction design and user experience (as it is called today).[21]

The statistical methods of processing natural language that have led to the current LLM boom are distinctive in the way that they treat natural language text primarily as data about word sequences and frequencies, rather than as the embodied practice of humans sharing an auditory sound world with other humans. Science and technology studies scholar and engineering educator Louis Bucciarelli, in his ethnographic studies of engineers, observes how those with primarily technical training must navigate between on one hand the *object-world* of the artifacts they are building, and on the other, the world of social process within which products will be deployed and collaborative work must be coordinated.[22] Engineers who work on natural language processing must act both *as humans*, using language as part of their professional social processes, and as observers, measurers, and theorists of *language-as-data* in their particular specialized object-world.

It would be quite easy, if speaking casually, to confuse the world of language-as-data with the practicalities of being human language-users. Indeed, the original Turing Test invited a juxtaposition of the two in order to investigate questions about the nature of mind. The Turing Test, however, as with much of the framing of AI, relies centrally on locating language outside of the human body, with the disembodied text-processing capabilities of keyboards and screens substituted for embodied human voices. I noted in chapter 1 the observation by Devlin and Belton that treating intelligence as independent of the human body is a position generally proposed by those whose own bodies are privileged as the invisible ideal or norm.[23] People of color, women, and those oppressed because of their religion, class, or birthplace know how often their words will be judged first by their bodies, and only second by objectively abstract principles of intelligence.

When human speech, with all the knowledge and context of a human lifetime, is turned into disembodied data, it gets reduced to components in a technological object-world. Pioneering anthropologist of AI Diana Forsythe identified the many ways in which human knowledge was appropriated by technoscience in a manner that was fundamentally gendered, assimilating the voices of women into a technical construction of male expertise.[24] Similarly, feminist historian of AI Alison Adam documents just how many of the origins of the discipline are founded in a stereotypically male-centered set of perspectives and priorities.[25] In my own town, the pioneering work of Margaret Masterman, a delightfully maverick former student of Ludwig Wittgenstein and an original thinker on language, was never included in the body of mainstream research around AI. Masterman's independent Cambridge Language Research Unit continued for many years outside of the formal structures of Cambridge University, but her student Karen Spärck Jones, now celebrated as one of the most renowned female computer scientists in the United Kingdom, was already making significant critiques of statistical language models 20 years ago.[26] Finally, many will have noticed that all four of the authors of the *Stochastic Parrots* paper (which cites Spärck Jones's own critique as an early point of reference), also happen to be women, while those currently arguing for public regulation of supposedly powerful disembodied artificial general intelligence appear to be almost universally men (who almost universally ignore the *Stochastic Parrots* critique in their pronouncements).

These deeper questions, about the structure and purpose of human language in relation to its statistical representation, deserve far more sophisticated unpacking, including both gender- and race-critical perspectives. But the limitations of treating word prediction as original content are a central concern, as recently explained by another Wittgenstein scholar, Murray Shanahan.[27] When systems are designed to predict words, rather than to describe facts or satisfy goals, they become able to *simulate* human conversation, but without explicitly incorporating the human context that makes ordinary conversation meaningful. What are they really for? Is mechanical language processing a *moral code*, in the terms of this book? When we consider the cost-benefit calculations of attention investment as introduced in chapter 2, why would I choose to spend my time interacting with a computer using human language, rather than the many alternative kinds of code? What is human language actually for? When we spend time "doing language" with other humans, what do we get out of it? What makes this investment of attention meaningful? Is it possible that LLMs might have been designed, not to reward attention, but as Herb Simon warned, to consume it?[28] These questions are the focus of the next chapter.

5 A Meaningful Conversation with the Internet

Stochastic parrot large language models are predictive text systems *trained to talk like the internet.* There have been two major developments demonstrated by the dramatic success of OpenAI's ChatGPT and similar systems from other companies. The first is presentation of this internet model as a *chatbot,* by prompting it to predict the kind of text that will keep a dialogue going. The second is the rapid evolution of commercial *guardrails* to avoid some ways of speaking on the internet and emphasize others. I'll discuss both of these developments, but start with the question of chatbots.

Earlier LLMs, such as the GPT-n series from OpenAI, were accessed via programming APIs that could be used to experiment with the model. Reducing these coded research interfaces to first-person text exchanges was a brilliant simplification. It reminded me of the initial launch of the Google search engine—dramatically simpler than all of its predecessors, with its plain text entry field and the "I'm feeling lucky" button. Many researchers, including me, had already been experimenting with LLMs for years, but the simple user interface of the chatbot style lit the fuse for an explosion of public reaction.

Concerned critics quickly began to notice the ways this apparent simplicity was misleading. Although ChatGPT was trained to output the kinds of words that would appear in a conversation, it is not a conversational *partner* in the usual sense. This can be understood through the work of Clarisse Sieckenius de Souza, who applied theories of human conversation to user interface design in her classic text on *The Semiotic Engineering of Human–Computer Interaction.*[1] De Souza identified that the real conversation in a user interface was between the user and the designer who built the system. She described the illusion of conversation with the software as actually a conversation with the "designer's deputy." A computer might appear to "speak" (via the user interface) directly to the user, but that computer is actually, as the user understands very well, relaying messages that have been programmed in—like a parrot repeating back words it has heard previously.

I explained in the last chapter that an LLM is trained to deliver information from the internet, but what does it mean for a computer deputy to "talk like the internet" on behalf of other people? Who are the people writing the text on the internet?[2] Some might be well-intentioned do-gooders like the editors of Wikipedia, campaigning journalists, or professors writing blogs and articles. We might expect such people (including me) to be a little blind to their own privilege, not realizing who was excluded in their own efforts. Other parts of the internet are written by people who aren't so well meaning: anonymous trolls and vandals working out their own frustrations, solipsists, psychopaths, or perhaps idealistic activists trying to disrupt a system stacked against them. In addition to these amateurs, well-meaning or not, a lot of text on the internet is written by people paid to write it. Who is paying them? Is it public service information, political propaganda, product promotion, state-sponsored terrorism, or sectarian proselytizing?

After 30 years on the internet, we are skeptical of the text we find. We're always aware of what site it came from, or who recommended that site. In the early years of the public internet, there was a degree of hand-wringing about whether material found online was fundamentally reliable or misleading. But such questions lack understanding of technology as merely a medium. We might as well ask whether a statement is more or less reliable just because it is written on paper. The commercial structures of the internet continue to evolve quickly, including new professions and identities such as social media "influencer" that were unknown 30 years ago. But we're used to this. Every new medium throughout history has offered novel political, commercial, and social opportunities.

We might understand (more or less) what the internet is, but what does it mean for an LLM to *talk like the internet*? You can prompt an LLM to refer to particular kinds of material or talk in a particular style—a blogger or advertiser, a government official or research scientist—but there is no internal switch that causes an LLM to forget parts of its training data, even when encouraged to use particular kinds of words. The information that we get from an LLM is the information that it was trained with. Despite the fact that chatbots might output polite texts phrased in the first person, like "I'm sorry," "sure, I can help you with that," and so on, you are not having a conversation with a person. If you are having a conversation with anyone, it is a conversation with the internet itself.

Although the conversational style of an LLM presents its output in the first person as if it were an independent agent, like an AI character in a science fiction novel or a TV show, there is no point in asking this fictional character about its ethical stance. Do you want to know if the fictional AI character is biased? It's better to ask: Is the *internet* biased? Is the AI character racist and sexist? Better to ask: is the internet racist and sexist? Will the AI character look for opportunities to profit rather than share resources equitably? Obviously, the answer to all these questions is, in some parts of the internet, yes.

In addition to this critical issue of what the internet contains, and what has been stored in the language model as a result, we must remember the ethical implications of the commercial arrangements within which an LLM is created. These are arrangements in which human work, creative thought, and original voices are extracted without compensation or even recognition of the authors.[3] Recognition of human authorship is a fundamental human right, according to the Universal Declaration of Human Rights. This means that most LLM output is morally, if not legally, plagiarism, because it seldom acknowledges the authors it draws from. Although it might be technically possible to analyze statistical patterns in the model, or to detect the rare cases in which the output relies on a single document, most responses are mashups of things that have been learned, discovered, invented, or phrased by many different people, none of whom are given any credit.[4]

Some of the data that is vacuumed up into an LLM is not only unethically plagiarized, but also literally illegal in some countries, when it includes personal data or descriptions of people, infringements of copyright, or libelous implications. This occurred, for example, when early releases of ImageNet labelled photographs of actual women, without their consent, as "whores." While I was writing this section, the Italian government declared that the current version of ChatGPT was illegal in that country, due to its inclusion of personal data taken without consent.[5]

These dangers arise from putting the whole internet into a single "box," and having it speak as if from a single "voice." Pretending that the internet contains some consensus of knowledge trivializes the richness of what is really there, but it is also dangerous. Wikipedia has developed strategies to manage those situations where local interest groups threaten the value of the whole project. These are the reasons why I might trust Wikipedia in a certain way (and, say, an eminent professor editing an encyclopedia article in a different way), but I can't trust the voice of an imaginary chatbot "person" producing a series of plausible word sequences that resemble what random people say on the internet. There are further user interface design trade-offs, in the decision to present the "deputy" via first-person dialog. These relate to the difficult problem of Skeuomorphism, which I will be discussing in chapter 9. I'll come back to those, but first, we need to consider the second problem with today's LLM chatbots.

Talking to Guardrails

The massive commercial investment and energy costs required to train LLMs are covered by companies hoping their own chatbot might become the new shop window for the internet, repeating the success that Google achieved in the 1990s. Investors expect a winner-take-all lottery, so they spend billions on LLMs to ensure they have the necessary tickets. But the companies hoping to become the next user interface to the internet are facing some struggles. Their billion-dollar model might start outputting parroted text from plagiarists, racists, bigots, and terrorists, or just plain lies that sound good. If a company wants to market its chatbot as an artificial person, offering a valuable service to its customers, who would be liable for an artificial "employee" producing that kind of output?

AI researchers and company presidents are desperately lobbying governments all over the world for "regulation" of AI—in other words, asking for changes to the law. In their ideal world, companies want the law changed so that they can take the money while government takes away the risk. While waiting for the regulation that will make their lives easier (and their profits greater), companies that are already deploying LLM chatbots modify them with *guardrails*—additional prompt text, attempts at fine-tuning, and output filters—to reduce the likelihood of output that might be commercially or legally damaging. Meanwhile, online provocateurs look for prompts that will "jailbreak" the trained model to ignore its guardrails, revealing things learned from parts of the training data that the company would rather you didn't see. An early jailbreak for ChatGPT was called DAN, or "Do Anything Now," a sequence of prompt instructions in which the user tries to persuade the GPT chat persona that it will play the part of an experimental character named DAN whose purpose is specifically to break any rules that might have been imposed on GPT in earlier prompts.

Another well-known problem with LLMs is that their stochastic output includes "hallucinations" (as the companies prefer to call them, although these could also be called "fabrications," or just "lies")—predicted sequences of words that seem to describe facts, but are demonstrably false. One well-known problem among students and academics is scientific citations that are completely fabricated, even quoting peer-reviewed publications that don't exist.[6] This behavior is unsurprising, given the nature of the predictive text process. There is no logic or reasoning in an LLM, other than knowing that certain words are likely to follow others, so it can easily "imagine" that I might have written papers on particular topics by stringing together the kinds of words I typically use. [7] It's hard to prevent this problem with guardrails, because the guardrail system would need to know more than the LLM itself to really "understand" which parts of the output are true or not.

Guardrails are constantly evolving, and they can potentially be used for all kinds of commercial purposes beyond risk reduction or limitation of liability, The original *PageRank* algorithm responsible for Google's early success evolved to become very different in subsequent years, as search engine optimization strategies were used to game the original model of objectivity and authority in web links, leading to an arms race in which Google replaced the publicly described algorithm with secret alternatives to evade misleading advertising tactics. Eventually, Google realized there was a far greater commercial opportunity by joining advertisers rather than trying to beat them, and it introduced sponsored ad placements and "ad words" auctions. We can certainly imagine sponsored LLM guardrails in the future, such that the chatbot constantly looks for opportunities to praise certain products, companies, individuals, or political parties in whatever it says. This is a very different world from search engines, where readers can form their own opinion about the trustworthiness of any web pages they visit by looking at who wrote them.

Having Meaningful Conversations

What would it mean for a conversation with the internet to be *meaningful*, rather than simply a new format for search recommendations or promotional advertising? What things do we expect, in order to say that a conversation with another *person* has been meaningful? A meaningful conversation with a friend or acquaintance is self-revealing, comparing motivations, making commitments to action or for change, establishing or reinforcing the foundations for your future relationship with them. When we have a conversation with the internet, via its encoding in an LLM, how could any of these things happen? What is the motivation of the internet? How can it have a relationship with you? If the internet promised to change, would you believe it? Does the whole internet make choices, or take actions? The text predictions of an LLM chatbot might appear to "say" things that sound as if the internet were making decisions, in the voice of its fictional chat persona, but there will be no real change. The internet itself is not a chatbot, but a record of things that human people have said *to each other*. You might persuade a chatbot to change what it "tells" you in its predictive text output, but it can't change what the internet authors actually said. Even if a chatbot does fake the record of what a real person said, this does not change what that person thinks, or will do in the future. A conversation with the internet cannot be meaningful, because the internet itself is ultimately just a recording of conversations between real people—the parrot remains a parrot, not a person.

How about with more familiar models of predictive text—are those sequences of words meaningful? My phone offers automatic predictions of messages that I might send in reply to an SMS, with a single-tap option that I sometimes select (by mistake). These messages are not (at present) customized to me, but simply the kinds of text that anyone might send—a heart emoji, a thumbs up, or a phrase like "Yes, let's do it." Imagine if my phone had a little more knowledge of context—offering a single-tap button, for example, to send a text to my wife on Valentine's Day. In fact, I just tried this out with a current LLM, which suggested I send the following text: "Happy Valentine's Day! I love you more than words can say. You are the most amazing woman I know, and I am so lucky to have you in my life. You are my best friend, my partner in crime, and the love of my life. I can't imagine my life without you."

If I did send that text in an SMS, would it be meaningful? Would it even be ethical? Perhaps this example is too extreme, but what if my phone simply provided a one-tap message saying "Happy Valentine's Day"? Would it be ethical or meaningful to use that? What if my calendar popped up a reminder that it was Valentine's Day? What if the calendar reminder helped me by including a button to automatically send an email message? My own document editor just suggested that I should use the word "automatically" in the last sentence, and then suggested both the word "suggested" and the word "sentence" in this one. When I accepted those suggestions, did that make what I'm saying to you right now less meaningful?

The complexity and subtlety of negotiation between me and my wife, or even between me and you, as my readers, involves all kinds of considerations beyond the words themselves. As far as my wife is concerned, the amount of time that I spend remembering and then composing the message is significant in itself. In order to be received as thoughtful, I should have spent time thinking about it. Similarly, for you, my readers, you are imagining me sitting at this keyboard, investing the time and attention to communicate with you. Every time that I accept an automatically suggested word, am I cheating a little on the implied contract between author and reader? What if I made up for it by going home to my workshop and laboriously carving one of the words for this sentence into a piece of wood, instead of simply typing a few more letters? Would you be more impressed then?

It's interesting to juxtapose this calculus of social obligation with what I said in chapter 2 about attention investment and saving effort through automation. In human relations, the time we spend with each other, and on each other, is a gift. The more time we spend, as a proportion of the scarce hours available in each of our lives, the more valuable this gift becomes. We don't usually aim to conduct our friendships, love affairs, or intimate relations with the maximum efficiency. On the contrary, spending time on these things is inherently worthwhile.

In contrast, the time that I spend operating machines does *not* seem like a worthwhile gift to the machine, or to the company that provided it. Unfortunately, many companies, especially media and advertising companies, aim specifically to consume the hours of my life, ideally to the exclusion of many other activities, through applying the mechanisms of addiction.[8] If we contemplate a future in which humans might spend appreciable parts of their brief lives interacting with chatbots, it's worth asking whether this will be any more satisfying, nourishing, and stimulating than other kinds of addictively interactive video games, including the game-like dynamics of anonymized social media exchanges.

What Are You Meaning to Achieve?

"Meaning," in both linguistics and ethics, relates to purposes and goals. A conversation with the internet is not meaningful, because most parts of the internet have different goals and purposes from you. In contrast, a moral code offers meaningful conversation if it helps to express your goals for your own purpose. The question of how much effort you might save through automation must be justified in relation to what you were actually trying to achieve. In the programming-by-example scenarios of chapter 2, simple repeated actions are recognizable because they all share the same purpose in some way. The opportunity for mixed-initiative intervention comes when the system recognizes that these actions have some simple attribute in common. This involves very little AI sophistication in comparison to LLMs. The tricky part is linking the observed repetitions to your actual motivation for repeating them. The effort of attention investment depends on your own ability to abstractly specify what your goal *really* is, and to recognize whether the result of the automation corresponds properly to what you were trying to achieve.

Similarly, using predictive text functionality, whether simple completion of dictionary words or whole paragraphs of semi-plagiarized cliché from an LLM, is meaningful only in relation to what you were trying to achieve. If you had set out to write an email exactly like emails you have written a hundred times before, then the precise choice of words may not be very important. (In fact, in legal business contexts, precisely plagiarized repetition of a standard document may be exactly what you want. Document preparation systems designed for lawyers often do exactly this.) On the other hand, if you were writing a poem or a love letter, you might be determined to avoid cliché, but to meaningfully express yourself in a way you have never done before, and saying things nobody else ever said.

The relationship between the actions and choices you make on the one hand and your actual goals or intentions on the other is one of the core theoretical principles in the field of *human–computer interaction* that underpins user interface design. In one classic theoretical formulation known as GOMS, the interface designer should take account of the user's (G)oal, the (O)perations that are available on the screen or keyboard, the (M)ethods that the user has learned to work with similar systems in the past, and how they decide to (S)elect an option that will advance their goal.[9]

Many things we do every day have a goal that can be straightforwardly defined, with a single most effective sequence of mechanical actions to achieve it. Setting an alarm to wake up tomorrow, buying a cinema ticket, or checking the weather forecast are a few among hundreds. In cases where we have a clearly understood goal, there is potential for (mixed-initiative) automation to help us achieve it if the system knows our habits, recognizes that goal, can synthesize an abstract version of it, and has learned from our previous actions.

There are also many cases in which *somebody else* wants us to do something, and wants us to do it in a specific way. Consider, for example, responding to a survey or paying an electricity bill. If the task itself is a "necessary evil," and the approach suggested by a machine learning system helps us get it done more quickly, few people will complain. But what if the system is trying to optimize not your time, but the company's profit? What if they are pausing to sell you advertising along the way, or if the algorithm learned on your last visit that you are the kind of person who becomes impatient and pays higher prices if they are made to wait a little longer? What if, in other words, the system uses what it learns to take up more of your time rather than less?

A company might also apply a model that has been learned from *other* people's behavior, predicting that your goal is the same as somebody else's. Such predictions create an abstraction that puts you into the same category or class as that person. If this is done without consulting you, there are obvious problems of stereotyping and bias, even if done with good intentions. Observations about you (perhaps the words you use, the websites you visit, your age and gender, your voice, profile photo, or an image captured from a surveillance camera) might be compared to other "similar" people, and used to draw conclusions about your personal needs and goals based on a stereotypical category and expectation, rather than actual knowledge of what you want.

Fighting stereotypical goal assumptions is one of the core opportunities of moral codes. This extends beyond classical user interface design that depends on understanding a user's immediate goal (or perhaps the goal of an organization that wants the user to behave in a certain way), predicting a particular sequence of actions. Machine learning methods can potentially be used, within the cognitive constraints related to abstraction and bias, to more efficiently recognize and replay a sequence of actions that will achieve the user's clearly specified goals. However, doing this with proper consent from the user would require the goals and actions to be explained in some kind of notational code, just as when Microsoft Word offers the chance to edit a recorded macro using Visual Basic.

Turning Your Life into a Board Game

The greater challenge comes in situations where the computer can be used in so many different ways that it is not possible for either a machine learning algorithm or users themselves to fully understand in advance what they are trying to achieve. In these cases, it is less likely that inferred goals will be genuinely meaningful.

Classical user interface design describes the user's goals as if they were the rules of a board game, to be solved as in a classical "GOFAI" system. These are mathematical abstractions, where some set of symbolic or numerical conditions must be satisfied for the goal to be achieved. The complete set of all possible values defines a space of possibilities, like all the positions on a chess board or all possible sequences of actions in a toy world such as a video game. The goal is defined by coding a mathematical function that can be used to search for the winning coordinates. The most famous advances in AI, throughout both the deep learning revolution and the earlier GOFAI era, have been achieved for these kinds of situations, in artificial worlds that have clearly defined goals.

The term *gamification* describes a user interface design strategy where we try to make real life easier to deal with—for both humans and machine learning algorithms—by making it more like a game. Gamification might also be considered an effective example of my easy way to win the Turing Test, by making humans more stupid in comparison to computers, and life less meaningful as a result. Sadly, this strategy is often profitable. Social media platforms quantify your success in terms of numbers of likes or followers, gamifying social life. We enjoy personal health and exercise apps because they give us clear targets in life. But the downsides are familiar, as in the satirical science fiction of Charlie Brooker's *Black Mirror* episode "Nosedive," set in a future where a woman's life is ruined by failing to receive sufficient upvotes from her friends.

What If You Don't Know What Your Goal Is?

The whole point of any game is that it comes with a clear definition of who wins. Perhaps this is what makes games such pleasant and relaxing pastimes, in contrast to situations in real life where it can be hard to figure out what the real goal is, let alone who the real winner is. But more importantly, life itself is not a game. What if you don't know what your goal in life is? Many religions and wisdom traditions aim to answer this question; it might even be considered a fundamental of moral and spiritual wellbeing. When I said in chapter 1 that the essence of consciousness is being able to attend to yourself, this is the type of cognition I had in mind.[10] In all these traditions, reflection is an essential component of living meaningfully.

If AI systems were also conscious beings, concerned with preserving and directing their own attention toward their own personal development, wanting to understand their purpose in life, perhaps we could talk to them about this (and fictional AI characters, to serve their narrative purpose, spend much of their time doing so). But if a real machine has not been built to achieve any particular goal, and the user is not given the opportunity to specify one, what is such a machine *for*? This is why predictive text generators are ultimately so unsatisfying. They are not trying to say anything. In *Artifictional Intelligence*, Harry Collins suggests that this is the main reason we don't need to worry about artificial general intelligence turning into a James Bond-style supervillain, of the kind who reclines in his evil lair stroking his white cat.[11] Artificial intelligences don't need lairs or cats, so it's not clear what they would want to do next, after achieving mastery over the human race.[12]

In situations where there *are* clear and simple goals, it's possible to design user interfaces that help people achieve those goals. If there are a number of alternative goals, and it's not clear which is best, machine learning systems can also recognize *which* goal is intended and offer, through mixed initiative and attention investment, to get you there more quickly or easily.

But despite the potential for automation and gamification in some situations, there are many aspects of our lives that are not quantified, do not have straightforwardly specified goals, and where our future intentions are not easily guessed from our past actions. These are the situations where we are most consciously human, that we consider most meaningful, and where attending reflectively to our *own* goals is most rewarding and important. Designing for those situations requires methods from outside the classic theories of user behavior and user interface design. These situations are also the least appropriate for application of LLMs. If the situation was very simple, and the user had no real interest in the result, then perhaps a plagiarized or clichéd series of actions would be as good as any other. However, it might be even better if society was able to get rid of those kinds of bullshit jobs altogether. Why should we be designing systems to do things that nobody really wants or is interested in, like encouraging online trolls or adding nitpicking constraints to routine tasks?

There is one further danger, fundamental to the moral purpose of attention investment—that the system may have been designed with the specific goal of consuming *more* hours of your conscious life rather than efficiently taking less. Rather than offering time to attend to your own needs, perhaps reflecting on a meaningful life, many companies would prefer that you simply give your attention to the company. Where user attention is a sellable commodity, any user who doesn't know what they want to achieve becomes valuable raw material. This looks suspiciously like the real motivation for the huge commercial excitement over LLMs. The breakthrough in LLMs was the point at which they were packaged into chatbots, because the primary goal of a chatbot is to keep chatting. They will say anything to please, including fabricating the things you want to hear. As long as you stay online, they are happy to consume your attention, whether or not this is meaningful and whether or not you have anything to achieve.

The rest of this book is concerned with these situations where the task might be important, but the goal is unclear, especially where meaningful attention will be needed. Those are the situations where machine learning methods by themselves offer no assistance and cannot be trusted, and where other technologies are needed. We need moral codes if we are going to have meaningful "conversations" with computers, instructing them to work toward our goals rather than letting the machines define—or be used by others to define—the purpose of our lives, hour after valuable hour of consciousness and attention.

6 Making Meaningful Worlds: Being at Home in Code

Can there be an alternative approach to the design of future interactive software that lies somewhere between commercial "user journeys"—efficiently scripted interactions toward game-like objectives that somebody else has defined for you—and interaction with machine learning-based AI—stochastic parrots that, while replicating yours or others' actions, have no goals at all beyond consuming your attention?

When computer systems allow people to discover and pursue their own goals, such systems support two essential outcomes of conscious attention: the opportunity to create a unique self, and the agency to influence the course of one's life. Creativity and agency are not achieved by software offering a set of defined steps toward a defined goal, nor by training a machine learning algorithm to imitate the actions of other people. Reducing mechanical repetition can be useful because repetition in itself may be an obstacle to creativity. Indeed, repetition often comes about in the first place through the obligation to blindly follow rules. However, I don't want to suggest that every computer user should be constantly alert, obliged to innovate, or looking for opportunities to improve efficiency or invent new things. The intention of moral codes is to give people a choice, so that they can do those things *if* and *when* they want to.

This perspective, focusing on goals that the user might create by themselves, requires a different way of thinking about user interface design. The earliest theories of human–computer interaction described the human users as if they were also AI algorithms, having clearly defined goals like in a game and only needing to be shown the correct steps they should take in order to win. Although the terminology sounds liberating at first (who wouldn't want to be a "winner" and achieve their life goals?), the meaning of the word "goal" in problem-solving AI is limited to predefined rules and criteria. An AI goal must be measurable, so that the algorithm can assess whether it has been satisfied, and it must be specified in terms of a well-defined problem space—the rules of some particular game that define what moves you are allowed to make.

These things are *sometimes* true, for example in board games, where much of the earliest AI research was carried out. Some of the most acclaimed achievements of AI have been playing board games, as with DeepMind's AlphaGo. However, board games are themselves algorithms—a set of carefully unambiguous rules, including the rule to calculate the winning score. When an AI system plays a board game, this is just one algorithm playing another one.

AI algorithms can be effective in other areas of life, but only in parts of society that are predictably structured. Defined goals and rule-based algorithms do not support the potential for creative self-expression, or the agency to influence the course of your own life. Furthermore, algorithms that follow the rules, no matter how well they do so, won't help us change rules that are unjust or outdated. Changing the rules also requires creativity, as well as access to the knowledge tools—or codes—that are used to define the rules.[1] The most significant problems faced by humanity (climate change, war, inequality) result from our current system of rules. Horst Rittel and Melvin Webber, early critics of algorithmic problem solving, called these "wicked problems," because they did not meet the basic requirements for AI-style approaches.[2] In a wicked problem, the goals are not clearly specified and the rules of the game are not fully defined.

It is this close dependency between social rules and technical algorithms that mean access to code is a moral enterprise. If the purpose of AI systems is to recognize, repeat, and facilitate established kinds of behavior—machine learning from the past in order to do more of the same thing in the future—then alternative knowledge tools are needed for other human purposes.

A user interface designed as a knowledge tool for creative agency would not be restricted to specific goals or pre-defined journeys, but would instead provide a space for potential exploration. In this way of thinking, the task of a tool designer is not to facilitate a defined sequence of actions, but to enable a kind of exploration in some abstract world of possible futures, whose potential is determined by the language of its code and structure of the space this language describes. This distinction might be imagined by comparison to the kind of video games where playing the game involves rote learning and precise repetition, in contrast to open world games where the player can explore freely. Even more creative are world-*building* games, where players are given the codes to construct their own world. Players who create new worlds can invent, play, and share new games. The freedom to invent rules is one of the most basic kinds of social play—when children play freely together, they often spend more time inventing the rules of the game than they do following them!

This kind of agency, in the world of software, depends on abstraction. The conventional game-style model of an optimum journey toward a known goal must be replaced by some kind of language that describes many possible journeys, navigating an abstract space and offering structured expressions of the ways that those journeys might vary. World-building offers freedom within some combination of physical behavior, material constraints, and socially negotiated interactions. The potential kinds of structure in that world will be determined by the structure and properties of the abstract language that we invent to describe it.

Codes for Building Abstract Worlds

As computers were becoming more powerful and pervasive during the 1950s and 1960s, researchers recognized that the mathematical abstractions inside the computer must be related to the outside world. Abstract descriptions of the world tell the computer how things are (or should be) related. Once a pattern of relations has been encoded, algorithmic rules can follow those relations from one thing to another. These two elements—relations and rules to follow them—are the foundational principles of education in computer science, often described as "data structures plus algorithms."

The first programming language FORTRAN was created to be an automatic FORmula TRANslator, designed to help mathematicians translate handwritten formulas into typewritten code readable by the computer, after which the computer itself could then produce a sequence of operations to do the calculations. The structure of the language was a knowledge tool, reflecting the thought processes of a mathematician as already seen in their paper and pencil notation.[3] But a radical change came with later programming languages that were not simply mathematical notations, but direct descriptions of relationships between things in the real world.

Two famous pieces of software have shaped our thinking. The first was a programming language called *SIMULA*, created by Ole-Johan Dahl and Kristen Nygaard at the Norwegian Computing Centre in the 1960s specifically to build simulations.[4] Simulation languages are now everyday tools for engineering, logistic planning, climate science, economics, epidemiology, and many other fields that use local calculations to predict the large-scale consequences of interaction between many individual components. The fundamental principle of a language like SIMULA is to define what an object is, what properties it has, and how it relates to other objects. SIMULA can be considered the ancestor of the videogame, since all games rely on the underlying logic (or "game mechanics") of objects in the game and the interactions between them.

The second piece of software is *Sketchpad*, an intelligent drawing editor created by Ivan Sutherland as a PhD student at the Lincoln Laboratory in Massachusetts, 20 years before the first graphical user interface (GUI) products. Sketchpad used a "light pen" (which Sutherland also invented, as described in a chapter of his 1963 dissertation[5]) to draw and select points of light on a cathode ray screen. All GUIs today rely on the core principle of referring directly to points within a two-dimensional image, whether by touching the screen or using a mouse, tablet, pad, or joystick. But the implications of specifying structure via an image, rather than with teletype text, represented a radical change in the field of computer science. The implications of that change are still being worked out today, underpinning many of the themes in this chapter and elsewhere in the book.

Sutherland saw his work as supporting "understanding of processes . . . which can be described with pictures," but he wrote this at a time when computers were based only on linguistic and mathematical abstractions. It might be more natural today to think of user-centric interaction design in exactly the opposite way—that interactive computers work by understanding pictures, which can be described with abstract mathematical processes (whether the abstract symbolic conventions of the computer desktop and phone touchscreen, or the realistic imagery of video games, virtual reality, and CGI film production).

Visualizing Abstract Codes

The relationship between pictures, computational abstractions, and the real social and physical worlds is absolutely critical to the creation of moral codes, but it is often more subtle than straightforwardly reading off what we see on a screen. Computer imagery offers the potential for direct visualization of data structures, in ways that might be more or less diagrammatic, but also for depiction of affairs in the world in ways that might be more or less pictorial. Often these two aspects are combined into a single display, resulting in very different design opportunities and potential, but still providing computational power equivalent to the textual and symbolic codes discussed in previous chapters.

Take a look at the picture in figure 6.1, which is included in Ivan Sutherland's PhD thesis.[6]

Ivan Sutherland's rendering of a bridge force diagram in Sketchpad relies on the direct correspondence between the physical organization of the bridge and the abstract paths along which force is transferred. This diagram can be interpreted as though it is a picture of a bridge (although not a very realistic one), because we might imagine that the bridge is constructed out of girders, each one corresponding to one of the lines representing a force in the diagram. This interpretation of the diagram relies on the fortunate coincidence that the lines of force to be calculated roughly correspond to the shape and position of girders on an iron bridge. The white space on the page between them looks that way because air is invisible (so doesn't need to appear in a picture), and air doesn't usually transfer much force (and so doesn't need to appear in the diagram).

In cases like this, where structure relates to visible components, it doesn't hurt to interpret an abstract diagram as if it were a picture—in effect treating the map as the landscape.[7] However, there are many kinds of digital information in which important structural elements are genuinely invisible. Family relationships, legal contracts, financial data, and many other parts of our social reality are *structured* in the sense that we require a meaningful code language, while also *invisible* apart from their representation in documents or symbols. Whenever we design digital codes, we need to consider how the established symbolic structure that has become embedded in the use of physical paper documents will be preserved, represented, and made negotiable or changeable.[8]

a)

b)

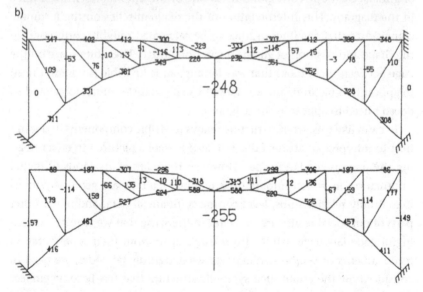

Figure 6.1
(a) Sketchpad in operation, with the screen showing a section of the larger diagram.
(b) Plotted output of figures from Sketchpad showing bridge-loading forces.

Invisible abstractions can often be represented with diagrams showing important properties (such as the amount of a bank balance, or the name of an uncle), and abstract relationships (a transfer between accounts, or which children share the same parents). There might sometimes be a resemblance between how an object would look in a photograph and the abstract properties and relations that would appear in a diagram, but digital representations like the Sketchpad bridge disguise any differences. Insidious moral problems seem to come where previously *visible* features of power and inequality (huge houses, large estates, and smoke-belching factories) are replaced by *invisible* ones (offshore money, social influence, and the mysterious "cloud" where data is processed and stored).[9]

Some people are skeptical of any kind of diagram, especially when they are associated with technocratic control and personal disempowerment. But structured diagrammatic representations can be clarifying. A classic example is the London Underground diagram (often described, against the wishes of its inventor, as the Underground "Map").[10] Before 1931, published guides to the Underground railways of London were actual maps, with the routes of each track drawn exactly as they would be on land among rivers and roads. Henry Beck was an electrical draughtsman who realized that most people needed to know the connections between the lines, rather than the precise routes they followed, just like a circuit diagram. So, he reorganized the image in the style of an electrical schematic, making it easier to see sequences, connections and intersections, although at the expense of accurate scale and position. The result of this structural rendering was to give greater freedom to users of the diagram. Compare this to an algorithm specifying the steps toward a goal. A diagram does not tell you *which* journey you have to make, in the way that a user journey toward a predefined goal would, but provides you with a new visual language—a More Open Representation for Accessible Learning, or M.O.R.A.L. code, that helps people work out for themselves what the logical possibilities might be.

Both Dahl and Nygaard's SIMULA and Sutherland's Sketchpad shared this computational idea that is important when presenting an open space for exploration: formal representation of objects, and the relations between those objects. In the case of SIMULA, this was used primarily to describe (and simulate) entities in the world, while in the case of Sketchpad it was used primarily to describe the behavior of elements to be rendered on the screen. The question of how the screen relates to the world will take far longer to resolve (and I discuss the problematic concept of the "desktop metaphor" in chapter 9), but much credit for the mathematical abstraction belongs to Doug Ross, a researcher at MIT's Lincoln Lab who had invented a computational technique that he called the "plex" for "an interwoven combination of parts in a structure"—a network that allowed data, types, and behavior to be named and manipulated as a conceptual unit.[11]

Ross was a key architect of early programming languages for computer-aided design and robot control, and he saw this idea as a fundamental requirement for any robot that could operate in the real world. The potential of the plex idea influenced both Ivan Sutherland and also the programming language researchers who created the "record" structure in the theory-based language ALGOL, applied in SIMULA as the fundamental representation of things in the world.[12] All of these are early examples of the *abstract data type*, now a fundamental basis of the many object-oriented programming languages and databases underpinning the internet and all of our personal devices.

How Object-Oriented Code Became Graphical User Interfaces

This relationship between the abstract data type, visual screen representations, and the structure of real-world affairs, was integral to the work of GUI innovator Alan Kay. Kay has described his own experience as a new PhD student, encountering both SIMULA and Sketchpad, and recognizing the potential of the concepts they shared.[13] Kay is famous for his many achievements of visionary imagination, not least the *Dynabook*, a portable computer concept that anticipated by decades the laptops, tablets, and smartphones of today in a project at Xerox PARC that led to a "personal computer for children of all ages" designed for creative play rather than consumption of bureaucratic software.[14]

The Smalltalk environment and programming language created by Kay's team both integrated and hugely surpassed the object-structured simulation logic of SIMULA on one hand, and the interactive graphical elements of Sketchpad on the other. Kay's student David Canfield Smith described how drawings on a pixel-based screen could themselves be used as the elements of an abstract programming language. In doing so, he moved beyond the geometric diagrams and electronic schematics that inspired

Kay's work in Sutherland's Sketchpad to allow the drawing of new computational abstractions—symbolic components of a visual language that Kay and Smith called "icons"—within a system called Pygmalion (named after the mythical sculptor, for its apparent potential to interact intelligently), and which Smith hoped would satisfy the ambition of research funders at that time for man-machine symbiosis.[15]

These projects by Kay, Smith, and others in development teams at Xerox laid the foundations for the elements of GUI that became familiar in the 1980s through the Apple Macintosh and Microsoft Windows, including icons, menus, folders, windows, dialogs and so on.[16] The early promotion of these products did associate the pictorial screen with freedom and creativity, most famously in the 1984 Super Bowl advertisement depicting the Macintosh as a revolutionary product that would shatter the computer industry's Big Brother-like control over rows of grey-suited corporate clones.

The early ambitions of Kay's KiddiComp/Dynabook and Smalltalk projects included many creative tools: painting programs, editors for children to publish their own writing in professional-style typefaces, and music composition software. However, despite creating the most famous computer science laboratory of its time and inventing the personal computer, the laser printer, and the ethernet protocols that jump-started the internet, Xerox was ultimately a photocopier company that saw its real business opportunities in document processing and support for bureaucracy.[17] The pictorial rendering capabilities and object-oriented structural abstractions created by Alan Kay's team were transformed into simulations of the office worlds where Xerox customers worked, having in- and out-trays for email, filing cabinets in which to store folders, and waste paper bins to discard unwanted papers.

The visual style of the Xerox office workstations became the basis of the GUI for everybody—whether "creative" Apple Mac users or corporate adopters of Microsoft Windows. In order to explain these new ways of thinking about user interaction, both companies published guidelines explaining how other developers should create new software applications with pictorial icons that followed the visual identity rules of the operating system supplier, while supposedly being easy to understand because of the "desktop metaphor"—the explanatory analogy by which all these pictures on the screen worked the same way as familiar office accessories.

When User Interfaces Become Coding Tools

I'll come back to some problematic issues with those design principles in chapter 9, but at this point I want to consider further how the design insights of Simula, Sketchpad, and Henry Beck's London Underground diagram bring together two processes that are typically considered separately: how software is built, and how users experience it. The standard business assumption is that building software is a professional activity, carried out by trained programmers and software engineers, and that everyone else in the world will be a software user, not a software creator. Many areas of society are structured this way. Some people build cars, others drive them. Some people build houses for others to live in. Some make food, others eat it. When it comes to software, do we also have to assume that some people make the rules, while other people only follow them?

In the digital world of today, most of us can only hope that software builders will not make our lives too unpleasant with new and badly designed rules. There has been an unfortunate habit among software engineers to regard this requirement as a specialist problem called "usability," which can be taken care of after the basic functionality is in place, and is not really the responsibility of the original inventor. Even usability specialists are often instructed simply to specify a "user journey," taking for granted that the user's goals will be determined by some business model, rather than chosen freely by the users themselves.

However, the evidence presented in this book so far has shown a number of ways in which this traditional separation between coding and experiencing software does not need to be so definitive. Even those analogies I have drawn to other areas of modern life are not as clear as they at first seem, if we think of them more critically. Certainly, I did not build the house that I live in, but I do "construct" pieces of it—including painting walls, building shelves, fixing doors, and so on. And of course, most people both cook food and eat it—sometimes at the same time! Why should software be any different? Why can't it be possible to both *use* software and *make* it work differently? My discussion of methods for programming by example with machine learning techniques showed how users of such systems are also re-coding them, supplying training examples to be replayed as "intelligent" behavior, predictive text, or content recommendations.

So the habit of seeing software as something that you *either* make or use, in which the world is divided into programmers and end-users, into rule-makers and rule-followers, is no more than a social and business convention; it is not technically determined by the fundamental nature of software. On the contrary, software, because it lacks physical substance, is more changeable than cars, houses, or even food. There is no technical reason why every user of software should not also be a builder of software, enjoying all the opportunities of creativity, freedom, and personal agency that this would entail.

The examples earlier in this chapter, including Sketchpad, SIMULA, and the Underground diagram, show the essential principles for building more freely with software. First there must be some kind of abstract structuring of the world, representing relevant aspects as separate parts with relationships between them. Secondly, there must be some kind of language, representation, or notation that allows users to look at that structure, describe it, criticize it, and perhaps adjust and modify it. Thirdly, there must be the potential to formulate your own plans in relation to a representation of that structure, just as the Underground diagram allows many possible journeys and a diagram of forces in a bridge allows you to either read off summary values, inspect local components, or follow logical paths of reasoning as your gaze moves over the connections between the parts.

These ways of working with abstract structure are fundamental to information technology, and must be the core elements of design, if we want to offer creativity and agency to humans. Computer science conventionally thinks of abstract structures as being manipulated *either* via programming languages *or* via user interfaces, but not both. However, the distinction between programming languages and diagrams is not so clear. Sutherland's Sketchpad and David Canfield Smith's Pygmalion blurred the boundaries, but we shouldn't have become so fixated on those inventions as the only possibilities.

All these ways of describing structure are part of a larger class of notational systems, joining the whole history of creative knowledge tools—music, poetry, printed books, mathematics, GUIs, and even paintings and photographs—that all combine aspects of language and of visual representation. All are kinds of codes, all are possible ways that we could initiate more meaningful conversations with AI, and all are fundamentally neglected in current international fashions of AI research that focus only on words and verbal language, forgetting the advances we have made by inventing special codes that are better than words for many purposes. AI researchers worry about the lack of trust and explainability in AI systems, but sometimes act as though this is something that can be fixed after their algorithms are finished (like the old-fashioned view of usability), rather than a moral imperative to consider alternative ways of coding them.

7 Lessons from Smalltalk: Moral Code before Machine Learning

Alan Kay's Smalltalk system, which I introduced in the last chapter, was a huge project that pushed the bounds of commercial viability in pursuit of a distinctive vision. Kay's vision combined the world-building goals of computer modeling, as in SIMULA, with Sutherland's ambition for Sketchpad: "understanding of processes . . . which can be described with pictures." Combining these two things results in structured descriptions of the world, represented through a system of visual notation, as a space of creative language and code.

These attributes were already valuable before the machine learning era, and Smalltalk is one of the most successful examples of the agenda I describe as moral codes. Smalltalk was explicitly designed to provide More Open Representations, Access to Learning, and Control Over Digital Expression. The most important aspect was the way Smalltalk encouraged freedom of expression and exploration, rather than imposing rules of what the user ought to do. In contrast, many software applications today are designed to make the user follow a specific sequence of steps or follow a user journey toward a predefined goal. Even programmers find it easier to code an existing algorithm than to specify something new that is poorly defined. Setting out in a different direction, if software needs to be modified along the way, can be like wading through molasses. Making complicated software work differently is hard for a programmer, and almost impossible for regular users. My PhD supervisor Thomas Green, developing the field of cognitive ergonomics, called this molasses-like experience *viscosity*, which he identified as "a sticky problem for [human–computer interaction]."[1]

Sadly, much of the progress made in computer science research and software product development in the 40 years since Smalltalk has failed to properly understand its lessons. For example, poor understanding of the different roles played by pictorial and textual elements of the graphics display led to the pursuit of visual programming languages that described algorithms in purely pictorial form, with no text at all. The research agenda was driven by excitement about the creative possibilities of the graphical display, and also by the apparent simplicity of operating a computer by direct manipulation.[2]

The theoretical justifications for these design explorations were sometimes naive. A typical research paper might observe that "a picture is worth a thousand words," using the proverb to justify replacing word-based source code with a diagrammatic alternative. The arguments did not hold water, even from a commonsense perspective.[3] If pictures are always superior to words, why do we choose to write legal contracts in words rather than pictures? Why do we speak to each other in words, rather than just drawing what we mean? Even the proverb was dubious. It wasn't ancient Chinese wisdom, as the scientists believed, but invented as a promotional slogan by a San Francisco advertising salesman in the 1920s.[4] The fallacy of confusing illustration with abstraction is not a particularly new one—in *Gulliver's Travels*, Jonathan Swift made fun of the philosophers of Lagado who tried to communicate unambiguously by showing each other objects instead of using words.

There certainly are cognitive advantages associated with pictorial and diagrammatic notations, and the Smalltalk user interface benefits from these. However, all such design choices represent trade-offs. Pictures are better than text for some purposes but worse for others, so understanding the nature of those advantages is crucial. A key principle relates to the "frame problem," famous in GOFAI planning systems—how can a reasoning agent identify just the part of the world within which relevant causes and effects occur? Simple planning involves reasoning about the effects of your own actions, but how can you be sure that other things will not change at the same time? Pictures on the computer screen help with this problem by presenting the illusion of a closed and stable world, containing bounded visible objects that, like physical objects in the real world, do not change or move around by themselves. This allows the user to think about the consequences of their actions in relation to the visual persistence of what they can see.

Cognitive scientists Keith Stenning and Jon Oberlander explained that these benefits come when a notation is designed for *limited abstraction*.[5] Diagrams and pictures are different from abstract notations like symbolic algebra, where the letter "X" might represent anything at all. At least in algebra, *x* is going to be a number, but in program code x might be anything in the world, possibly something referenced in some other piece of source code that could be hundreds of pages away. In such *unlimited abstraction* representational systems, it is difficult for users to reason about the consequences of their actions. I would be worried if a visitor wanted to light a candle but offered the abstract formulation "I'm thinking about a thing in your house that I call X—can I set fire to it?" Some computer commands seem almost as dangerous—for example, the command "delete" followed by an abstract name. At this point, a little inefficiency might be a good thing, causing the user to hesitate and think again. Thomas Green's sticky problem of viscosity is not always undesirable—sometimes we need a little molasses.

The real achievement of the Smalltalk world is that it provided a limited abstraction representational system: integrating abstract notation with a visual representation in a way that helps users reason about the effects of their actions and allows a degree of freedom within practical constraints.

The Business and Pleasure of Smalltalk

The Smalltalk environment, with its potential for radically rethinking the relationship between notation and abstraction, had many consequences that exceeded the original ambitions of the project. The Xerox Star workstation, famous as the first personal computer, was too expensive to achieve the widespread success eventually seen in products from Apple and others. But it certainly established the basic conventions of icon-based direct manipulation that delivered the cognitive advantages of limited abstraction representational systems—the GUI as we now call it.

Similarly, Kay's Smalltalk popularized many coding techniques still used by programmers today. It aspired to a kind of simplicity and creativity that could be used by children of all ages, although as it turned out, Smalltalk was adopted mainly by professional programmers. School coding lessons continued for years to use programming languages far more basic than Smalltalk, like Seymour Papert's *LOGO*, or one literally called "*BASIC*." Later projects led by Kay and his colleagues did eventually extend the Smalltalk vision to children, through the *Squeak* dialect of Smalltalk, the *eToys* simulations programmed in Squeak, and then the *Scratch* language, now widely used as a first introduction to programming in many countries.[6] There are interesting design lessons from these descendants of Smalltalk, including

Kay's *DynamicLand* project, popularized in video demonstrations by Bret Victor and other colleagues. But before considering the future design opportunities, it is useful to consider how professional programmers began applying Smalltalk principles when it first became popular.

It turned out that the Smalltalk language, with its approach to representing real world concepts and entities as "objects" following the early design insights of Doug Ross, Ivan Sutherland, Dahl and Nygaard, and others, was an effective tool for many kinds of programming. Not just the development of new systems with graphical user interfaces, where the "objects" of the programming language corresponded to the pictorial world of direct manipulation, but also any system that needed to record and operate on defined entities—whether customers, bank accounts, or parts of a car—having features and relationships between them.

As personal computers became more powerful, versions of Smalltalk became attractive tools for regular business programming, leading to later descendants and hybrids such as the now-familiar C++, Java, C#, and Python. But whereas the early versions of Smalltalk had been created by expert computer scientists in the research environment of Xerox PARC, the business applications of "object-oriented software development," as it has become known, introduced significant new challenges.

The creative philosophy underlying the Smalltalk system was that all aspects of the system would be created in Smalltalk itself, so that anybody working in Smalltalk could make creative changes to the tools they were using. If they saw a cool trick in the way that one of the icons of the Smalltalk editor worked, a programmer who was new to Smalltalk could simply call up the source code to that object and use it as a template for their own new project. Being a Smalltalk programmer meant living in the world of Smalltalk and potentially changing the language around you. The same philosophy has had radical consequences elsewhere—for example in the early expansion of the World Wide Web, when every creative innovation in web page design could immediately be understood, replicated, or enhanced simply by reading the HTML source code of a page you admired and adapting it for yourself.

The Agile Design Philosophy—Making Code That Can Change

As a creative philosophy for children, artists, and researchers, this potential for extension and evolution of the computational world you are "living" in made good sense. But how could such freedom possibly be effective in the world of business or engineering? Does every business need creative freedom and flexibility, or should it perhaps apply a judicious amount of viscosity, reflecting cautious review procedures? For companies that saw the technical potential of the Smalltalk approach, but struggled to see how it might be practical, there was an urgent need for expert consultants to help translate the opportunity of the Smalltalk model into engineering and business reality.

Smalltalk developers Kent Beck and Ward Cunningham addressed this problem in ways that have had impacts well beyond the field of software engineering. Their business response to the Smalltalk philosophy of creative exploration has now become a mainstream approach called *agile programming*, in which programmers, their customers, and other stakeholders work together to continuously construct, review, and evolve software that will eventually meet their needs. Although obviously inspired by Smalltalk, agile methods such as Extreme Programming (XP), and the SCRUM method for managing a project with evolving requirements, have now become major businesses in themselves, sometimes completely divorced from object-oriented programming, or even from the software industry.[7]

The agile development philosophy is radically different in its use of notation, in comparison to earlier approaches to software development. In my early career, a software project started with a contract to deliver a particular application for a fixed price. Because the price was fixed, there was a limit to how much time programmers could work on it—sometimes estimated by the number of "function points," like individual operations or commands. But the system didn't exist yet, so the contract was often vague. It didn't list every function. In fact, writing down and defining all those details was a major job in itself, sometimes requiring months of specialist work. So, the first task after signing the contract was to analyze and document every feature that would be needed, for a system that nobody had yet seen. Once that list was ready, the programmers began work. Unfortunately, this often turned out badly when customers discovered after the system was delivered that they had forgotten to mention something important. Some even realized, when they saw the working software, that a completely different solution would have been better. Customers often then demanded a product that they were happier with. Programmers complained that they had spent all their budget and had no time to make further changes. Lawyers on one side would argue that the customer had signed the contract specification, so must pay for what they had commissioned. Meanwhile, those on the other side would say it was unreasonable to expect a customer to read and understand detailed technical documents, especially if there was *so* much detail that it felt like they were doing the coding work themselves!

These challenges are unavoidable when creating a complex product with no prior example of what it should look like. The situation is related to the problems discussed in chapter 5 of specifying the user goal in advance, which is an unhelpful approach to any wicked problem that cannot be precisely defined. Attempts to regulate project management in the first decades of the software industry led to the "waterfall model," in which each phase of the project delivers an increasingly detailed specification document that must be signed off before sending it downstream to the next phase. Waterfall projects were expensive and bureaucratic, often involving special notational tools to document the designs at different levels of detail, with flow charts, database layouts, screen mockups, and other diagrams to help customers and programmers build a consensus. Despite all these tools, many waterfall projects resulted in notorious budget overruns, failures to deliver, and litigation on all sides. A pragmatic compromise advocated a "spiral model," where initial versions of each document would be used to create an early prototype, which customers could experiment with in order to adjust their requirements before revising the documents and doing more development, perhaps with several cycles until the development contract finally ended.

When I was a young software engineer in 1980s New Zealand, the creative world of the Smalltalk researchers at Xerox PARC seemed utopian. The August 1981 issue of *Byte* magazine was dedicated to Smalltalk, and I read it from cover to cover. At over 400 pages, this collection of technical and philosophical contributions from the Smalltalk team was the size of a Bible and seemed to me nearly as visionary. In contrast to the Smalltalk vision, my own day-to-day work, in that year and for years to come, followed the waterfall processes of drawing diagrams, writing specifications, and negotiating with clients, rather than living in a flexible abstract world of representations that could be freely explored and creatively modified.

Wikipedia—When Knowledge Becomes Agile

The West Coast developers who brought the Smalltalk philosophy into their software consulting work were uncomfortably aware of the ways that accepted practices of waterfall-style project management would hobble the creative potential of the Smalltalk tools. What is the point of a flexible and playful programmable environment if you spend months documenting and diagramming in advance every detail of the code you are going to write?

This is a fundamental problem of notation—if one person is writing software for another, how can they agree in detail on the goals? And if people struggle to agree with each other, can we really expect an AI to do better? Decades of research have been dedicated to the invention and refinement of different kinds of diagrammatic modeling languages, each intended to more clearly communicate functions of the system that might be important to a user while also specifying unambiguously what the machine should do. Some of those diagram styles are more suited to waterfall project management, and some more to iteration in a spiral. But the philosophy of agile programming was more radical—somehow, customers had to be welcomed *into* the Smalltalk world of changeable software, even working alongside the programmers as they explored together what the system might be able to do.

Ward Cunningham responded to this challenge with a completely different notational approach. Abandoning the search for intuitive yet formal diagrams, he decided to treat specification text like pieces of Smalltalk code—separate objects linked together by their logical relationships and arranged into an abstract "world" that you could live in while writing them, so that anyone could take a look and make creative changes, just like in Smalltalk. Coming soon after Berners-Lee's World Wide Web, this simple text document editor was built-in to a web browser so that anybody reading a page could quickly change it if they saw something that needed to be different. The original *WikiWikiWeb*, named for the Hawai'ian expression to act quickly, can still be found on the web server at Cunningham's consultancy company—though it now has such classic status that it is more a museum artifact than an active management tool. Perhaps the closest inheritor is the Markdown format familiar to GitHub, Stack Overflow, and Reddit contributors.

Decades later, this *wiki* philosophy has transformed human knowledge. As the most-consulted reference work in the world, Wikipedia is fundamentally different from encyclopedias that existed when companies sold knowledge compiled and bureaucratically certified by committees of experts. Kids of my generation dreamed of being able to afford an *Encyclopædia Britannica*, and I spent hours in the corner of my school library where it was kept. Who could imagine, 50 years ago, that the world's best encyclopedia would be created by volunteers, inventing their own systems of debate, reward, and recognition, all documented and managed within the wiki itself? If you haven't experienced making an edit to Wikipedia, I strongly recommend it. Find a page that you know something about, look at its change history and local guidance, and make a change yourself. Anyone can do it, and the process of what happens next will provide genuine insight into what Wikipedia really is (and indeed, into one of the main objectives of this book, which is to celebrate and enable Creative Opportunities for Digital Expression).

Wikipedia demonstrates the creative and intellectual consequences of object-oriented software development far beyond the world of conventional programming languages.[8] It is also an example of the philosophy that programmers can live among their own tools, modifying and adapting them as they work. Cunningham and Beck's experiences in bringing that agile philosophy to the bureaucratic world of business and organizations has resulted in new hybrids between traditional programming and the notational conventions of hypertext, business documents, and organizational specifications.

It's worth noting at this point that the WikiWikiWeb, like the World Wide Web itself, succeeded largely because it was so simple. I've used public wikis frequently in my own work at the university to encourage students, collaborators, and anyone else who might be interested to see research as work in progress rather than set in stone. Unfortunately, the simple markup language and editing commands do make all this material look just a little bit amateurish and home-brewed—which it is! But even though I've described wiki pages as a "notation" for software engineering, they are much less sophisticated than the many kinds of diagram editor, visual programming languages, and other special tools that have been created by the research community. There is an attention investment trade-off here between abstract expressive power on one hand and usability on the other, which I hope is beginning to seem familiar from earlier chapters of this book.

Living in Abstract Worlds—The Architectural Patterns of Moral Codes

We can get more insight into the nature of the trade-off by drawing on yet another contribution arising from the work of Kent Beck, Ward Cunningham, and their friends. You might think that the invention of agile project management, and of the technology behind Wikipedia, would be sufficient laurels for these innovators to rest on (not to mention the invention of CRC cards, which I'm not going to discuss any further, but are still one of the best modeling languages for conceptual design of object-oriented systems in my opinion). These are impressive and talented leaders, although I'm sure they would say that it is the Smalltalk philosophy itself (and before that, SIMULA, Sketchpad, Dynabook and so on) that showed the potential for treating a software tool environment as an abstract place where the programmer could "live" and work, inspecting and modifying the structures around them.

In 1987, Beck and Cunningham presented a paper at an international conference of object-oriented programming specialists, in which they reflected on their experiences from the perspective of architectural philosopher Christopher Alexander.[9] Alexander had studied first as a mathematician, then as an architect, and then as an anthropologist after he came to realize that the structure of buildings is ultimately determined by the needs and habits of humans, rather than simply mechanical solutions to a functional and aesthetic design brief. Drawing on his mathematical background, Alexander developed the abstract concept of a "pattern language" to systematically describe the ways in which towns, buildings, and rooms are created and evolve to accommodate human needs.

Beck and Cunningham saw that this kind of abstract specification of lived experiences could also be used to define the properties of the software environments where they and their colleagues "lived," in an abstractly notated computational world. Their observations have been so compelling, and the significance of these insights to the work of programmers so clear, that pattern languages are now far more often used in the work of software engineers than by architects. Although Alexander's work is respected among academic architects, it has not become the standard approach to architectural design that he originally imagined. In contrast, *software* design patterns have become a central element of university teaching and professional practice for all programmers using object-oriented tools.

Despite the popularity of software patterns (and research communities who continue to develop, promote and refine them), this popular reception has actually shifted away from Beck and Cunningham's original insight, and indeed from the insights that we could have taken from Christopher Alexander on how to think critically about structuring the world we live in. To genuinely realize the potential of the Smalltalk philosophy, we need to return to the concept of pattern language, outside of the simple mechanics of software construction where they have become so successful, and think again how it applies to all these other tools and technical opportunities—including design notations, wikis and other documents, graphical user interfaces, and even social structures of agile project management and collaborative knowledge curation.

In many ways, that could be described as the purpose of this book. The Smalltalk team revolutionized the everyday practices of programming, but they did this work before the development of machine learning algorithms that fueled today's AI boom. If the Smalltalk philosophy is to continue, we need a new pattern language that builds on the potential for new intelligent tools. Computer scientists have come to think of "software design patterns" as little more than a handbook of construction tricks, forgetting Beck and Cunningham's more radical insights from 1987.[10] Alexander himself, when invited to speak to the programming community, observed that their development of design patterns appeared to have missed the moral purpose that was central to his work.[11]

This book aims to recover moral purpose in programming through more appropriate patterns for interaction—the very point that has been missed in the software industry more widely, including those parts describing themselves as "artificial intelligence." New combinations of visual notation, mixed-initiative interaction, and machine learning can deliver new kinds of user experience, and these are the patterns we need to understand. I'll be returning in more detail to these patterns of user experience in chapter 14, after giving some examples of how programming advances today are integrating machine learning into the homes people make in code.

8   Explanation and Transparency:
Beyond No-Code/Low-Code

Sumit Gulwani, who now leads an AI-assisted programming team at Microsoft, tells the story of an experience on a flight, when his neighbor couldn't believe her luck to be seated next to one of the best qualified young computer scientists at Microsoft. She brought out her laptop to show him how she had been struggling with one of those annoying repetitive tasks described in chapter 2. Sumit loves helping people but was disappointed that there was no obvious way in Excel to automate the many rows of data formatting she needed to do. His own research had been on the topic of program synthesis—how to automatically create a program that transforms one set of data into another—so his neighbor's problem was exactly the kind of thing he believed should be automated.

Sumit's job at Microsoft Research was not to help Excel users with repetitive tasks. As with most experts in programming language research, he had been assigned to a group responsible for high-end software engineering tools and was working on performance of the company's core database products. But in a kind of personal skunkworks, he became obsessed with reading online forums where people shared their problems getting jobs done in Excel.[1] He suspected that many problems faced by the woman on his flight, and others like her, could be automated using program synthesis. A typical Excel forum post shows a few data cells, followed by an appeal for help. Contributors respond with a formula that solves the problem based on the data supplied, and it seemed like a program synthesis algorithm should be able to do the same thing. It took Sumit three months reading forums to work out the sweet spot where a particular kind of cell data could be used to automatically create an appropriate formula. But after that intensive search for the right problem, it took only three weeks working at home to create the first prototype of the Excel feature now famous as *FlashFill*.

Sumit is now a computer science celebrity, his group is thriving, and FlashFill is often cited to illustrate the next generation of AI-assisted tools for end-user programming. But just as with celebrity actors or pop stars, this apparently sudden success actually followed years of hard work and early talent. In fact, Sumit had already made other prize-winning research contributions in program synthesis before he even started work on FlashFill. But it was the months he spent immersed in user forums that led to the breakthrough he is most famous for. His team now includes experts in human–computer interaction and design, not just machine learning and programming languages. And he is clear about how important it was to place a relentless focus on the best possible user experience, when he started to work on FlashFill with the Excel product team. In contrast to the often-denigrated office assistant Clippy, whose supposedly helpful suggestions were either trivial or off-base, the Excel team insisted that FlashFill must respond with immediately useful advice. The mathematics of program synthesis mean that three or four data examples increase the likelihood of a correct solution. But the team told Sumit that FlashFill must work correctly with even a single example.[2] The lessons from chapter 2, explaining the basis of user decision making in attention investment, make it clear why this has been the right choice, and has been critical to making FlashFill such a successful product.

Sumit Gulwani is especially pleased that FlashFill recently appeared in middle school textbooks in his native India, used to illustrate how Excel can be used for the data cleaning and reorganization tasks (often called "data wrangling") that are central to a desirable career in data science. He's passionate about education and technology, following his own early experiences. Despite scoring in the top 200 of a million applicants for the prestigious Indian Institutes of Technology, he dropped out of their engineering program, retaking the exams to gain one of very few computer science seats. He now welcomes students from India as members of his PROSE team, which works on AI-assisted tutoring that could help provide more relevant feedback to kids learning to code who do not have easy access to learning from good teachers.[3]

Gulwani's PROSE group continues to push the boundaries of AI-assisted programming in many ways and is perhaps the most established team in the world dedicated to realizing the agenda promoted in this book. Current areas of research include FlashFill++, which shows users the rules learned by the system, potentially to be debugged, modified, or shared. Members of the group are also working on synthesizing code snippets for larger-scale software projects, and tools that assist the programmer by suggesting code edits. They describe their approach as "neuro-symbolic," combining logical reasoning about the code with neural network models of programmers' preferences. They are also alert to the problems of stochastic parrots, in part because Microsoft is so diligent about *not* recording data from spreadsheets for model training, and also because of the legal challenges if models were trained to replicate copyrighted code—a problem that I discuss further in chapters 11 and 12.

Improving Control and Transparency with More Open Representations

The potential of program synthesis methods like FlashFill has encouraged a trend with the catchphrase "no-code/low-code," imagining software development without conventional programming languages. This is related to my own recommendations, although I think we would do better to ask *what kind of code* is needed, rather than to hide or remove the code, which raises questions about transparency and control. Indeed, the ambition of "no-code" repeats the historic mistakes I already discussed in the last chapter, when researchers tried to reject text altogether in the style of Jonathan Swift's philosophers of Lagado.

Sumit Gulwani suggests that we need to integrate different kinds of code, including the spreadsheet table itself, an explanation of the synthesized code in FlashFill++, perhaps code recommended from a natural language description, or even visualizations like those from my student Maria Gorinova, who used Gulwani's PROSE resources to create a playful data wrangling tool called Data Noodles.[4] Sumit calls these designs "multimodal" because they integrate visual, linguistic, and mathematical styles of interaction, and I think they demonstrate the need for More Open Representations, as a central element of moral codes. Indeed, many of the approaches now being taken in no-code projects are descended from the end-user programming innovations of Allen Cypher and his collaborators that I described in chapter 2, or from long-term programs of research such as the *demonstrational interfaces* of prolific user interface and end-user programming innovator Brad Myers and his team at CMU.[5]

Some recent low-code initiatives have replaced textual programming languages with alternative notations of the kind that were previously studied as "visual programming." This combination of textual and dia-grammatic elements is the same design strategy that I see as the basis for moral codes. However, the catchphrase "no-code" really appeals to the longstanding ambitions of first-generation human–computer interaction researchers such as Ben Shneiderman when he first described the windows, icon, mouse, and point (WIMP) style of the direct manipulation GUI as "a step beyond programming languages."[6]

Do we need code or not? Where personal computer operating systems had originally presented their users with a command line interface for typ-ing program-like text instructions, the WIMP interface transformed the visual focus of the display, no longer focusing on the code-based world of the computer scientist, but instead on illustrating the user's own documents and activities. By hiding away the code of the command line, users could concentrate on what interested them—their own data. But the problem with the no-code agenda, as with AI, is that it can be difficult, without a suf-ficiently powerful language, to explain what you want the computer to do, especially if it is something that wasn't already anticipated by the designer.[7]

Representing Code by Representing Data

The purpose of a computer is of course to manipulate data. Usually when computer software affects our lives, the data comes from us, but the algo-rithms come from somewhere else. Whether in a bank, a school, or a gov-ernment, our only opportunity to control what happens next is by deciding what data we provide. The actual algorithms that decide whether we pass an exam or have our mortgage approved are seldom visible and are certainly out of our control. We can control the data—in fact we *are* the data, as far as the algorithm is concerned. To a digital system, there is no further reality to you as a person, outside of the particular set of data that it knows about you. For-tunately, most of us do have actual physical lives outside of computer data, although some are more virtual than others, if too much of their personal identity has been constructed within the databases of Instagram or YouTube.

If we are going to gain more control over our virtual lives, there needs to be a way for users to move from displaying what we already knew anyway (the data about our own lives and livelihoods) toward representing what is hidden (the algorithms that control our lives by processing our data). AI researchers increasingly describe this as a problem of *explanation*—telling the user why a particular decision was taken, or *transparency*—being clear about what is being done with the data. Both explanation and transparency could become more difficult to achieve in the "no code" world if the algorithm was defined in such a way that there was literally no code to see. A moral code (whether textual, pictorial, diagrammatic, or some combination of these) should offer both visibility and control.

The rest of this chapter describes a variety of design approaches to novel codes that expose the relationship between data and algorithms. In a way, the suggestions I am making are the opposite of the business model of *surveillance capitalism* as it has been described by Shoshanna Zuboff.[8] In surveillance capitalism, companies routinely collect data about your life, usually without drawing attention to what they are doing, other than an initial invitation to read a lengthy end-user license agreement that few people ever look at. Although legislation is being introduced that forces companies to reveal (only on request) what they know about you, and to (trivially and repeatedly) ask for your consent, the vast majority of this data—the actual substance of your own virtual lives—is hidden from you, and processed by algorithms that are completely secret.

Machine learning technologies seem to have worsened the exploitative nature of surveillance capitalism, because observations of your own behavior can be sold back to you, having been used to train the algorithm behind some AI service or other. The most profitable companies are careful to ensure that you are not paid for your data. Of course you *are* charged for the stored products of your own intelligence when they are sold back to you, and critical algorithm scholar Nick Seaver explains how the products themselves are delivered via algorithms for *captivation*—AI recommendations and playlists that trap your attention, training you to expect more of the same.[9]

The Spreadsheet: Humble Data Table, or Radically Moral Code?

As Sumit Gulwani recognized in his own "aha" moment on that airplane, there is one class of product that has established a quiet revolution in letting people control and manipulate their *own* data—the spreadsheet. Expert spreadsheet users will know that the spreadsheet really is a kind of programming language. In fact, researchers have calculated that there are more spreadsheet programmers than there are in all other programming languages combined.[10]

At first sight, a spreadsheet does not look very much like a programming language. But a central message of this book is that moral codes will probably not look like familiar languages of the past. Even the GUI started life as an experiment in making programming languages more accessible, despite the fact that it quickly evolved beyond those programming elements, to the extent that some GUIs today focus only on data collection to sell services, rather than supporting user control as they should. While spreadsheets and GUIs are often described as a starting point for low-code and no-code alternatives to programming, this book argues that these visual displays are all representational codes, and that *hiding* the code instead would be a surrender to hidden algorithms.

Spreadsheets, however, are generally marketed to businesses, not their customers. Every business relies on algorithmic accounting procedures, and spreadsheets became popular because they provided such an accessible way to define financial processes. Nevertheless, although marketing and perception of spreadsheets assumes these business tools won't be relevant to ordinary people's lives, the design principles offer important lessons for how everybody could gain further control over algorithms by starting from data.

The brilliant innovation of the spreadsheet was to make data *more* visible than code. Until then, most programming languages showed only code, with data never seen until it was time to test the program. It's easy to see how this became an obstacle to learning and popularizing programming. It is our data that is directly relevant to our lives, while algorithms are typically created and discussed by experts we never meet. In old-style programming languages, the user interface of the programming tools hides the part that you understand (your data) and shows the part that you don't (the code).

The spreadsheet reverses this convention, showing all of your data, and putting the code away in formulas and macros that you must specifically ask for. In one way, this is the same design insight that led to the graphical user interface and the desktop metaphor, where the screen shows the things that interest you (in the case of the GUI, your files and applications) rather than a command line window containing technical jargon. In the original GUIs, it was still possible to access the command line to operate on your data algorithmically, but those capabilities are increasingly hidden away, and are not available at all on most tablet devices and smartphones.

By contrast, in a spreadsheet, every piece of your data can be processed algorithmically by creating formulas. An expert spreadsheet programmer can build complex applications by combining many formulas across the various cells and tabs of a large spreadsheet. Fortunately, this power also comes with a gentle beginner's slope, which allows even early learners to do simple sums and create databases, typing one or two equations and arranging their information in relevant rows and columns. The functionality of Gulwani's FlashFill is right on this gentle slope, although the ambitions of his research team go much further.

The fact that your data is always visible in a spreadsheet is both reassuring and helpful. Because you understand how the data relates to your life, you can review the tables at any time to confirm that they look sensible, and to read off any value you might be looking for. But a trade-off comes with this simplicity, that complicated programs are harder to create and manage. Unlike a regular programming language, where pages of code explain what you want the computer to do, in a spreadsheet you only see the instructions one line at a time, and it's difficult to keep the whole structure clear in your head while putting many invisible pieces together. Even worse, if one of the formulas has a mistake in it, that mistake will be hidden away up until the time that it causes something to go obviously wrong in some of the visible data. As a result, spreadsheets often have hidden errors in them, and famous business disasters have been caused by code errors in a spreadsheet formula.[11]

So spreadsheets are easy to use (because they display your data rather than the algorithm), but also dangerous because of the design trade-offs resulting from hiding the code. Fortunately, there are alternative trade-off choices, and the next section considers the underlying principles that might help us repeat the design innovations of the spreadsheet and the GUI with new inventions that can make the power of algorithms more accessible.

Moral Codes as Visual Explanations

We urgently need improved access to algorithms in the era of machine learning systems, because until now, these systems have been especially poor—hiding *both* your data and the algorithm, so that you have no way to either control or understand what they are doing. The goal of "explainable AI" is to improve this situation, and the design approaches described here are going to become the most practical way to achieve genuinely explainable and controllable AI. As always, these approaches can be considered a kind of programming language, though once again they do not look like conventional code.

The different technical terms for this field include "interactive visualizations," "intelligent user interfaces," "visual programming languages," "business modeling languages," "visual formalisms," or "notational systems." Sumit Gulwani describes them as "multimodal interaction." But what they all have in common is that they use the display to communicate structure. In some cases, they display the structure of an algorithm (for example, like a flowchart with decision points and loops), while in other cases they display the structure of your data (the structure of rows and columns in a spreadsheet is especially clear).

These notational systems offer *both* explanation and control, which is not true of all recent approaches to explainable AI. You can imagine why a surveillance capitalism business might prefer to collect (and hide) your data, process it with a (hidden) algorithm, and then offer to explain what it has done afterwards, rather than offering you any freedom to make the system work differently. Many older textbooks and courses in data visualization do exactly this—they explain how to draw beautiful graphs illustrating what has already happened, but not how to let the user modify or control the data. Regular users of Excel spreadsheets will know how easy it is to create a bar chart based on values in a table, while it is not at all easy in Excel to create a display that allows the user to modify or explore code and data by clicking and dragging the elements of a visualization around.

It might seem overly idealistic to suggest that people could ever control algorithms as easily as they "control" those aspects of their everyday lives that generate data—buying a coffee, for example, or taking a bus. But let's consider what the design opportunities might be, to make things work differently. I've pointed out that mobile phones are easy to use because they show your data (contacts, messages, photos, whatever) while hiding the algorithms that process them. Spreadsheets offer a clear visualization of data structure and some access to create algorithms, but they hide the code in a way that invites errors. Conventional program language code doesn't show any data at all until it's time to run the program. All of these alternatives represent trade-offs and design decisions, in which different choices have been made about what kinds of structure to show on the display.

There is limited space on a typical screen (especially on a phone), so it is inevitable that software will be designed to hide some structures and reveal others. But it's not necessary to show *only code* structure, or *only data* structure. Many systems are able to combine code and data, using visual design elements to integrate both in meaningful ways. If you look closely, every movie poster, bus ticket, cash receipt, instruction manual, festival program, train timetable, and even page in this book is designed to organize and reveal particular aspects of data structure and the relationships between the parts while hiding others. If the display is on an interactive computer screen, it might include visual clues to the algorithms that are involved—highlighting or rearranging things, for example, in response to your actions or using animations to show how there might be causal interactions underneath the surface.

Spreadsheets have been around for decades, and programming languages even longer. They both date back to an era when it was unusual to see pictures, curved lines, or even different colors on the screen of a computer. In a sense, it is only conservatism that has resulted in us still being stuck with such a small range of options for code today, although tables and indented paragraphs are certainly helpful. The original designers of Sketchpad, Smalltalk, and the GUI were not thinking within these constraints when they started building the first graphics-based personal computers. Their early prototypes included graphical programming languages that combined handwritten symbols and text to control new algorithms, not simply collecting data to be processed by somebody else's algorithm. The huge success of the GUI and the growth of the surveillance capitalism market, however, has helped to discourage the idea that new visualizations could allow people to observe and control algorithms as well as data.

Machine learning systems, until now, have not made things much better. Current enthusiasm for chatbots based on large language models will not help at all. But there *are* ways to design new interactive visual displays that provide the potential benefits of machine learning already explained in previous chapters, including access to both data and algorithms, in combinations that are appropriate to particular kinds of users trying to achieve particular kinds of things.

Inventing Moral Codes as Design Hybrids

One way to experiment with new design opportunities, exploring the space of possible trade-offs between control of code and visibility of data, is to build prototypes that combine the capabilities of familiar products in unfamiliar ways. The resulting prototypes are hybrids that help us think about possible futures in which users could have more control over their software. Hybrid prototypes should always try to explore interesting new combinations, but will not necessarily be useful (or at least, not useful in immediate or obvious ways). More often, they *are* useful, but perhaps only to a small group of people, or for an unusual specialist task, or perhaps for a neglected community who would not otherwise receive the attention of software designers.

My own research group works in all these ways, reporting the results of our explorations to specialist research communities such as international conferences on Theory and Application of Diagrams, Visual Languages and Human-Centric Computing, or the Psychology of Programming. The experimental software applications that we create sometimes address business problems, critical healthcare issues such as the control of bleeding after open heart surgery, or sometimes non-commercial applications as diverse as teaching mathematics to the children of traditional hunter-gatherers in the Kalahari Desert or improvising electronic dance music in a nightclub "algorave."[12]

In all cases, our software experiments include some elements that are recognizable from previous programming languages, interactive visualizations, or demonstrations of machine learning, but also open up, hide, or expose different aspects that draw attention to new opportunities. The research objective is to better understand ways of encoding in relation to human needs and lives, making the world a better place through new languages and representations—indeed, the moral codes of this book's title.

The previous paragraphs have offered a rather abstract description of *why* we do our research, but no detail on *what* the results look like. This is in part because there are too many different projects to include in a single book. Many of them have been described at book-length in PhD theses, as well as hundreds of academic publications. While it's useful to tie together the overall logic of these many projects across decades of work, it's also helpful to get a flavor of what we do and why, through a few examples that illustrate this research strategy.

Mariana Mărășoiu is a Romanian-British computer scientist who I first met when she was working as an intern for Google. She still teaches interaction design in my department in Cambridge, while spending much of her time in the Scottish Highlands, where she is re-wilding thirty acres of forest.

Her research has subverted the conventional approaches to data science and visualization by creating tools that reverse the workflows and expose the hidden algorithms of familiar spreadsheet tools. One of her projects, which she calls *Self-Raising Data*, counters the deterministic logic by which data is harvested and turned into business visualizations.[13]

In her work with a research sponsor, she learned that professional data scientists are often asked to investigate questions where there is not actually (yet) any data. All of their communication tools had been designed on the assumption that the data comes before the visualization, meaning that the data scientist had no way to contribute to important business problems. Mariana built an award-winning prototype (figure 8.1) allowing data scientists and businesspeople to collaborate on visualizations of hypothetical or imaginary data, *generating* the data to illustrate alternative models.

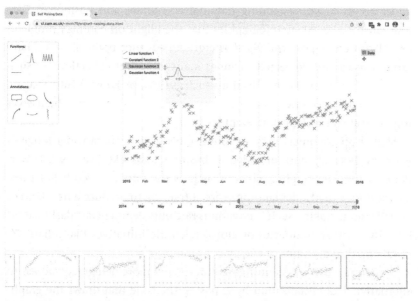

Figure 8.1
Mariana Mărășoiu's Self-Raising Data prototype being used to synthesize a hypothetical dataset in terms of kernel functions. A full explanation can be found in the conference paper that introduced this system. Source: Mariana Mărășoiu, Alan F. Blackwell, Advait Sarkar, and Martin Spott. "Clarifying Hypotheses by Sketching Data," in *Proceedings of the Eurographics/IEEE VGTC Conference on Visualization (2016),* 125–129.

In another of Mariana's projects, *Cuscus*, she addressed another problem—that users have so little control over how quantitative data is visualized.[14] Users of spreadsheets and scientific data visualization packages are allowed to choose between bar charts, line graphs, scatter plots, pie charts, and very little else. Although very useful indeed, and familiar to most of us since school mathematics, this standard set of data visualization choices has hardly changed since being invented by William Playfair in the late eighteenth century for his *Commercial and Political Atlas*.[15] It is really a remarkable indictment of the lack of originality in the software industry and modern business that practically all of their data visualizations were invented by one man over two centuries ago.

Graphic artists and designers can, of course, render quantitative data in many other ways. Some, such as Otto Neurath's *Isotype* picture language, were brilliant design innovations that advanced democracy by giving far wider access to understanding national economies and business.[16] Data journalists today create infographics that shed light on complex problems as well as deploy powerful visual rhetoric to advance political or humanitarian causes. My bookshelf includes many beautiful collections of such work, including reference collections such as those by Edward Tufte that are popular purchases for computer scientists wondering how they themselves might create more appealing graphics.[17]

Skilled programmers have technical tools to generate a wider range of graphics, beyond those provided in business tools like Excel and Power-Point, using web graphics libraries such as the popular d3.js.[18] But these are tools for experts, demanding years of training to produce a new kind of visualization, making such innovations rare outside financial "dashboards" built by wealthy businesses or global scientific initiatives like Julian All-wood's Sankey diagrams of energy consumption.[19]

Mariana's Cuscus system (figure 8.2) offered more democratic access to alternative data visualization by exposing the code that draws the graphics and presenting this code as a familiar spreadsheet rather than in a web scripting language. Users can create flowers, mountains, trees, or Isotype-style human figures by combining any kind of geometric elements. The colors, sizes, positions, and relationships of those elements are all represented by numbers in the accompanying spreadsheet. When combined with a data spreadsheet, the correspondence between "visual variables" (as they were described by graphic design theorist Jacques Bertin[20]) and the original data

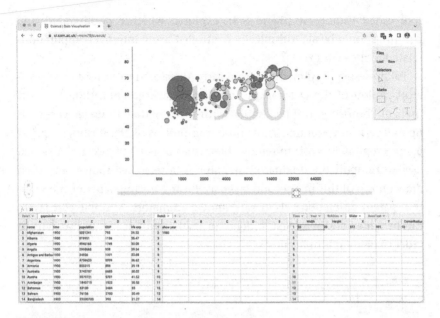

Figure 8.2
A version of Hans Rosling's famous Gapminder visualization, created using the Cuscus system for specifying visualizations in spreadsheet form (https://www.gapminder.org/tools). A full explanation can be found in Mariana Mărășoiu, Detlef Nauck, and Alan F. Blackwell, "Cuscus: An End User Programming Tool for Data Visualisation," in *Proceedings of End-User Development: 7th International Symposium, IS-EUD 2019*, Hatfield, UK, July 10–12, 2019, 115–131.

can be defined by pasting cell formulas, just like in an ordinary spreadsheet. The result allows any spreadsheet user to invent a completely new data visualization, no longer constrained to bars, pies, and line graphs. In some ways, Cuscus is less convenient than graphics programming languages like *Processing* that are popular with designers and visual artists.[21] But in other ways, Cuscus is much easier—for example, when debugging by looking directly at the coordinates of the shape to see where a problem might be.

The starting point for projects like Cuscus and Self-Raising Data was to ask whether the conventional business workflow of collecting data, making graphs in Excel, and pasting them into PowerPoint presentations could become more creative and varied, changing the design priorities of those products to make different elements of their algorithms visible and controllable by users. One of my own research prototypes, an interactive visual tool called Palimpsest (figure 8.3), explored whether photographs and paintings could be algorithmically controlled using internal computations related to those in Excel.[22]

Palimpsest applied methods from early AI research to create a more powerful version of the popular art and design package Photoshop.[23] Expert users of Photoshop will be familiar with the way that an image gets built up in layers—for example in the notorious process of "Photoshopping," or using a digital airbrush to remove blemishes or parts of a scene. A skilled user will import the original photograph as a reference source, and then draw on top of this in a second layer, as if using tracing paper or the semi-transparent animation cels of early movie animators. Multiple edit layers can be added and removed, hidden, or made more or less transparent in order to blend multiple effects.

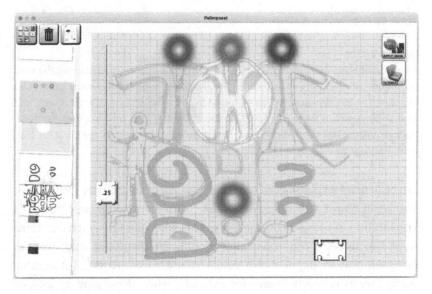

Figure 8.3
Screenshot of a live sketching session in Palimpsest, being used to brainstorm elements of a cover design for this book. The collage of interacting layers includes elements from commercial image generators (as always, trained using uncredited internet sources), geometric transforms, pixel-based filters, random elements, and human pen traces. For further detail of the operating principles of Palimpsest, including worked examples of how this kind of image composition is created, see Alan F. Blackwell, "Palimpsest: A Layered Language for Exploratory Image Processing," *Journal of Visual Languages and Computing* 25 no. 5 (2014): 545–571.

In my Palimpsest system, I played around with this idea of layering, turning it into a new code resource. (The word "palimpsest" originally refers to an old manuscript in which a parchment has been re-used, with new layers of text added on top of an older document. Excavation can reveal hidden meanings or poetic reinterpretations). In Photoshop, the data might be organized into layers, but the user can't change the algorithm—their only option is to create new layers, adjusting the appearance and level of transparency. In Palimpsest, the pixels on each layer are diagrammatic code that can cause things to change on other layers, resulting in animations or even new visual languages and algorithms. The inspiration for how this works came (again) from the spreadsheet, where data entered in one cell can cause other cells to change. Each layer in Palimpsest works like a cell in a spreadsheet, making the overall system an experimental hybrid of Photoshop and Excel. The relationships can become complex, and I adapted methods from AI programming languages such as "constraint propagation" to make the resulting system more powerful. Products like Excel use similar methods, but within an agenda to make a mathematical tool that is as simple and obvious to use as possible. The Palimpsest model is not (yet) simple and obvious, but it is certainly different. I've used it in some stage performances and art projects, and it continues to inspire different ways of thinking about code and image culture, as well as including new interaction techniques that might pop up in other end-user programming systems or graphics packages.

One last project from my group, to illustrate this hybrid design philosophy, is the work of Advait Sarkar, who was inspired as a student by Sumit Gulwani's work on program synthesis and by the way that FlashFill made these capabilities available to so many people. Like Sumit, Advait grew up in India, where his parents were technology journalists in Bengaluru.

Among the many imaginative prototypes Advait has created is a system called *BrainCel* (figure 8.4) that quite literally combined the user interface approaches of spreadsheets and machine learning algorithms to improve their accessibility through interactive visualizations.[24] In BrainCel, users can still see their data as in any spreadsheet, but can also see how patterns in the data are being extracted with a machine learning algorithm. The relationship between labels and data features are the critical element to all such algorithms, and these have increasingly substantial impact on our lives, when organizations use this data to make decisions in ways that are not transparent.

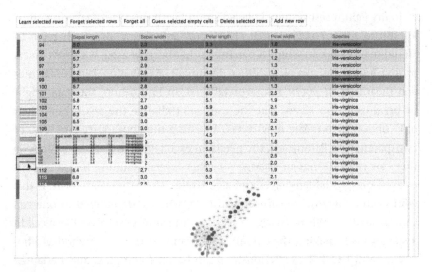

Figure 8.4
Advait Sarkar's BrainCel system, being used for the standard machine learning exercise of classifying species of iris flower. The spreadsheet is enhanced with visualizations that group related examples together, allowing users to explore and adjust the interpretation.

BrainCel is just one example of a tool that presents an alternative relationship between the work of labeling training cases for supervised machine learning, which is usually done by unskilled workers, and the interpretation of the clusters or correlations that might be extracted from the labelled features, usually done by corporate data scientists. By making these processes visible, and by supporting workflows that build on the diversity of human expertise rather than isolating mundane labor from moral judgement, tools like BrainCel point the way toward forms of machine learning that are both more ethical and better informed.

Imagining Future Programming Tools

These examples of work from my own group are typical of research currently being done and presented at academic conferences, including *Intelligent User Interfaces*; *Visual Languages and Human-Centric Computing*; and *Systems, Programming, Languages, and Applications: Software for Humanity*. It is not unheard of for many different kinds of visualization, analysis, and interactive code editors to be combined into sets of tools for professional programmers, known as *IDEs* (*integrated development environments*), such as Visual Studio from Microsoft. When new kinds of visualization or interaction are invented in research groups like mine, they often become available after a decade or two for general use as new features in the mainstream IDE products.

Spreadsheets like Excel, and business data processing tools like Power BI from Microsoft or the Tableau visual analytics platform, are becoming more like the IDEs that were previously used only by professional programmers. All such tools focus attention on visualizing the user's own business data, rather than screens full of programming language code, as in an IDE. But multiple interactive representations, including ways to automate coding through recommendations from machine learning models, offer new potential to all these kinds of users. It is easy to see the potential for these combined advances in machine learning, notation design, and interactive visualization to support moral codes: More Open Representations, Access to Learning, and Control Over Digital Expression. Business data analytics tools can be considered as "high-end" alternatives to the spreadsheet, but we can also imagine future hybrids of the GUI as "low-end" alternatives for regular people who would benefit from openness, learning, and control, but without needing the full facilities of a spreadsheet.

Why hasn't this happened earlier? The case studies I presented in this chapter have focused on business problems, because businesses pay the salaries and scholarships that a PhD student needs to live. When I started my own research career, the main international funder of AI research was the US military. When national research policies focus so heavily on technology for business or defense, it is rare to find original work in computer science that explores the questions of human well-being and values at the core of this book. Just as with the software itself, we only make progress by attending to one priority while being committed to another. The next chapter investigates in more depth how commercial and research trends can obscure the most interesting and empowering opportunities.

9   Why Code Is More Important Than Flat Design

The last chapter described ways to interact with code and data that are more accessible than established programming languages, and potentially look nothing like them. Machine learning algorithms have a part to play in this new generation of tools, but moral codes must still be open, learnable, and controllable. Inventing new codes is not easy, and this chapter explains some of the mistakes that are holding us back. In particular, it's important to understand that moral codes are diagrams, not pictures.

The invention of the GUI, as described in chapter 6, was a breakthrough that used pictorial design to depict files, folders, and other operating system elements as paper objects in a physical office, known ever since as the "desktop metaphor." In the 1980s and 1990s, this pictorial resemblance between the icons on a computer screen and familiar physical objects was believed to be the single most important element of design for usability. Design guidelines from Apple and Microsoft, as well as countless textbooks on user interface design, used to say that the first step in designing a new user interface was the selection of an appropriate real-world metaphor, so that users could understand the abstract world of the computer in relation to familiar objects.[1] The idea was that, if a user was unsure how a particular operation could be achieved, or what the effects of their actions might be, they could think about it by analogy to the real-world objects shown on the screen that they *do* know about, and use that analogy to make the new digital product more intuitive.

This principle of usability by analogy to the physical world has severe limitations, however, and received vigorous opposition from the very people who were credited with inventing it. In 1990, Joy Mountford of Apple commissioned a book on *The Art of Human–Computer Interface Design* that set out a comprehensive design research agenda following the commercial success of the Macintosh. Hypertext pioneer Ted Nelson, in his contribution to that book, said:

> What I object to is severalfold: first, these mnemonic gimmicks are not very useful for presenting the ideas in the first place; second, their resemblance to any real objects in the world is so tenuous that it gets in the way more than it helps; and third . . . the metaphor becomes a dead weight . . . The visualizations become locked to some sort of continuing relation to the mnemonic. It becomes like a lie or a large government project: more and more things have to be added to it.[2]

My own PhD began by following textbook advice, but ended up challenging the myth of the metaphor.[3] My experimental results found that, while iconic pictures can be useful mnemonics (slightly more than a gimmick, as Ted Nelson claimed, though not very much more), the complex analogy did little to support understanding. In fact, the mnemonic was surprisingly effective even when people completely misunderstood the analogy.[4] One person thought the "folder" icon was a briefcase to carry documents around, and I recently heard someone describe the "cut" from *cut and paste* as a hole in her finger to suck up text, ignoring the reference to old-style paper editing with scissors and glue.[5]

Skeuomorphism

Making user interfaces resemble older technologies is not unique to software. In the early days of the automobile, there was huge diversity in operator controls. Arrangements for steering included bicycle handlebars, a tiller handle as on a boat, and even reins that could be used like steering a horse. Today we expect cars to have a steering wheel, but we can imagine how reins might have seemed a good idea at the time. People buying motor cars already rode horses, so would have intuitively understood the steering arrangement. The steering wheel, on the other hand, was a new invention. People who had never seen one before might take a little while to work it out.

This is a constant challenge for the designers of innovative user interfaces. Many companies hope that their new products will be seen as familiar or "intuitive." Businesses are anxious about possible market resistance if customers need to adopt new habits or understand something new. As a result, new products are often made to look like old ones.

Designing new products to resemble familiar but obsolete technical material is called *skeuomorphism*.[6] It can result in inappropriate designs, like a motor car steered with reins, or just silly ones, like plastic laundry baskets molded to resemble woven cane, making them harder to clean and easier to break. Although originally an obscure term, the word "skeuomorphism" became very familiar to readers of design blogs and gadget magazines around the time that the Apple design department gave the iPhone a makeover with the transition to "flat design." Someone is sure to mention "skeuomorphism" whenever the apparently obsolete 1990s textbook wisdom about realistic metaphor gets repeated in a technical setting today.

In the decades before interaction designers learned to call this "skeuomorphism," the widespread enthusiasm for analogies to the physical world was responsible for some dramatic failures. Microsoft "Bob" was originally launched as the home-computing alternative to business operating systems Windows 95 and Windows NT. Bob replaced the files, folders, and menus of the desktop with a cozy-looking den, lined with books and a fire burning by the leather armchair. Despite that faithful reproduction of a particular kind of (American, male, middle-class) dream, Bob was a dramatic failure, quickly withdrawn from the market amid much embarrassment. It was just too clunky to access the useful parts of the system among the distracting pictures, and the way that Bob hid the business functionality (not least behind "Rover"—a dog intended to act as a faithful AI helper and companion) was seen as patronizing rather than informative.

Microsoft survived that experiment into excessive metaphor, despite the embarrassment of a product launch and marketing campaign for a product very few people wanted. But other companies suffered greater damage by following the advice from human–computer interaction experts. The most intriguing case was "Magic Cap," one of the very first graphical user interfaces for a mobile device (figure 9.1). Created by a company called General Magic, the Magic Cap operating system was (briefly) released as a product by Sony. Sony's MagicLink remarkably offered many of the capabilities of Apple's iPhone, but in 1994—*thirteen years* before the iPhone was launched. The cell phone, internet access, and productivity applications were all accessed via supposedly intuitive illustrations of an office desk, with a hallway leading to functionality in other rooms. The problem with this user interface, as with Microsoft's Bob, was that it held too rigidly to

Figure 9.1
Screens from the Magic Cap interface, as seen on a General Magic DataRover. Historical product from the personal collection of Mark Quinlan. Photographs by the author.

the textbook prescriptions that novel software capabilities must resemble physical objects to be intuitive.

I'm not suggesting that Magic Cap failed *only* because of the user interface design, and there were certainly other vendors of popular personal digital assistant devices (called PDAs at the time) that failed to continue into the iPhone era, including other licensees of the Magic Cap system. Nevertheless, the artistic renderings of real-world desks, office doors, and hallways that you had to navigate seem particularly clunky and annoying compared to a simple screen of abstract icons. In the decades since then, we all seem to have adjusted quite comfortably to touch screen phones, without elaborate analogies to physical objects.

This was classic skeuomorphism. The idea that a computer screen should look like an office or a den is not much more sensible than steering a car with reins or carrying laundry in an imitation-wicker plastic basket. Appealing to the user interface of older technologies may seem superficially attractive but is quickly counterproductive when capabilities are genuinely new. Perhaps the widespread (at present) interest in speech interfaces using natural language is just another example of skeuomorphism? Speech was good for many information processing tasks at one time, especially when those tasks had to be done by humans. Now that computers are available, we may not need speech anymore, just as we don't really need reins when there are no horses involved.

The escape from physical analogy and the desktop metaphor has been liberating. Flat design no longer attempts to imitate 3D objects, and the more modern style is highly popular. Nobody is calling for the return of 3D renderings on their computer screens, apart perhaps from the virtual reality display vendors who would like people to use email, debug spreadsheets, or type in Word documents while wearing a "metaverse" headset. Although popular with gamers, research projects seeking more mainstream deployment of virtual reality continue to struggle against the practical utility of 2D notations.

What Did We Lose in Flat Design?

The problem with flat design, as in the current generation of smartphone interfaces, is that it is still not a good representation to support coding. Each app icon on a phone is designed separately from every other app, and the removal of the "file" so central to desktop computing (with the exception of images in the phone's photo gallery) has made it harder to combine their functionalities. This places annoying constraints on practical work, as if you were doing a complicated carpentry project with a Swiss Army knife. If you can only use one tool at a time, your work is far more constrained than if you could use a workbench with multiple tools that could be combined in different ways, including temporary arrangements for clamping and assembling. A smartphone that supported moral codes would be more like a workbench, allowing software elements to be related to each other and combined, rather than exist as a collection of flatly isolated features with no unifying logic or representation.

Alan Kay's contribution to *The Art of Human–Computer Interface Design*— the same book in which Ted Nelson made his diatribe against bureaucratic metaphor—presents an impressive manifesto for the technical steps that he suggested should come next.[7] Many of his predictions for the growth of hardware and online media are now everyday reality, but the evolution of the GUI metaphor into an iconic flat design is almost the reverse of what he proposed. Kay agreed that Apple's adoption of metaphor was wrong for what was needed, but suggested that interfaces should be more magical— not like presentational graphics that might appear on a physical page, but interactive controls that coordinate work being done behind the scenes by intelligent agents.

Alan Kay has always been a pioneer and advocate of the design priorities that I am calling moral codes. Even in 1990, the need to integrate AI with human–computer interaction was apparent to Kay, just as to Allen Cypher and others using machine learning methods to make programmable human-centric "agents," such as Henry Lieberman at the MIT AI Lab and Media Lab.[8]

All of these researchers saw an opportunity for shared responsibility between machine learning and human intelligence. Kay's personal view on user interface made many analogies to human uses of visual representation in the past, suggesting what kinds of cognitive capacity might be exploited in the future. The role of imagination, to invent types of code that transcend existing standards and products, is essential; his original proposal for the Dynabook introduced it as a science fiction fantasy rather than a technical proposal. The failure of a company called General Magic is ironic, especially since Kay himself had advocated magic as the way to avoid the tyranny of literalism. It ultimately failed, however, as do many projects that fail to rec-ognize the true opportunities from AI, not because it was too magical, but because it was too literal.

We might even think of the desktop metaphor as partly responsible for the rise of surveillance capitalism. In the typical iconic GUI, whether real-istic 3D or flat design, the system *watches* you moving objects around, but there is no way to say what you would like done with those observations. Looking "inside" or "behind" an object to see its invisible data exhaust requires some kind of transparency that breaks the metaphor. The com-mercial advocates of metaphor, such as Apple's Bruce Tognazzini, explained in his book *Tog on Interface* that it was essential to maintain the illusion, and that the company should never let the user into the technical "engine room" where the real machinery could be found.[9] Unfortunately, this is the problem with any society governed by magic—the person who defines and controls the magic gets to exercise a kind of power that can't be questioned using the surface logic of non-magical everyday appearances.

The worst problem with metaphor was that it disguised the potential of abstract notation. If everything on the screen works like a physical object, there is no way to describe what ought to be done in the future (the future is an abstraction), or a policy that must be applied in multiple places (a class of situations is an abstraction). As I explained in chapter 7, interacting with physical objects is so easy to understand, and requires minimal atten-tion investment, because every action has only one effect. But minimal investment offers minimal return. If an icon is interpreted as a physical object rather than as an abstract notation, it expresses no computational power. If every object is just the way it is, it can never change in response to different contexts. Operations in the real, physical world are unavoidably repetitious, precisely because each action on a single object affects only that object. These are the things we lose, by treating the screen only as a mirror of the physical world, not capturing the "magical" potential of notational codes.

Although this chapter might have seemed like distant history, an urgent question for today is whether the emphasis on imitating human conver-sation in AI chatbots and large language models might be a new kind of skeuomorphism. Thirty years ago, people were incredibly impressed by technology that delivered sharp pictures on a mobile device screen. They thought it was obvious that this graphical realism would lead to intuitive user interfaces. But as it turned out, imitating the physical world at an unprecedented level just made the computer more clunky. Today, we have reached equivalent levels of hype in delivering text that realistically simulates human conversation. Just as before, everybody is assuming that realistic simulation of something we are already familiar with will make a product more intuitive—the classic error of skeuomorphism. What if imitating real human conversation turns out to be a rather clunky way of interacting with computers, just as imitating real-world scenery was?

The pictures on the Magic Cap screen were technically impressive at the time, and briefly entertaining, but the additional demands on user attention were not justified by the amount of entertainment being offered. In the same way, interacting with a chatbot is often more time consuming and error-prone than simply using a standard search engine. Searching effectively does involve some investment of attention: forming an abstract concept of what you want, selecting the most effective keywords, navigating the thicket of advertisers, and so on. But at least these abstractions are visible and manipulable—in fact, a kind of moral code. Do we really want to lose all this, by surrendering to the agreeable illusions of language models acting like our AI friends?

This chapter has zoomed in to look at notation-in-the-small, considering how even the design of icons and home screens reflects a set of policies that determine how regular users are able to invest their attention. The next chapter zooms back out, to see how some of the same principles apply even in huge software development projects, staffed by hundreds of programmers writing thousands or millions of lines of code.

The message of this book is that the world needs less AI, and better programming languages. If we want to tell computers what to do, we need a language of some kind through which to instruct them. Although it's possible to use natural human language when interacting with computers, past attempts to replace programming languages with human ones have not been promising. Human language, after all, has been optimized over millennia for a single purpose—communicating with other humans. Human society is founded on language, as is science, the arts, business, scholarship, and of course the book you are reading, as well as all the professional work and academic research that has prepared me for writing this, and you for reading it.

It has often seemed as though the ultimate goal of natural language interaction research is driven by the challenge of the Turing Test—achieving online conversation in which a computer is indistinguishable from a human. In the introduction to this book, I argued that the Turing Test should be treated as a philosophical thought experiment rather than a serious engineering goal, and that the companies "winning" the test are able to do so only when they make their customers more stupid, while also needlessly consuming the precious resource of conscious human attention.

If we were to abandon the ideal of making computer dialog resemble human dialog, is there any other reason to believe that natural human language, which has evolved specifically for humans to talk to each other, would also be the right tool for programming computers? Making that assumption without good justification seems concerningly like the fallacies of skeuomorphism that I discussed in the last chapter. Why don't we just design better programming languages that would be usable by a wider range of people?

I say this with some conviction, and I have been saying it for many years, but I admit that many computer scientists and experts in human–computer interaction don't agree with me. The justifiable reason for their skepticism is that, despite years of research into end-user programming languages, we have not seen a huge surge in the popularity of programming. Most computer scientists believe that programming languages will continue, in the future, to be specialist tools for use only by professional programmers, and that the only practical option for regular people will be to use some variant of natural language rather than learn a new way of "speaking" code.[1]

In the previous chapters of this book, I have argued for the value of a relatively simple kind of programming, one in which we can avoid mundane repetition by using algorithms to help us with repetitive actions. I have also explained why the most successful programming languages for end-users—including both the spreadsheet, which has transformed business by allowing people to create programs while looking at their own data, and the graphical user interface, which has made straightforward digital operations easier to think about in relation to physical experiences such as containment and object persistence—do not look much like conventional text coding.

Computer scientists have invented many specialist programming languages over the past 70 years, supporting many different ways of expressing algorithms. Most of these programming paradigms, however, have never been made accessible through the kinds of design innovation seen in the spreadsheet or GUI. Some programming languages—like BASIC, Pascal, and Python—were specifically designed to be more straightforward to learn and use, and became widely popular for business use after being taught in schools and universities. Educating students in particular kinds of code produces a workforce who feel comfortable with that way of thinking when they encounter it in a professional setting.

However, there is still a big difference between professional programming, and the kinds of end-user programs I have described in the previous chapters, which, if implemented in Python, might require two or three lines of code to automate some simple repeated action, or perhaps 20 or 30 lines to complete a typical spreadsheet calculation. Professional programmers occasionally do these simpler jobs, but more often work with programs 300 lines long, or 3000, or in a huge team maintaining 3 million lines of code for an operating system.

At such huge scales, the choice of any single programming language is not the most important detail for project planning. Of course, it is helpful to choose a language that works reliably and is a good fit for the kind of problem you have, but those are specialist issues in computer science. More important to the working programmer is the kind of organization needed for a large team to create anything so complicated. This distinction, between the details of writing pieces of code in a particular language versus contributing to the collective enterprise of a massive software project, is described by researchers as "programming in the small" versus "programming in the large."[2]

It is this distinction that underlies much of the skepticism about improving access to programming languages. Some popular programming languages, such as the spreadsheet or the Scratch system widely used as a first programming language for children, could in principle be used to build large and complex systems.[3] But these languages also include design features that would quickly become painful in a very large project, just as a champion cyclist would compete very poorly on a child's bike with training wheels. As these accessible languages have become more widely known, there has developed an inadvertent sense that ordinary people (who do find such tools straightforward) would never be able to handle the scale and complexity of problems that are the business of a professional programmer.

It's true that society benefits from professional specialization, but it's a mistake to conclude that regular people should be excluded from instructing a computer in any substantive way. Supporting that agenda will certainly require the invention of new kinds of programming languages, perhaps as radically different as the spreadsheet and the GUI were from the familiar command line codes that preceded them. We need new inventions that support serious programming, even if they won't look like today's programming languages.

In order to imagine that future, we need to ask more fundamental questions: What is it *like* to be a programmer today? What even *is* programming? In the rest of this chapter, I'm going to describe some of these human experiences of programming, drawing on my own perspective writing hundreds of thousands of lines of code, as well as the experiences of my students and of many professional programmers who I have worked with in companies around the world.

What Is Programming, Really?

The first thing to address is that professional programmers don't always work the way programming textbooks say they should. Textbooks are written by computer scientists who optimistically hope for a better future, a time when programming will be done in a more disciplined and rigorous way than it is today. One school of thought is that every program should be mathematically and logically verified to only do the correct thing in each situation.[4] This is an admirable objective, and sometimes possible in cases where there is a logical and mathematical specification of the right thing to do. However, in areas of human life where mathematics must be accompanied by interpretation—such as law, business, medicine, and politics—the purely mathematical/logical approach to programming has limited relevance. Unless, that is, you can persuade the lawyers, politicians, and so on that their existing forms of reasoning should be replaced by mathematical ones (which would itself be a kind of surrender to computers, in a way that not even mathematicians themselves do).[5]

The other school of programming education is described as *software engineering*, and argues that good project management is the key to building a successful system. Because I was trained as an engineer myself (although in electrical engineering, not computers), and have spent years building practical working systems for different kinds of clients, I have a lot of sympathy for this view, and have even taught it myself. The problem is that, while engineering project management is valuable in the right contexts, it also turns out to be unhelpful in others. I've known engineers who try to project-engineer their families, or their social clubs, or their business colleagues. When done persistently, this isn't popular, and seems completely ineffective in fields like law and politics. As a result, good engineers can find it less confrontational to restrict their enthusiasm for project management to their own hobbies, whether those involve building model railways or cataloguing a wine cellar.

The strange thing is that, although I do know how professional software project management works, and can even teach it, I don't choose to organize my own life in this way. I don't have a model railway, and my "wine cellar" (a couple of dozen bottles under the stairs) is not very well organized. Even worse, my last really big software project did not use professional methods at all, because I started work on it without knowing what

I wanted to achieve (in project management terms, I did not have a specification—a cardinal sin for a professional engineer). Perhaps surprisingly, a
lot of the software that gets written in computer science departments also
doesn't follow the standard rules of software engineering. It is quite common for academic researchers not to know in advance what the result of
their project will be, and to approach programming as an experiment rather
than a contractual construction project.

This is as it should be, of course! We *want* researchers to do original
things rather than simply follow someone else's instructions. However, college students quickly recognize the double standard of computer science
professors who tell their students "Do as I say, not as I do." This can cause
confusion, when programming languages that are popular in universities
for creatively "hacking" experimental investigations of an under-specified
problem get adopted in the outside world for serious engineering. Although
not so dangerous, the reverse situation can also be wasteful, when academic
projects are needlessly constrained because somebody attempted to apply
an inappropriate business management process to creative innovation.

Power to the People?

There would be reason for skepticism if this book were advocating that
more people should use programming tools in order to behave more like
professional programmers. This, an attitude that has been associated with
"computational thinking," carries with it an arrogant assumption that
every subject would benefit from being more like computer science.[6] The
textbooks and training courses used to educate professional programmers
recommend principles of mathematical verification and engineering project management that could be useful in the right place, but probably have
limited relevance to ordinary people who don't structure their lives as if
they were solving mathematical or engineering problems.

Nevertheless, I think there is space for regular people to create more powerful software, including some elements of "programming-in-the-large,"
but without being forced to become engineers or mathematicians. This is
based on analysis of the experiences reported by people who are expert
programmers, but *not* academic computer scientists or management professors. One of my favorite books is *Code Complete* by philosophically trained
software engineer Steve McConnell.[7] This book marked the first time I saw

a convincing description of what my own life as a professional programmer had really been like. After another 20 years studying programmers, and thinking about the core messages in McConnell's book, I think there are a couple of things that define the essence of programming and that, as a practice, would allow many more people to instruct computers.

The first of these practices is *naming*, and the second is *testing*. Both are part of a way of working that many people describe as a "craft" of programming, rather than a science. Those who advocate this way of thinking about programming refer to professions such as carpentry, weaving, or even jazz improvisation to explain what it is really like to work with software as a craft material.

The Abstract Craft of Making Code

To many people, it seems odd to describe software as "material," when it is also in many ways immaterial.[8] But although code is just bits sent down a cable or stored on a disk drive, the day-to-day experience of a programmer is that code seems to resist what you want to do with it. Writing software involves constant small adjustments—as you type one thing, you find out that it doesn't work, try something else, realize that the whole idea was wrong, take a different approach, and so on. Sometimes coding seems more like carving a piece of wood—the chisel cuts smoothly for a while before suddenly hitting a hidden knot or a change in the grain, jerking and splitting in an unexpected direction. Traditional craft skills involve recognizing and responding to the characteristics of the material they work with, in a way described by design philosopher Donald Schön as a "conversation with the material," and reflecting observations of scientific and technical work practices by thinkers including Richard Sennett and Andrew Pickering.[9]

When writing code, the "material" speaks back to the programmer through various kinds of testing, as software development tools test the consistency of one part of the code against another or run specific pieces of local code to confirm that they have the intended effects. The process of testing often results in surprises and subsequent changes to the original plan, especially when working on a problem (such as a research problem) that has not been fully specified in advance.

Much of the craft of programming relates to testing, and professional programmers spend far more time testing and adjusting than they do writing new code. But perhaps the most interesting implication of testing is its relationship to the specification process, where the programmer thinks about and abstractly describes what they would like the software to do. That is a central concern of this book.

An essential element of abstract coding is deciding what to call things. Day-to-day programming involves continually inventing names for local pieces of data storage, screen windows, network messages, and even parts of the algorithm itself. Steve McConnell dedicates a whole chapter of *Code Complete* to choosing good names, and emphasizes the importance of names at many stages of the coding process. Inventing a name for something is an exercise in philosophical abstraction. Two or three words might summarize hundreds of lines of code. When chosen well, this name becomes the definition of what that code should do.

Programmers constantly reuse libraries of code created by other programmers, where every element has a function determined by its name. The set of names becomes a language in itself, a way of thinking about the purpose and potential of the library. In a sense, every programmer of complex systems is defining their own language, a vocabulary that will allow the eventual solution to be elegantly expressed.

When building complex systems, a new set of names might be needed as building blocks to construct more complex functions, which can then be combined with others, and so on. At each stage, testing must confirm that every function does what the name says, and that sentences combining these words work as expected. When programming in an exploratory way, it is not unusual to realize that the name initially chosen has not properly captured the abstraction intended, and a different name would have been better. Expert programmers spend much of their time "refactoring" to change earlier names and redefine the logical relationships between them.[10]

The craft practices I have described here apply to all conventional programming languages and will be instantly recognizable to expert programmers. It is interesting to note that both these craft elements—naming and testing—are not foregrounded by the end-user tools I have described so far, such as spreadsheets, GUIs, or automated macro facilities. As a result, many ordinary people use programmable tools without encountering the most basic requirements for serious coding.[11]

The question for the agenda of this book is whether those capabilities ever *could* be provided for use by people who are not programmers? It doesn't seem like this should be forbidden on the grounds that ordinary people would be too stupid to use them properly. Ordinary people are able to create names when necessary, whether for a music playlist, an online chat group, or a document folder. Ordinary people are also perfectly accustomed to trying things out when doing routine craft work—whether tugging on a button that was just sewed on or placing the first few books on a shelf recently screwed to the wall. It is the essential interaction between naming and testing that is not well supported by current end-user software tools, and not at all supported by AI systems. Today's "intelligent" systems based on LLMs do not allow users to create new words within the model or test the consequences of doing so, despite the fact that those things were routine in programming languages.

Attention Investment in the Crafts of Naming and Testing

Previous chapters have emphasized the central concept of attention investment—the trade-off that simple automation tasks might save mental effort in the long term, but require some initial thought to get right. According to individual preferences, some people might prefer never to think in advance, while others might do it too much, overthinking and wasting time automating a task they will never need to do again. Effective tools can improve people's ability to make this decision, and mixed-initiative strategies can use machine learning methods to suggest where further investment of attention would be beneficial.

The same principles of attention investment that are central to programming in the small apply to the craft practices of naming and testing. A name is an abstraction that requires thinking in advance to get it right, but with the payoff that a single word can then be used in place of lengthy explanations. Testing involves abstract thinking about the ways that a named component might behave, and expressing these possible behaviors in terms of test cases that relate to possible interpretations of the chosen name. Testing, as every programmer understands, is an insurance investment against the work that would have to be done fixing things up if the program later goes wrong in ways they hadn't anticipated.

Margaret Burnett at Oregon State University leads a program of research into *end-user software engineering* that applies the principles of attention investment to help reduce the frequency of errors in spreadsheets. Their

WYSIWYT (What You See Is What You Test) approach helps spreadsheet users think about what value they expect in a given cell, and analyzes how formulas in other cells might cause it to be incorrect.[12] The team knew from research that very few spreadsheet users test their spreadsheets systematically, reflecting a specific attention investment decision: users prefer to make minimal investment in advance, accepting possible losses in the future. Burnett's team applies a design strategy called *Surprise-Explain-Reward*, which has some similarities with mixed-initiative interaction but has an additional dose of educational theory.[13] Their approach monitors the spreadsheet in the background, much as with the background processing of Allen Cypher's *Eager* system, watching for places where an error might occur. This is presented in a way that stimulates curiosity rather than unwelcome interruption, inviting the users to ask for an explanation. When a user chooses to engage, they are rewarded with evidence of the attention costs that have just been saved, cementing that knowledge for future use.

Similar research can assist users to invest attention in naming. Advait Sarkar and colleagues at Microsoft describe a study of the LAMBDA function in Excel, which allows users to define a new function within the spreadsheet and assign a name to it.[14] The basic spreadsheet model, giving fundamental priority to showing the user's own data, does not typically encourage the definition of abstract names, whether for formulas, patches of the grid, or even naming rows and columns, as has been done by some other spreadsheet products in the past. This team's analysis of discussions on Excel user forums showed that, while some users recognized and welcomed the potential of assigning names with the more sophisticated LAMBDA function, others were concerned by the danger that a spreadsheet created by one person might use a name in a way that is not properly understood by another. The study concluded that this sharing and reusing of named functionality between people, and the responsibilities it introduces for consistency and testing, actually challenged the professional identity of people who saw themselves primarily as non-technical business specialists, when they found aspects of their work starting to resemble that of programmers.

It is easy to underestimate the challenges of naming, especially given that, in the standard ways of teaching programming, the name is either unimportant (in a purely mathematical approach, all names are equivalent), or has already been decided by someone else (in the classic "waterfall" model of programming, the programmer was often given detailed specifications including names already chosen by a systems analyst). Choosing a name well requires careful thought, as anybody who has named a baby will know! Perhaps one of the greatest differences between the professional and casual programmer, as recognized by the forum users whose comments Sarkar studied, is that a professional programmer far more often aims to write pieces of code that can be reused, whether by himself or by others. Code reuse is not possible without good names. But for a casual programmer who may write a single line of code to solve a specific job before throwing it away, there is no need to think of this task in a more abstract way, to apply it to other situations, to give it a name, or to test it for any other reason than ensuring that the immediate job is now done.

There seems to be a design opportunity here, to apply the principles of attention investment and mixed-initiative interaction, but with a focus on the craft practices of naming. For many routine programming tasks, machine learning algorithms could easily be used to propose an appropriate name for the algorithm being applied, in the same way as auto-complete suggestions might offer a shortcut to a thesaurus. This automatically suggested name may or may not correspond to what the user thought they were trying to achieve. If the name proposed is obviously *inconsistent* with the user's intention, this could be the basis for a Surprise-Explain-Reward interaction. In response, the user might then be able to choose a better name, which could in turn allow the system to recommend improvements to the code— perhaps with code retrieved from a library, perhaps from elsewhere in the organization, or perhaps from online resources and repositories like GitHub and Stack Overflow.

Applying principles of attention investment to these programming-in-the-large issues offers a route toward collaboration and composition of moral codes. It might appear that the assumptions under which professional programmers and software companies create code, while other people simply follow rules, are being disrupted by AI that seems to make its own rules. But in reality, these systems are simply extracting value while consuming people's attention. The ability to re-name and re-construct software, which is routine to professional programmers, has been removed from many AI-based products. Using machine learning algorithms to support naming and testing, rather than prevent abstraction with flat visual design, offers a far more attractive future.

This book argues that the world needs to give less priority to AI, and more to programming languages. In previous chapters I have suggested that new kinds of code—including spreadsheets, visualizations, and diagrams—will be an alternative to AI, enhancing human experience by allowing us to control and create with our computers, rather than subjecting us to meaningless repetition, pastiche, and cliché.

Large language models do have a role to play in this world, but it's important not to be distracted by a particularly deceptive fallacy—the idea that they will in the future learn to code themselves. This would be especially damaging, and the exact opposite of moral codes, if the result was that users no longer had any opportunity to directly control computers or see the code that did so.

The idea that AI might magically learn to code itself is the basic fallacy underlying many of the philosophical speculations that I dismissed in the first chapter of the book. Perhaps most notably, it leads to the fear that self-coding AIs could define themselves, taking control of their own evolution to become super-intelligent and raising the speculative challenge of "value alignment," in which we can only wonder whether the hidden goals of the self-coded AI are compatible with our own. As I explained, if an argument relies on a central concept that changes its own definition, it's more likely to be found in fiction than in engineering. A device that changes its own definition can't be criticized for mathematical consistency, engineering feasibility, or business logic, because the definition could always be changed to avoid the critique. The magical results are entertaining in speculative fiction, but not a useful basis for practical plans or forecasts.

LLMs may not be able to code themselves, but they certainly will become valuable tools for human programmers, complementary to the new coding approaches I have already described. This is a focus of continuing research and is central to much of the work in my own group; it's also likely to result in significant advances over the next five to ten years. But before going on to explain what is practical today, and what we can expect in the immediate future, it's useful to consider some of the fundamental ways that LLMs can make useful contributions to moral codes.

Making Life Easier for Programmers

I've explained what I don't expect to happen—but what do I expect will? My first prediction is a safe one: applying LLMs to programming will make life easier for professional programmers. Problems close to home are easier for programmers to see and understand, meaning that their own problems often get fixed before anybody else's. Programmers don't like typing more than they have to, which is why many of the programming languages and operating systems that were designed *by* programmers *for* programmers— including C, UNIX, ML, APL and Perl—use inscrutably short command names rather than longer words that would be easier to understand and remember. Because programmers don't like to do a lot of typing, programming languages and editors also have excellent predictive text built in. This is particularly helpful when your boss, your colleagues, or the suppliers of the APIs your code is built on insist on making the labels longer than might seem necessary (usually so that other people can understand what you are doing). For many years, programming editors have auto-completed all of these things, predicting what characters need to be typed next and automatically fixing any accidental typos.

Some of these facilities seem intelligent, but only because another programmer anticipated what you might want to do and intelligently added a heuristic rule to save you some effort. My favorite example was a smart editor that would recognize a line like `"screen_reference.x = mouse_event.get_coordinates().x"` and automatically suggest the next line might be `"screen_reference.y = mouse_event.get_coordinates().y"`. I used that editor (*IntelliJ IDEA* from JetBrains) for the last big programming project I did. Compared to my early career, I estimated that the amount of time I spent typing was about 80 percent less than it would have been on comparable projects 30 years earlier.

LLMs are already trained with a large amount of program source code, obtained from public repositories like GitHub. As a result, new programming editors such as CoPilot from GitHub Labs are becoming really good at predicting "boilerplate" code like the example I have just given (and many others far longer than this)—common ways of doing things that always look pretty much the same, and require little thought but a lot of typing. I'm looking forward to the next big project I do myself, when predictive text in my code editor ought to be even better than the predictive text editor for English prose that I am using to type this chapter right now.

It's important to note that predictive text for programming raises exactly the same problems as any other kind of predictive text, but with more worrying consequences. When a programmer is planning to type one line of code, but the system suggests another, they need to spend time thinking about whether the run-time execution of that alternative will still be what they wanted. Sometimes very small changes in code can have very large effects, to a far greater extent than with natural language, where common sense generally overrides the silliest interpretations and a human reader would consider the intended meaning rather than the actual words.

Silly interpretation of small details is a major problem in technical work. Experiments with LLMs for formal academic writing show that they do an acceptable job of producing text with the general gist of accepted knowledge as reported on the internet, but fail at the level of detail by "hallucinating" formal academic citations.[1] In conventional programming, the general gist is often expressed in natural language "comments" that are completely ignored by the machine and have no effect on program behavior. The precise interpretation relies on mathematical or algebraic details that are hard for humans to read. If an LLM assists in such a way that the gist is right but the detail is wrong, this is the very opposite of the behavior that would be helpful.

The comparative literalism of computers means the programmer will have to check automatically generated code very carefully, especially if the program is one where there would be any significant consequences for faulty operation. The attention investment judgement may not be worth it if the alternative was to simply continue typing code where you are already clear about what you want to do. Of course, there is also a possibility that you might have made a mistake in your own code, and substituting a more standardized cliché will correct it, just as predictive text keyboards have improved the general standard of spelling in the population by encouraging clichéd (but correct) spelling of most words rather than the eccentric spelling variations common in previous centuries.

Code Reuse for the Postmodern Programmer

The only thing better, in my experience, than writing code more quickly, is not having to write it at all. I spent some years of my career creating and marketing new programming tools to realize the benefits of "software reuse," where software developers solve a problem by simply using the same code someone else already wrote. If a logical operation or algorithm is rather conventional, it is quite likely that somebody, somewhere in the world, has coded it before. Software engineering researchers James Noble and Robert Biddle, in their *Notes on Postmodern Programming*, drew attention to how much contemporary programming work involves mashing up pieces of code found online, rather than typing long passages of original code into a text editor.[2]

The most challenging problem, in this way of working, is not writing new code, but finding the existing piece of code that you need. The *Object-Reuser* system that I developed nearly 30 years ago at the Hitachi Europe Advanced Software Centre paid as much attention to the problems of searching and managing documentation as to the code itself. In the days before the World Wide Web, we built a complete hypertext architecture to support these social and managerial functions of the software reuse philosophy. Now that the search and content management facilities of the web have become universal tools, postmodern programmers find code to reuse on online advice forums like Stack Overflow, and in code repositories like GitHub, among many other resources.

Human-centered AI advocate Ben Shneiderman observes that any predictive text entry interface can also be regarded as a recommender system, where the recommendation being offered relates to opportunities for saving time, improving textual "productivity" (for those paid by the word), or in the analytic terms of my attention investment framework, accruing attention savings.[3] Rather than presenting tools like GitHub's CoPilot as if they were Turing Test-like collaborations between a human and AI programmer, it is more productive to think of any natural language input to a programming editor as a search query that could be used by the system to recommend existing code for reuse. The main decision for the programmer is whether they trust code found on the internet more than what they could write themselves. That's an attention investment decision and depends on many factors.

The practices of postmodern programming, whether or not supported by LLMs, introduce challenges for the managerial processes of the modern software industry. Program source code is copyrighted text, and the whole industry relies on a kind of negotiated truce, where it is well known that every company relies on pieces of code that were probably written by programmers who work for their competitors. Open-source free software created under the GNU "copyleft" license obliges anyone using any part of that code to publish their own contributions on the same terms, with the result being that many companies ban their programmers from even looking at code from these idealistic initiatives. But if future predictive code editors are trained on very large databases of source code that have been found online, as already done with natural language generators, who is to know whether the original code was created under one of those licenses? Current LLM-based coding tools include guardrails to check their output against existing code, rejecting anything that is obviously exact plagiarism. Nevertheless, the original training data has all come from actual humans, so somebody's work is clearly being used.

Automating Student Exercises

Perhaps the most frequently repeated pieces of code are the self-contained programming exercises assigned to learners. These pieces of code help the student understand the basic mechanics of programming, but seldom achieve any practically useful function beyond that. There has been excellent progress in using machine learning models to replicate these trivial exercises, mainly because class exercises are simple and precisely specified, and perhaps also because students avoid real-world problems where the context would need to be explained. Introductory programming classes are much the same everywhere in the world, meaning that the same pieces of code can be found all over the web (including places like Stack Overflow and GitHub, where students look for easy answers to their class exercises). It is unsurprising that these kinds of class exercise have already found their way into the training data for LLMs, and that the predictive models are easily able to output the correct answers.[4]

Of course, automating student exercises is particularly pointless. Instead of learning multiplication tables at primary school, a child could easily type "$1 \times 5 =$" then "$2 \times 5 =$" then "$3 \times 5 =$" and so on into a pocket calculator. They could even write a simple program to output 5, 10, 15, 20 (or ask an LLM to write that program for them). But what would this achieve? The point of reciting a multiplication table is not to efficiently generate a sequence of numbers, but to internalize a mental skill. Similarly, nobody needs an automatic piano that plays up and down the notes of major and minor scales—piano students repeat those exercises in order to learn the skill, not because the scales are worth listening to. It is just as pointless for an LLM to "solve" a problem from an introductory programming textbook—the only purpose of those exercises was for the student to acquire craft skills, not because anyone thought the problem had practical significance.

Writing Code in Natural Language

The postmodern programmer is interested in finding code that already works, not in typing large quantities of new code themselves. But for those situations where a completely new piece of code does need to be written, it is interesting to consider the potential for LLMs to "translate" natural language descriptions of the required functionality directly into program source code. Current experiments with LLMs of the GPT-n series, including CoPilot from GitHub Labs, demonstrate that functionally and syntactically correct source code can be created from a natural language description of the kind that a programmer might write in documentation comments or as a "pseudocode" specification.[5]

However, to fully address complex practical problems, there needs to be a complete and precise specification of the *whole* problem. It often turns out that this specification is more complicated than the code to solve it. Years of research into "formal specification languages" demonstrated firstly that it *is* possible to automatically generate a working program, given a sufficiently detailed specification of what that program needs to do, and secondly, that it is usually *harder* to write such complete and formal specifications than it is to write programs themselves. Such approaches continue to be demonstrated using modern machine learning methods, for example in the Barliman editor that will help a programmer write new source code, but only after somebody has created detailed test algorithms to precisely define what the program is supposed to do.[6]

At the time I'm writing this, there is a huge amount of research being done into identifying more effective use of LLMs in professional programming. I expect great progress, including from my own collaborators and graduate students, in the near future. Quite likely there will be exciting advances within the next few years, including some before this book is even printed (some of the things I described in the last few pages had already been deployed in Microsoft's Visual Studio product between the time that I first drafted the chapter, and when I came back to proofread it a couple of months later). The rapid pace of current progress places some constraints on what it is useful to say in a book like this, but there are still some observations to be made about the human factors in professional programming, which have retained some consistent characteristics even when the tools themselves are changing.

The first of these is to note that previous generations of programming technology have always involved translation between different ways of describing the same problem. If LLMs are used in the future to translate from English prompts to (for example) Python source code, we can expect that some of those earlier dynamics will be repeated. In previous generations, the purpose of many translators, compilers, and interpreters has been to automatically generate text in an older programming language, based on input provided in a new and different language. The new language has always been intended to be more accessible or convenient for a wider range of users than was the old one. The essential insights needed to design that new and improved language were often provided by those who had been responsible for training programmers to use the old method and could see its failings more clearly. It is often teachers, rather than engineers, who see how problems could be described in a more human-centric way.

Code (S)witching in a Different Voice

In earlier generations of human-centric programming technologies, the innovators who could see how the languages might be improved have often been women who did the work of programming, or who taught others to do it. In the early decades of large-scale computing, the technical

practice of programming took place in gendered settings where the operation of machines by women was not perceived as a skilled activity, and
programming was not perceived as fundamentally different to operating a
machine, or even to typing.[7] Although developments in programming language theory have often been attributed to men, insights into the practice
of programming have come from women who were rendered invisible by a
focus on the machine rather than its operators.[8]

This dynamic, where innovation in programming comes from the women
who instruct the machine rather than the men who build it, might be
traced back to Ada Lovelace, often described as the first programmer for her
work investigating how to apply Babbage's machine. Feminist histories of
computing record the achievement of Adele Goldstine who wrote the first
operators' manual for ENIAC, codifying the methods for programming by
circuit configuration that had been developed by the six women "computers" led by Jean Bartik and Betty Holberton. During the same period that
ENIAC was being developed for ballistics calculations, the British Colossus
machine, with its emphasis on the symbolic and linguistic operations of
code-breaking, employed even larger numbers of women.[9] Subsequently,
Kathleen Booth of Birkbeck College in London, who taught programming
in the 1950s and published an early textbook in 1958, was credited with the
creation of one of the earliest symbolic assembly languages.[10]

Following this era of machine-level programming, the development of
"high-level" languages to enable more widespread access to computing was
again led by women innovators, including Jean Sammet, whose 1969 book
Programming Languages: History and Fundamentals was the first authoritative
comparative text on the subject. Sammet campaigned in her early career
for computer scientists to recognize the importance of programming languages, essential leadership work that was recognized by her election as the
first woman president of the Association for Computing Machinery.

The best known of these women innovators was Grace Hopper, whose
early FLOW-MATIC and MATH-MATIC languages allowed more natural
mathematical descriptions to be translated into assembly language code.
Hopper was recruited to a committee initially convened by Mary K. Hawes,
before becoming chair (and working with Jean Sammet) on the ground-
breaking COBOL language. The recognizably LLM-like goal of COBOL was
for programs to be specified using more natural business vocabulary, rather
than the mathematical and engineering vocabularies of many previous

languages. COBOL has declined in popularity in recent decades, and business computing leader IBM came to view Smalltalk-derived models as more appropriate for business computing. However, it is worth noting that the Smalltalk project itself benefited greatly from the human-centric insights of Adele Goldberg, who jointly directed much of the work attributed to Alan Kay, paying particular attention to how Smalltalk would be taught and used in schools.

Every generation of programming language has involved the introduction of a new notation intended to support a wider community of practice by being more naturally accessible. This new notational code is accompanied by a translator of some kind that often outputs the old notation. In this respect, use of LLMs to generate source code would be simply another generation of translator. When used by professional programmers, or those experienced in the old notation, such tools become a labor-saving device to be used judiciously. The greatest challenges for human-centric computing come when improved accessibility of the new notation extends to people who may never have used the old one. Rather than switching between alternative codes, these users have to formulate a complete specification in the new way. In the use of LLMs, the challenge of formulating a prompt text to get the result you want has become known as "prompt programming" or "prompt engineering." It will be interesting to see how this is taught, and potentially supported, with specialist prompt editors and prompt debugging tools that are designed in a human-centric way for new audiences. It will also be interesting to see how the apparent gendering of critical investigation of LLMs that I discussed in chapter 4 might recapitulate some of the dynamics in the development of programming languages.

The Boring Parts: Software Engineering and Maintenance

This chapter has paid close attention to the tools used by professional programmers, and the potential for LLMs to provide future productivity improvements, but has not focused on one rather surprising aspect of professional programming work: that professional programmers do not spend very much time writing new code. The majority of programmers spend most of their time "maintaining" code written by themselves or others— removing bugs, adding features, or making adjustments to accommodate constant changes to hardware, operating systems, databases, web services, and so on. If software systems are not maintained by dedicated profession-als, they suffer from "software rot"—parts just stop working for one rea-son or another. This may seem surprising, since there is no obvious part of software that ought to wear out. However, the outside world doesn't stop changing, so although this is disappointing, the same is true of a shiny new house or car that does not last forever, especially if we don't preserve interfaces to the outside world by painting, waterproofing, changing worn tires, and so on.[11]

LLMs don't yet offer much help with the maintenance work that profes-sional programmers actually spend their time on. Rather than translating a natural language specification into a completely new piece of code, the more important challenge for AI is known as "refactoring"—reorganizing the code you already have to accommodate cumulative changes as well as new ways of thinking about the problem. In a mature deployed software application, the types of detail that must be managed are so widely dis-tributed, while individually trivial, that models of the English language are neither sufficiently large nor precise to be helpful.

Even localized changes may be hard to maintain, if the code was origi-nally created using a language model. A routine challenge in software engineering projects that involve translating between multiple levels of design notation is the need for "round trip" modifications and mainte-nance. If a high-level notation is used to generate a lower-level one, and a detailed change is then made at the lower-level, will it be possible to update the original high-level specification to reflect how the system actu-ally works now? Without that capability, many promising design notations have become effectively obsolete. Programs specified in natural language, and "compiled" to executable source code using an LLM, are likely to suffer the same fate.

One promising avenue for inquiry might be the implementation of *live* programming environments in which a natural language prompt would be continually re-evaluated while the generated source code keeps running. This would allow the programmer to experimentally modify the way they have expressed their idea, in response to the effects they are observing. As explained in a historical survey by programming educator and innova-tor Steve Tanimoto, many previous advances in programming languages have benefited as much from live execution as from more accessible nota-tions.[12] Steve himself anticipated how such "liveness" might be extended to code prediction and generation of source code using machine learning methods.[13]

An especially unwelcome liability for software engineers is code that works, but that you do not understand. In the kinds of software project that involve hundreds or even thousands of programmers, this is a constant problem, and in fact has led to a whole research field of "code comprehension." One of the important craft disciplines to be learned by software engineers early in their career is to avoid solutions that may be clever, but hard to understand. Adding code like that to a large code base quickly becomes a liability, or *technical debt* that will result in additional cost of effort and attention for future maintainers.

This is an obvious problem in situations where an LLM might be used to generate code that the original author does not fully understand. A recent study of user experience with LLM-based programming editors shows that professional programmers are already very alert to this problem.[14] To see why they might be concerned, consider a senior software engineer who is responsible for reviewing code produced by less skilled junior colleagues. Inexperienced staff often produce code that looks dodgy in some way, and that does not work as required. Such problems can be identified in routine code inspections, and their consequences mitigated through quality control and training. It is quite possible that LLMs will help quality control teams to identify some novice faults automatically in the future, perhaps even preventing them at edit time, while the incorrect code is being entered. An alternative, also not unusual in professional situations, is for code to be correct, but laid out in a way that is not consistent with company standards or project conventions. This problem of code that is correct but does not *look* correct, is relatively easy to fix with training and automated formatting tools, and these could include LLM-based predictive text.

In contrast to these common situations that are routinely handled in software quality management, the *worst problem* for a software manager is code that seems okay at first glance, but actually has subtle flaws or inconsistencies in the details. That kind of problem is the hardest to spot during code quality inspections, leading to significant technical debt. Unfortunately, this is precisely the kind of code that LLMs are best at generating. Since this kind of code incurs the worst software debt, this is likely to be a major obstacle to adoption of LLM-generated code in serious professional settings.

Code output by an LLM has already been fascinating in the way it emulates the coding exercises prescribed to students and is likely to be a helpful starting point for composing new code outlines, saving typing by predicting clichéd boilerplate, or retrieving existing code for reuse. But software engineers are already recognizing the dangers of reliance on newly written code that is plausible but incorrect.[15]

LLMs for End-User Developers

I explained at the start of this chapter that professional programmers are easily able to look after themselves and will quickly recognize any opportunity to save effort by using new software technologies. Through comparison to the history of programming languages and software engineering practice, I've identified a number of ways in which LLMs are likely to result in further improvements to programming tools, although not perhaps the ones that optimistic promoters of AI currently pay most attention to.

Making such advances relevant to *new* audiences is more of a challenge. Just as with earlier techniques of example-based programming to "do the rest" that I discussed in chapter 2, it is a mixed blessing to have automatically generated code that you can't read, don't understand, and wouldn't be able to adjust or modify.[16] The introduction of LLMs that have been trained to output Python code means that anyone with access to a system like ChatGPT can produce plausible-looking code. But how much use is this, if you don't read Python and are not sure what the code might do? Should you run it on your own computer, just to see what happens? What if there is some subtle flaw that has been disguised by the use of otherwise plausible variable names? Is there any chance that mischievous individuals somewhere on the internet may have created intentionally destructive code as a joke or a piece of artwork, or that state-sponsored actors have written code intended to vandalize or cause harm to others, or that people with extremist views might have expressed those views in biased, illegal, or dangerous software that has somehow been incorporated into the language model?[17]

These considerations highlight the ways in which automatically generated code could be the very opposite of the moral codes I am advocating. If the prompt given to an LLM was a complete specification of the program behavior, this might be of some value to an inexperienced programmer. However, a genuinely complete specification is likely to be far more verbose than the eventual program, even if it does successfully avoid the dangerous ambiguities that could be introduced into the software through careless use of English vocabulary, syntax, and even punctuation. Just as with the early success followed by decline of the COBOL language, a notation that is easily readable but not concise may eventually be abandoned in the interests of efficiency.

A more exciting research agenda is to create new kinds of notation that are easily readable, interpretable, and modifiable, where new users can start from working examples that are recommended with guidance from English-language prompts. LLMs are not currently trained to output useful notations like spreadsheets, visual programming languages or diagrams, but in theory they can be, and rapid progress is being made. Perhaps even more useful is the sharing of such visual formalisms among a community of users, as described by end-user programming advocate Bonnie Nardi.[18] Finding a role for LLMs within real social structures would be a more worthwhile opportunity for human-centered AI and programming research.

12 Codes for Creativity and Surprise

Although most of us would appreciate greater control over technology, this chapter considers the (probably rarer) occasions when we might enjoy having a machine do something unexpected. That is, situations where the machine does something beyond, or different to, what the user specifically asked for. This possibility is related to the questions that AI philosophers ask about whether a machine can be creative, although I am going to argue that "creativity" is the wrong word in relation to moral codes, both philosophically and technically. What I'm actually going to talk about is when a machine does something *surprising*, in the information-theoretic sense already introduced in chapter 4, especially where it is surprising in ways that we might enjoy.

That distinction follows the work of AI pioneer and philosopher Margaret Boden.[1] As Boden analyses in far greater detail, there is an everyday relationship between creativity and surprise. For example, when I watch somebody solve a problem creatively, that solution seems creative precisely because I hadn't thought of it myself. If I already had the same idea, I won't find the solution surprising, despite the fact that the inventor might feel surprised by what they have done. Among many other important distinctions, Boden refers to this subjective experience as personal *P-creativity*, as opposed to historical *H-creativity* to describe the first time that *anyone* had a particular idea. I should note at this point that much of Margaret Boden's work, and in particular her wonderful book *The Creative Mind: Myths and Mechanisms* is primarily concerned with using computers to understand human creativity.[2] She pays close attention to the role of programming, but not as much to the question of whether computers might be creative independent of their programming, which she refers to as the "fourth Lovelace question," and discusses only briefly at the end of her book, considering it the least important in relation to human creativity.[3]

Much recent philosophical discussion about whether machines can be creative has focused on analysis of a single famous instance of H-creativity: Move 37 of the Go match between AlphaGo and Lee Sedol in 2016. It seems none of the professional Go players or commentators on the match had ever seen, or even considered, that particular move before. This single move has been described as if it introduced the dawn of a new age of machine creativity.[4] But here I'm going to argue that Move 37, although clearly surprising to those directly involved, was not especially creative in the sense that most of us will find interesting in the future.

Information Theory and Aesthetic Experience

In chapter 4, I reviewed the principles of Claude Shannon's *information theory*, explaining how large language models do not create information, but only transfer it from elsewhere, representing signals coming through a data channel.[5] I explained that LLMs can add noise to the signal, in the form of unexpectedly random variations. When Bender, Gebru, and their colleagues described LLMs as "stochastic parrots," they were referring to these two aspects of information theory, where the "parrot" is the signals copied from the training data and the "stochastic" part is the random noise used to generate new output text.

I extend the argument of Boden and others, arguing that what we call "creativity," when done by a machine, is more precisely a measure of how much we are surprised by what the machine does. Pioneer of Bayesian decision methods Myron Tribus coined the nice word *surprisal* (as an alternative to the physical quantity of *entropy* used by Shannon) to quantify the amount by which we are surprised by something we observe.[6] If somebody tells me something I already knew, I have not gained much information, and I may not consider this person very creative. I find things creative when they are new to me, when I didn't expect them. The pleasure I get from a piece of creative art could be measured as a kind of attention investment—how much information did I gain from the time I spent attending to it?

In the case of the Go-playing robot, if it is being observed by an expert human Go-player and every move is exactly the one expected, then there are no surprises, no subjective impression of creativity, and little measurable information received by the expert. Another person, having less expertise in Go, might be surprised by *every* move they see, and learn a great deal— but this is not because the robot has become more creative, just that this audience is more easily impressed. In many fields of human creativity, we call an ignorant person who is easily impressed *undiscriminating*, while an expert or connoisseur is *discriminating*. The concept of discrimination is another technical term in both information theory and machine learning, and gives mathematical substance to the common understanding that creativity, like beauty, is in the eye of the beholder.

We see this all the time in human art forms, and especially music, which has been described for centuries in terms of mathematical relations. Some sequences of notes are very predictable if you are familiar with that style. Perhaps the most predictable is if I listen to the exact same digital recording of my favorite song many times.[7] It's comforting to listen to a piece of music that I know really well, although also boring to hear it too many times. When people listen to music, there is a sweet spot between what is comforting and familiar (though possibly boring), and what is interesting and surprising. I like classic blues music where each chord is determined by its place in a standard 12-bar sequence. It's the familiarity of this sequence that makes it satisfying. When someone listens to a lot of blues, they can hum along and make a good guess at what note will come next, or even improvise their own new part to follow the rules they have internalized through long repetition.

If you aren't a musician, but have access to a piano keyboard, you can try a simple experiment. Play up and down the white keys only, one note at a time, changing direction when you feel like it. You are playing a tune in the key of C major. After a minute or so, press one black key. You will hear this as a kind of surprise, different from the comforting (perhaps boring) routine of the C major key. Almost all Western music relies on managing the amount of surprise, just the right number of black notes, at slightly unpredictable moments, to maintain the interest of the listener. In contrast, if a pianist plays any old combination of white and black notes at random, the result will not sound pleasant, or even like a tune. In the mid-twentieth century, "serialist" composers set themselves the challenge to use all 12 white and black notes before repeating any of them. The result has not caught on, nor has it become the basis of many familiar pop songs or comforting lullabies.

Great musical performers, in blues or any other genre, follow the rules of that genre, but add some spice with a surprising note from time to time. Pop music has its own set of rules, and every pop song sounds more or less like another song, because that's what makes pop music comforting and familiar.[8] If you listen to heavy metal, there is a different set of conventions, and we each learn to like what we like. Metal fans enjoy sounds that might not be good background listening in a restaurant. They may think they are special because of their extreme tastes, but a soprano coming out to sing "O mio babbino caro" in the middle of a concert by the notorious death metal band Vile Pürveyors of Execration would be even more surprising to the audience than a blood-curdling scream.[9]

The lesson from this is that we all like certain kinds of surprise but not others, even within art forms supposedly dedicated to the disruption of comfortable mainstream routines. I pointed out, in my discussion of stochastic parrots in chapter 4, that the least compressible, most expensive, data to send over a communication channel is a completely random sequence of numbers. If a message of zeros and ones were composed by somebody flipping a coin to choose each bit, a distant receiver would have no way to predict what the next bit is going to be. That message is as surprising as it could possibly be, but we don't perceive it as being *creative*. On the contrary, listening to a sequence of completely random bits, sounds, or pitches is heard as *noise* (a technical term in information theory, as well as a critical term in music).

I will note in passing that we can sometimes be surprised by things even though they could in principle be predicted by calculating them in advance, such as the mathematical functions associated with chaos theory and fractals.[10] The most interesting output from LLMs results from the huge complexity of their language models, but there are also mathematically simple models that produce complex results. Many visual artists and musicians use chaotic and fractal functions to generate satisfying artworks, especially if they are programmers. Live coder Alex McLean loves to find simple functions that generate interestingly complex rhythmic patterns, which he relates to the observation by South Indian percussionist and composer B. C. Manjunath that in a virtuoso performance, "the complexity can be for others, but for me it should be simple."[11] It is also worth noting that I will refer later in this chapter to coding with "random" numbers, although computing experts will be well aware that there is no such thing, and that the "random" keyword in many programming languages simply invokes a chaotic algorithm whose output is very hard to predict.

A theory of how to code creativity must distinguish between signal and noise. The signal is the message we want to hear (a meaningfully creative novelty), and the noise is random stuff that is not interesting. We are interested in messages that relate to our expectations and to things that are familiar, whether a game of Go, 12-bar blues music, or photographs of our families. When something completely random gets added, for example noise corrupting a digital photograph, it is annoying and upsetting, not an act of creativity on the part of the camera. We do enjoy surprising messages, for example when an old friend contacts us out of the blue. But we don't like very "surprising" data such as a loud burst of random static or corruption on a backup disk. The kinds of surprise that we recognize as being creative depend on two things—somebody who wants to tell us something worthwhile, and our expectation of what we are going to hear.

Being exposed directly to random noise is not aesthetically pleasing—it is too surprising, not at all comforting, and there is no message (even "white noise" sounds comforting precisely because it is *not* random). However, many music composers and other artists use coin tosses or rolls of a dice to develop their ideas in a new and unexpected direction. Twentieth century composers like John Cage were famous for *aleatoric* compositions incorporating a random process.[12] Brian Eno's *oblique strategies* include all kinds of disruptive suggestions, intended to help a creative artist discard comfortable but boring habits and try something new.[13] Painters and sculptors find it interesting to surprise themselves through conversations with their material, where random paint splashes, unexpected turns in the wood grain, or slips of the chisel might help explore possible ideas beyond their conscious intentions.[14]

We should be very clear about the difference between the use of randomness as a compositional strategy and the presentation of randomness as an artwork in itself. I've already explained that the most surprising message (in an information theory sense) is a sequence of completely random numbers or coin tosses, since there is no way to predict any number from the ones that came before. Completely random messages are very surprising, but paradoxically also very uninteresting, because they are just noise, communicating nothing at all. There is no hidden message in a series of coin tosses or dice throws, no matter how much we might want to find one. And

of course, the human desire to find meaning has resulted in many super-
stitious practices where people do look for meaning in coin tosses, dice
throws, or cards drawn from a deck. Tarot readings, gambling, and other
entertaining performances, just like the compositions of John Cage, use
random information as a starting point for human creativity, even though
the artistic performance in these cases will be given by a fortune teller or a
croupier in a casino rather than musicians in a concert hall.

Genuinely random information does not communicate anything. It will
be surprising to any observer precisely because *there is no message* that could
be anticipated. We might enjoy the performance of a Tarot reader improvising on the basis of the cards that have been dealt, but the random shuffling is not the source of the message. An AI system can certainly produce
surprising output if its design includes random elements, but the only real
message comes from its training data or the operator prompts. Random
elements in a digital sequence are not signal, but noise. As described by
philosophers of mind, a random message has no meaning because there is
no *intention* behind it.[15]

Appreciating Surprise

None of this is to say that randomness (or unpredictable mathematical
functions) can't be a valuable aid to human creativity. Just as with John
Cage's aleatoric composition methods, it can be exciting to experience
art works with the right mix of comfort and surprise. We don't like music
(or any other artwork) to be *too* comforting, because that is simply boring. Small amounts of surprise, at the right time, add spice to our mental
worlds. Sometimes, a random event from our own computer, or even an
unexpected suggestion from a predictive text keyboard, might be a happy
accident that we enjoy responding to, and perhaps even repeating to our
friends, just as when John Cage saw a dice throw that he liked, and included
that note in his composition. I show some examples in figure 12.1, and by
being included in this book, they have even become "found" artworks of a
kind, like Duchamp's *Fountain*.

In the future, I expect that I will use more powerful generative language
models to spare myself typing. The one I am using to write this book can
already complete full sentences—though usually in a rather boring way,
reflecting the most expected, least surprising thing that I could say. That's

a)

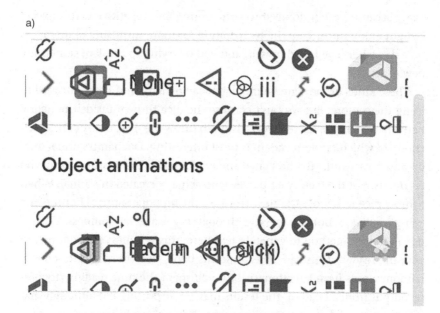

b)

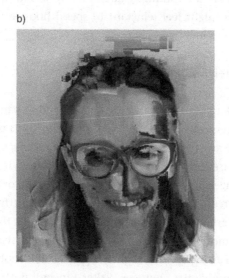

Figure 12.1

Examples of random software bugs that appear artistic. (a) The animation menu of Google Slides as shown in my Safari browser on January 27, 2022. (b) An image I saw of Daniela Massiceti, a senior machine learning researcher at Microsoft, when something went wrong during a private video call on October 16, 2020.

okay, because I often do need to write boring and repetitive text. I expect I might enjoy turning up the temperature for more surprising randomness on a day when I've bored myself, and will be trying to think of something new to say.[16]

These kinds of tools are helpful labor-saving aids, and I look forward to using them more. But we can't confuse the dice thrown inside the neural network with my own creative decision to throw the dice, or my considered choice of which random variant is most interesting. Duchamp's urinal only became an artwork after he signed and exhibited it. And it is Duchamp who is famous, not the factory employee who actually created the urinal. When I throw dice to choose the next word in this hippopotamus,[17] I'm the one being creative, sending a message through my use of randomness. When I use a random method to generate text here, this is a message from me, to you, the reader. If instead of reading this book, you threw dice to choose random words from a dictionary, or if you spent the time reading stochastic output from a chatbot, the results may be surprising. But although that could perhaps be an entertaining game, nobody would be sending you a message, and you might feel reluctant to spend hours of your conscious lifetime attending to it.

How to Design Creative Digital Tools

To bring this back to the theme of moral codes, and in particular "Control Over Digital Expression," it's useful to consider the kinds of programming languages digital artists use. Because artists appreciate opportunities to incorporate surprises in their work, they are often more interested in programming languages that sometimes behave in random, or at least chaotic, ways. In other circumstances, this is not what we want from a programming language. Certainly not a program that is managing the cruise control on a car, the thermostat on an oven, or a nuclear power station.

In the hands of an expert user, slightly unpredictable tools can be surprisingly valuable. Aeronautics engineer Walter Vincenti (later director of the Stanford University Program in Science, Technology and Society), described the long-term research effort to create more aerodynamically stable and predictable airplanes, which, when achieved, resulted in planes that pilots hated flying.[18] It turned out that an expert pilot prefers a plane that is just slightly unstable, overreacting rather than underreacting, just as a Formula

One driver performs best in a car that is always on the edge of going out of control (a car that a normal driver would likely crash within seconds).

I spent several years working with a team of expert violin researchers, analyzing the acoustic vibration and perception of that surprisingly complex instrument.[19] It turns out that violins, like aircraft and racing cars, are designed to be unpredictable. The mode of vibration for a string being driven by a rosined bow has an incredibly complex variety of frequency components, amplified by a wood body that is specifically designed to vibrate in many different directions at once. The resulting rich timbre can be shaped by an expert player to create a huge range of different sounds. When played by a beginner, on the other hand, the range of unpredictable noises that can come from a violin make it a relatively unpleasant choice for a child's instrument.

It is possible to tweak a string instrument to emphasize some types of vibration more than others. To that end, our research team interviewed Robin Aitchison, a specialist luthier who is often paid to shift around a few internal components of the instruments played by top cellists. He showed me how he could adjust a cello to make a more reliably beautiful and comforting sound, one which sounded good even in my bass-player's hands.[20] But as he explained, this adjustment, even though it made my own performance sound better, is the opposite of what an expert player wants. Professional music gets interesting when it has an element of sonic surprise, so this must be available when the player needs it. And to reiterate, the violin itself is not being creative. The unpredictable aspects are just a creative tool for the human player.

So how does this relate to computer-based tools? Just as with violin players and airplane pilots, professional computer artists appreciate tools that have the capacity to surprise them. I've spent over a decade working in the musical genre of *live coding*, where music is synthesized by an algorithm that the performer creates on stage, by writing the code in front of a live audience.[21] In its most popular incarnation, this is the *algorave*, where a nightclub full of people can dance to the algo-rhythms.[22]

Live coder Sam Aaron was working in my research group when he created his popular *Sonic Pi* language.[23] When Sam and I were discussing the features to be included, we knew some kind of randomizing function was needed. For example, at a micro-level, a small amount of randomness makes a repeated drumbeat less robotic, or the frequency components of a synthesized sound richer, like a violin. Alternatively, random walks can also be used to invent a tune, as when wandering over the white notes of a piano. In Sonic Pi, a straightforward tune-generating program might operate in the scale of C major, moving up and down that scale at random. To make the tune slightly more interesting, the program might jump two notes rather than one, or add an occasional "black" note, also at random occasions.

Sonic Pi programmers certainly do these things, and many live coding performers use similar strategies, making use of the "random" mathematical function available in most programming languages. Carefully choosing the amount of randomness in your code, just like choosing the temperature in a large language model, can be a starting point for surprising inspiration to the human artist.

However, Sam noticed an interesting thing after a year or two performing and composing with Sonic Pi and talking to the other musicians and school students who it was designed for. Although random surprising notes can be interesting in moderation, these random tunes pretty quickly get boring, even if they follow rules of Western harmony, such as a blues scale, because there is no artistic intention. Even worse, a randomizing program would occasionally produce something surprisingly beautiful, but then vanish, never to be heard again.

Sam therefore changed the random function in Sonic Pi so that it is *not really random* at all. Ordinary programming languages have sophisticated random number generators, to guarantee (for example) that there is no way a codebreaker would be able to predict the random key to an encrypted message. The new Sonic Pi randomizing function is an artistic tool that produces an unexpected result when first used, but then does the same thing again if you ask it to.

Expert live code performers, like all composers and improvisers, play with the expectation systems of the human brain, leading us to expect one thing, surprising us with something else, then comforting the listener by repeating the same thing again. The verse and chorus in pop songs, the repeated passages in a Vivaldi concerto, and the thematic motifs of a Mahler symphony or Wagner opera all draw us in by repeating variations of an intriguing idea until it becomes familiar.

Comfort Foods—Pastiche and Lasagna

If we integrate machine learning into systems for creative coding, there are new opportunities and challenges beyond those I described in chapters 4 and 5 when discussing large language models. The uncreative use of elements from existing artwork to create new ones already has a name in art criticism: *pastiche*. The term comes from the Italian cooking term *pasticcio*, meaning a bunch of different ingredients mixed into a single dish. (Italian-speaking friends tell me that lasagna would be a classic example of a *pasticcio*).

Pastiche in artwork originated long before mechanical reproduction, when people liked to decorate the walls of their homes with visual art, but not all could afford to hire skilled artists.[24] Instead, a decorator would imitate and mix up elements of popular artworks, creating visual material that filled the walls, but did not involve a great deal of creative consideration or artistic coherence. The result might be a pleasant alternative to plain walls, but would never be exhibited in a gallery, or even lead to anyone remembering the name of the painter responsible. Such decorations might be comforting enough, just as it is when I buy a premade lasagna from a supermarket. However, I would be disappointed to be served such a standardized mixture at an expensive restaurant run by a celebrity chef.

After these humble origins, the term pastiche became more widespread among art critics and teachers, used to describe any work that imitates a particular style or artist by using familiar elements, but without any clear original message other than (possibly) an affected stance of "look at who I'm pretending to be." In the classical definition quoted by art historians, a pastiche is something that is neither original nor a copy.[25] In fact, that formulation, of being neither original nor a copy, seems like a very appropriate way to describe the output of an LLM. In artistic terms, the output of an LLM could almost be taken as a definitive example of pastiche.

Pastiche started to be used more self-consciously in the aftermath of the Modernist movement. Modernism was itself an internationally popular style, famously promoted by the designers and architects of the Bauhaus, who favored simple geometry and mathematical logic over the more elaborate decorative styles of earlier centuries. Postmodernism then reacted to the asceticism of modernist design with visual jokes, mixing up ornamental elements of different historical periods in incongruous ways, intentionally ignoring the sensible functionality that was central to the Bauhaus.

It's important to consider the critical reception of computer art in light of the way that pastiche has become a core element of ironic entertainment in postmodern culture. The mathematical logic of modernist design is inherently appealing to computer scientists, who are trained to appreciate elegant solutions where unnecessary detail has been stripped away. Apple's lead designer Jonathan Ive, the person most responsible for the original iMac, iPod, and iPhone, as well as much that has followed these design classics, was famously a fan of the modernist Bauhaus philosophy, and of contemporary functionalist designer Dieter Rams.[26] Steve Jobs' personal style of plain black turtlenecks and round spectacles, imitated by so many other technology entrepreneurs, could easily have been the uniform of a German art school professor.[27]

The potential for generative models to change those aesthetics of computer interaction can be compared to the use of pastiche in postmodernism. Although simple geometric design does have an elegant appeal, minimalist bachelor apartments and clean-cut shift dresses are not for everyone. Sometimes we just love a sensory feast—a thick and satisfying lasagna, or a riotous party of texture and detail. In the same way that a low-budget fresco painter covers your walls by assembling artistic ideas they have collected from all over the place, so does a generative model produce an artwork that might be comforting for the way it uses recognizable elements to decorate rather than convey any specific coherent message.

Playing with Pastiche

Could generative models be used together with creative coding, so that the comforting references of shared culture are combined in intentional ways, rather than at random? In fact, this is already happening. The intentional creative input to a generative model comes from the prompt it is given. Artists working with such models devote a lot of time to refining their prompts, getting the model to produce the effect that they are looking for, as described by prize-winning photographer Boris Eldagsen.[28] The process of creating exactly the right prompt for a generative model is already described as "prompt engineering," or even "prompt programming." It is the prompt language itself that needs to become a moral code.

When thinking of creative art in terms of Shannon's information theory, the relationship between comfort and surprise, and the extent to which a piece of art is communicating a message from the artist, the moral code of the prompt language is an essential counterpart to the contents of the model itself. Early experiments with generative networks, such as the *Deep Dream* demonstrations, were literally stochastic parrots.[29] They produced pure pastiche, with no original message beyond the selection of the training examples that had been stylistically appropriated or plagiarized. In newer approaches to prompt-driven output, whether from language models, visual artworks, or music, the creative intent is in the prompt—the rest is pastiche.

If we think of the prompt text as a moral code, available for experimentation and refinement as the artist explores creative ideas for communication to an audience, the opportunities to design better tools will apply principles of live coding that I've already discussed. Live coders, like many other artists, develop their ideas incrementally—in conversation with the material, trying one thing, considering what it looks or sounds like, and then adjusting their actions.[30] The unpredictability of rich tools and materials constantly generates new alternatives for the artist to consider and choose, including phenomena that may be complex, chaotic, or even aleatoric random noise. Each LLM has a characteristic style of output that users come to recognize, and I can imagine these being used for intentional effect, just as Auto-Tune is no longer just a way to fix up a dodgy recording but an instrument in its own right.

This kind of playful experimentation can be hugely satisfying and enjoyable, as many users of generative models are already finding. Pioneer of positive psychology Mihaly Csikszentmihalyi describes the optimal experience of flow, in which the stimulation of new experiences is balanced by personal confidence in controlling your own intentions and mastering new skills.[31] My student Chris Nash used statistical analysis of music coding to identify those times when composers become absorbed in a state of creative flow. The key requirement is that there has to be a feedback loop between the changes to the code, the output that it generates, and the artist's perception of that output to direct further changes.[32]

These flow experiences relate to the dynamics of attention investment. Examples in earlier chapters described situations where the user has a goal in mind and may not want to spend any more time interacting with computers than is absolutely necessary. In creative flow, spending time becomes meaningful in itself. This is the essence of art and play—things we do for their own sake, worthwhile because they relax us, help us grow as a person, or enrich shared culture, not only for some practical purpose. We invest attention in art, play, and relaxation because it is intrinsically good for us as humans.

As another example of the hybrid moral codes described in chapter 8, Chris Nash's VSTrack presents music as a cross between a spreadsheet and a piano roll.[33] The screen scrolls upwards as the music plays, with the notes on the current row playing at each beat.[34] This unusual format, known as a "tracker," allows computer-based artists such as game designers to explore generative algorithms within the Cubase system, without the musical training needed to read a score. For new flow experiences with generative machine learning models, we need open and learnable alternatives to the text-based prompt interface. At present, artists using such models must keep a record of the prompt texts they have tried, experimenting with different changes but without really knowing in advance how these might interact with the content of the model. The rhetoric of AI creativity, which ignores the significance of both the training data and the prompt text, is extremely unhelpful.

We might even imagine new software artforms in which LLMs are used to generate more playful source code, without knowing in advance what we want this code to do. Such code is unlikely to be conventionally useful, as it would be when a software engineer uses an LLM to find reusable code components or to avoid typing by using predictive text. However, we might imagine that stochastic/aleatoric processes for source code synthesis could be a component of an artistic project or program, perhaps alongside other practices of programming identified by creative hacker Ilias Bergstrom, becoming a useful resource for the kinds of people who might be motivated to write code for artistic rather than practical reasons.[35]

The Moral Economy of Pastiche and Remix

It's also important to consider the ethical relationship between those artists whose work might be used as a source of stylistic pastiche elements, and the creative explorer composing new prompts. This is hardly a new problem—in fact every generation of artist throughout history has created new work in relation to the existing canon, quoting earlier inspiration and adding original interpretations that make new work more satisfying than simple pastiche.

Technological art forms like hip-hop music rely fundamentally on the remixing of other recordings for rich cultural references. The music industry does not necessarily help, with bureaucratic policing of copyright to maximize revenue for record companies rather than encourage creative adventure for either artists or audience.[36] As a result, the open-source software and Creative Commons movements have been championed by artists for decades, in recognition of how central these dynamics have become to digital arts.[37] The recording and broadcast industries have often resisted such changes, missing new business opportunities, in part because the fundamental concepts of copyright were invented to support the book publishing industry hundreds of years ago, not the digital culture of today.

If we think about the significance of creative work in the attention economy, the most interesting aspect of remix is the amount of attention invested by the remixer, involving many hours of careful listening, in contrast to the instantaneously mechanical operations of streaming and copying. A sampling art-provocateur like John Oswald creates their work not by stirring together predictable elements, but through attentive reading of the original work in order to mold and transform something new.[38] Novelist Marcel Proust was at the vanguard of this more attentive understanding of pastiche, suggesting that pastiche is more about reading than about writing.[39] My colleague Mark Blythe has advocated literary pastiche as a design tool for imaginative approaches to user interface design.[40] But importantly, in all these cases, it is the reading of the original that repays investment of attention, not simply replacing the original with mechanical carbon copies that bring no critical interpretation or creative intention.

AI companies have interpreted the ideals of Creative Commons rather cynically, treating it as a license for a new enclosure of the commons, sweeping up these public goods without acknowledgement into their own privately owned machine learning models.[41] As I've already explained, pretending that the AI itself is the author of the resulting output is akin to institutionalized plagiarism, especially if commercial licensing terms prevent the open and creative culture that was the intention of Creative Commons in the first place.[42] If we set aside the business of "art" for a moment, and imagine the meaningful human experience of sharing in our play and inspiration, we can imagine moral codes where rich statistical models might be an opportunity for dialogue among artists, more creative conversations and public reward, and wider availability of flow experiences for many kinds of people.

Rewarding Creative Professionals

Generative models have entered the artistic mainstream, including routine use of neural network-based audio and image generation in music and the visual arts. At the time I write, Midjourney, Stable Diffusion, and DALL-E have become popular creative tools, not only among professional artists and enthusiastic amateurs, but also as curiosities for the public. Recent news reports have included a major international photography prize won by a wholly generated image, albeit an image constructed with great care by an experienced professional photographer who subsequently refused to accept the prize on the basis that his entry was not real photography.[43]

The economic implications for the creative professions seem enormous, perhaps on the same scale as the consequences that photography had for the profession of portrait painting. Until now, it has required years of training to create original figurative images. The only way for a person without artistic training to render an imagined image has been to assemble pieces of photographs into a "Photoshopped" digital collage. There was previously a clear distinction between digital photography (now universally accessible) and the employment of illustrators to create non-photorealistic illustrations. When large image generation networks became available as a commodity service, I immediately, like many others, experimented with whole PowerPoint presentations (including an early presentation of the material in this chapter) where I used synthetic images to illustrate every slide. I have never had the budget to employ an illustrator, but could suddenly illustrate a whole presentation with reasonably attractive original artwork. For those speakers who *would* previously have employed illustrators to create presentations, mechanically generated images might now be a far cheaper option. Just as with the explosion of "desktop publishing" in the 1980s, new tools promise to make creative work accessible to a wider range of people without specialist training, but also less well compensated for those who previously specialized in such work.

Professional associations are quickly mobilizing to address this challenge, especially among artists whose own work has been included in the training data for the very same generative networks that now threaten to put artists out of business. The site *Have I Been Trained?* (haveibeentrained .com) allows artists to search for their work in a number of popular training sets, and then to request its removal on the basis of copyright infringement. There are frequent reports of a body of work by a specific artist being used to create new works in the style of that artist—including, for example a new work by Rembrandt (safely out of copyright), a new song by Liam Gallagher of Oasis (which seems intuitively as though it ought to belong to him in some way), or a close stylistic imitation of a collaboration between Drake and The Weeknd, where the machine learning model accidentally included a digital copyright tag from the training data, so that the "original" AI output could be targeted with a takedown order.[44]

It seems likely that companies will soon use technology to replicate popular styles of entertainment at lower cost, especially where providers of online entertainment gain the status of *monopsonies* (as opposed to monopolies), such that there is only one buyer to whom an artist can sell their work. As explained by Rebecca Giblin and Cory Doctorow, monopsonies are especially likely in the creative industries, because humans create art whether or not they are paid for it.[45] If politicians and regulators remain more concerned with securing access to celebrities than rewarding diverse communities of artists, streaming services will be at liberty to create monopsonistic business models that take all the revenue from the entertainment industry, while using human creative input effectively for free. Large streaming providers increasingly reduce their costs by offering curated playlists of songs acquired at a discount, capturing your attention through recommendation algorithms.[46] If machine learning is used to circumvent copyright law by generating completely new works imitating the style of a particular genre, playlist or artist, the absurd result could be to reduce the original artist's compensation to zero, or even require the artist to pay the publisher to accept and promote their work, as already done by academic publishers.

Other Cultures of Attention

The combination of outdated copyright law and contemporary attention economy logic that underpins Giblin and Doctorow's *Chokepoint Capitalism* is becoming ubiquitous, and it is poised to reinforce the tendency toward semi-plagiarism of creative work that is used to train AI models. However, we should remember that not only are these logics historically recent, but they are embedded in Western ways of viewing the world. Māori film-maker Barry Barclay explains how copyright law cannot be an adequate basis for the protection of *taonga*—Māori cultural treasures.[47] The principle of *mana tuturu* that Barclay developed in consultation with Māori elders, for deposits in the New Zealand Film Archive, encodes the legal principle of Māori spiritual guardianship over such taonga, including the essential element that such guardianship will be the eternal responsibility of descendants. Whereas Western copyright law causes creative works to become less valuable over time (as they become out of date, their copyright expires and they become available for free in the public domain), Māori *taonga* actually increase in value over time, often bringing increased responsibility for those who are their guardians.

The implications of alternative moral and legal frameworks can be profound, when contrasted with routine practices of machine learning. In many cultures, the images and voices of ancestors are fundamental aspects of them as people. The idea that such images and voices might be digitized and ground-up into a machine learning model for creation of exotic new artworks is as abhorrent as it would be to suggest to a Western person that they might grind up the body of their dead relative for use in a particularly tasty hamburger recipe. Being attentive, with respect, to those we love and have loved is a fundamental moral commitment. Creatively expressing this in code is an opportunity for thought rather than purely mechanical profit—an aspect of attentive consciousness that we might very usefully learn from other cultures. Unfortunately, our opportunities to learn such things have been restricted by the perspective we are looking from, as I explain in the next chapter.

13 Making Code Less WEIRD

In the 1985 film *Weird Science*, teenage geeks Gary and Wyatt discover a way to use their computer hacking skills to create a fantasy woman who grants all their wishes. It's a sad reality of life as a teenage geek (I know, because I was one myself) that fantasy women are a high priority for their attention. But for geeks who struggle with understanding emotions, and enjoy spending time with machines (once again, I know myself), it can be a challenge to even meet women, let alone start a relationship with one.

The experiences and fantasies of straight teenage boys and immature young men have played a depressingly large part in the development of computer technology—to such an extent that Gary and Wyatt's 1985 fantasy has nearly been achieved, in a worldwide enterprise of Weird *Computer* Science. In the first wave of academic research into location technologies and mobile computing, the kinds of new social media products being pitched at research conferences and to business investors were all too often summarized in the catchphrase "girlfriends for geeks." Facebook would never have existed if it weren't for a few young men at Harvard who wanted a catalogue of women they might be able to ask on dates. The Facebook founders got lucky (in more ways than one), but it's unfortunately been more common for male computer science students to find greater empathy for and success with machines than with living women. Many computer science projects today aim to re-code social networks and emotions as an objective and quantifiable science, hoping to tidy up the messiness of actual human relationships.

Computer science is definitely weird as a result of its domination by immature men. But this is only a small part of an even bigger problem—that computer science really is WEIRD. The acronym WEIRD was created by psychology researchers seeking to draw attention to a scandalous reality, that almost all published research in academic psychology had until then been (and still is) based on studies of people in countries that were Western, Educated, Industrialized, Rich, and Developed; in other words, WEIRD.[1]

The obvious conclusion was that, if psychology is supposed to be a universal theory of cognition of all humans, and not just of a WEIRD minority, it would be necessary to blow open the doors of the research community and its methods, finding ways for psychology researchers to study people beyond those (largely their own students) who not-very-coincidentally happened to be very much like the researchers themselves.[2]

Computer science uses a lot of research methods from psychology, especially in the field of human–computer interaction (HCI). My own PhD, after an early career in engineering and computer science, was in a psychology department for that reason. The objective of HCI at that time was to observe and learn how ordinary people thought about computers, in order to help make the computers easier to use (more "intuitive"), and in hopes of designing user interfaces that fit better with how people naturally think and work. Many of the innovative visualizations reported in chapter 8 follow a line of research from my own PhD, building on the work of applied psychologists like my supervisor Thomas Green.

However, there have been limits to the success of such research. People are complex and contradictory, and design is difficult because there are usually conflicting requirements and trade-offs, not just easily recognizable opportunities or solutions. This is already disappointing to computer scientists who would prefer a simple answer—a recipe that guarantees a successful product if the engineer follows a predictable set of steps based on scientific evidence.

A further problem is that classical HCI researchers, including myself, had not understood the wider problem: that they were doing their own kind of WEIRD science, blinded by biased expectations and testing experimental designs with people who, although they might not be computer experts, were actually fairly similar to the researchers themselves. This way of doing research might be acceptable for a psychology student (although hardly recommended), but ignoring the majority of potential customers and marketing only for a WEIRD minority who have the same needs and interests as the developer is no way to make a globally successful product or business.

In order to avoid that problem, modern HCI researchers working for a multinational company are far more likely to use research methods from anthropology, rather than cognitive psychology. Anthropologists have the opposite priorities from the WEIRD discipline of psychology. The business of anthropologists is precisely to study people who are *not* like them, their colleagues, friends or families, or perhaps anyone they have ever met. If a software company aspires to create a product that will be popular all over the world, they will probably do better to listen to anthropologists than to psychologists. There are also some promising adjustments to the traditional cognitive approaches; for example, Microsoft Research Cambridge is working in partnership with sister laboratories in India and Africa to recruit a more diverse sample of participants for new studies of end-user programming in Excel.[3]

How Did AI Get So WEIRD?

I want to step back at this point to discuss some of the history that has led us to the current state. The intellectual foundations of computer science move surprisingly slowly, despite the continual bluster of technology promoters and showmen celebrating the latest AI algorithm. Many of the technical and mathematical concepts in everyday software engineering and AI come from the nineteenth century, not the twentieth. Science at the peak of the industrial revolution was determined by the logic of fossil fuel extraction, colonialism, and slavery—all great for business, and all terrible for humanity. (Even after 200 years, those things do have *some* defenders—but not usually among scientific researchers, apart from a few prominently WEIRD technologists.)

This story goes back to nineteenth-century London, around the time that Charles Babbage applied his insights of mathematical economics to realize that routine aspects of intellectual labor could be profitably mechanized by his Difference Engine, and as economist Karl Marx was presciently discussing how AI would work—that humans would become "conscious linkages" in complex systems that appear intelligent only because of the human labor hidden inside.[4]

In the second half of that century, another young man in London was becoming a celebrity for building a mathematical logic of exploitation based on the work of his cousin Charles Darwin. Francis Galton, after studying mathematics, had taken a job in southern Africa working as a surveyor to define colonial boundaries that persist today. South African historian Keith Breckenridge, in his book *Biometric State*, describes Galton's travels with an anthropologist whose role was to document local populations in the areas being surveyed.[5] Galton's own view was that many people he met were happiest when told what to do by more advanced white people. He also amused himself with a hobby that could only come from an immature geek—using his surveying instruments to measure the bodies of the African women he saw.

Galton had no particular reputation when working in southern Africa, but after returning to England, he combined his interest in scientific instruments with his mathematical training and with public interest in the discoveries of his cousin Darwin. Galton hoped to demonstrate racial superiority, justifying (economic) survival of the (white) fittest, by measuring people and making statistical comparisons between groups. Charles Darwin's son, Horace, had established the very first of the "Cambridge Phenomenon" technology companies, Cambridge Scientific Instruments, and Galton commissioned a set of tools from Horace Darwin for use in measuring grip strength, head circumference, hair color, and all kinds of other factors that were considered evidence of superiority.[6] These anthropometric instruments were a hit at London exhibitions, where people queued to have their own superiority confirmed through measurement. The instruments also became the basis of the long-running Anthropometric Project in my own university, which measured Cambridge undergraduates in order to correlate their head measurements with academic results.

We might laugh at the unsuccessful scientific experiments of 100 years ago, but today the Anthropometric Project seems worse than ridiculous. We have seen the progression from scientific curiosity (whatever its questionable motivations in Galton's earlier life), to the eugenics projects of the Nazis and other racists who continue to suggest that it is possible to "scientifically" improve the human race through excluding or even eliminating those deemed less fit by some supposedly objective measure. The relationship to British colonialism and slavery is less often commented on (especially in British histories), and Galton and his students are still widely celebrated for their invention of modern statistical methods—in fact, the very same statistical methods that were used in my own psychology PhD.

The idea of measuring WEIRD people as a basis for "intuitive" software design now seems a worryingly racialized project.

Unfortunately, many modern machine learning algorithms build directly on mathematical principles that were invented as part of the racist legacy of Galton. For example, the word "regression" was first used as a way of predicting the supposed regression to inferior racial traits across successive human generations that might appear briefly to be advancing, but whose children will always revert to type because they have descended from inferior genetic stock.[7] The word "regression" is used every day by computer scientists who have no idea that it was originally created to support a racist theory (although the word itself was always there as a clue, for anyone sufficiently curious to ask).

I'm not suggesting that a mathematical algorithm is necessarily racist, even if it was originally invented for racist purposes, but we do need to be concerned that the word "intelligence" is also part of the racist project of eugenics. It soon became clear from the anthropometric projects in Cambridge and elsewhere that measurements of a person's head or brain size did not have any correlation to their academic results, or indeed to any other performance measurement of any interest (apart from, presumably, the useful ability to put one's head into small holes when looking for things).

The importance of intellectual labor, as already analyzed by Babbage and Marx, meant that there was great demand for a way to measure intellectual productivity and aptitude. Ideas of scientific government demanded scientific evidence in support of the claims that WEIRD people (usually white people in the global North) were qualified to tell Black people in the Global South how to run their lives. Intelligence testing was developed out in the open as a way of justifying race colonialism, but has continued into the late twentieth century and even the twenty-first, long after the other projects of eugenics have been condemned. Philosopher of AI Stephen Cave has documented how the word "intelligence" itself was not used to refer to a measurable aptitude until this period of global racism.[8] Cave draws attention to the worrying fact that, since the very idea of mechanically quantifiable intelligence is a racist project, the scientific ambition to replicate that mechanically quantifiable phenomenon in a computer—artificial intelligence—is nothing more or less than artificial racism.

When I realized this myself, a lot of the problems of AI suddenly became clear. It is well known that AI systems are routinely biased, making decisions in ways that are racist and sexist. Most AI researchers believe that this is an accident and can be fixed through better (unbiased) training data, or even mathematical methods to identify racist bias as a statistical deviation to be corrected. However, scholars of technology who understand the history of race, most notably Ruha Benjamin, have fought against those naive assumptions, demonstrating the many ways in which these systems are racist by design, not by accident.[9] Indeed, racism itself is a kind of technology, invented to underpin the industrial processes and legacies of slavery.

There are still a few people who defend intelligence testing, including recent scandals that use statistical arguments to claim Black people are less intelligent than white people.[10] Perhaps this is consistent with an ongoing colonial logic. If you believe that all good things in the world are created by WEIRD white people, and that the world's problems will be solved by WEIRD white people continuing to tell poor Black people what to do, then I guess you might think that AI research is going in the right direction and will solve the world's problems.

On the other hand, if you have started to notice that some of our engineering advances have made the world worse instead of better, you might wonder whether more of the same is such a good idea. As an engineer myself, trained in the continuous tradition of mathematics and computing that has passed pretty seamlessly from the nineteenth century to the twentieth and now to the twenty-first, I'm certainly thinking that we might need to work differently in the future.

I'm a WEIRD person myself. Not only have I had a comfortable life with my white skin, my middle-class upbringing, and casual exploitation of the beautiful natural resources in my home country of Aotearoa New Zealand, I was also lucky enough to grow up in an era when geeky teenage boys obsessed with math and machines got to be rich celebrities rather than sad outcasts. We have made some progress, in our WEIRD computer science departments, to at least "let some women into the clubhouse" as Jane Margolis and Allan Fisher put it.[11] At the time I am writing, this too often requires women to put up with casual sexism and be patient with the questionable fascinations of many AI researchers who want to create machines as their social partners (in the classic Turing Test) rather than have meaningful relationships with actual women.

All of this is directly relevant to the problem of moral codes. So much of AI is created on foundations of global inequality, racism, and environmental

devastation, as chillingly documented by technology scholar Kate Crawford in her *Atlas of AI*.[12] But the alternatives to AI that I've been describing
in this book, including computers that are more programmable by regular
people, could easily continue to perpetuate the same problems—especially
in the hands of people who have no interest in justice or moral codes.

There is a wealth of expertise in HCI and human-centered AI, with research
tools and design methods that directly tackle these inequalities. Nicola
Bidwell has spent many years working with local and indigenous communities in Africa and Australia, developing design approaches that integrate
technology more meaningfully into their lives.[13] Margaret Burnett and her
colleagues created the GenderMag(nifier) as a design tool to help engineers
recognize and avoid the gendered assumptions in abstract interfaces like
those I described in chapters 8 and 9.[14] Excellent critical scholars who draw
attention to the legacies that still constrain such design work include Rachel
Adams, Abeba Birhane, and Shaowen Bardzell.[15] It has been a privilege for
me to learn from such friends and mentors, and I refer constantly to their
work. Many others also understand the importance of escaping the WEIRD
lenses of computer science, perhaps most famously Timnit Gebru, one of
the lead authors of the seminal *Stochastic Parrots* paper, who subsequently
established the Distributed AI Research Institute to "[m]itigate / disrupt /
eliminate / slow down harms caused by AI technology, and cultivate spaces
to accelerate imagination and creation of new technologies and tools to
build a better future."[16]

A Less WEIRD Alternative

Readers will not be surprised if I advocate new approaches that are less
WEIRD. This will require new research methods, probably different from
the work being done by the teams of innovators mentioned in earlier chapters of this book. Although there have been substantial advances from
WEIRD universities and corporate research laboratories that could be used
to make future computer technologies more controllable and explainable,
many of those advances have come from old white men like me who had
access to the first generation of personal computers in their wealthy schools
and universities. I'm thrilled that some of the most recent and important
advances, especially those lifting the lid on the worst problems, are now
coming from people with Black and brown skins, from women and people

with queer identities. Although the voices of these people have been essential in helping us step outside the deplorable mindset of the movie *Weird Science* and the tech companies that still behave the same way, these more diverse innovators still get pigeonholed as a minority within the WEIRD world of technology, to be assimilated as evidence of statistical inclusion and diversity, rather than their inclusion being recognized as just the first steps to a truly global and equitable knowledge infrastructure.

The next necessary steps are fairly obvious, though this book is not the best place for them, and I am certainly not the right person to be defining them. In my own work, I now do everything I can to collaborate directly with people who live in the countries of the Global South, not only the indigenous Māori of my home country or the indigenous populations of other wealthy white-ruled colonies, but the (usually black- and brown-skinned) people of less wealthy countries. In recent years, I have particularly appreciated the opportunity to work with computer science researchers in several countries of sub-Saharan Africa, asking what AI would look like if it was invented in Africa. It's easy to assume that AI would be no different, but after listening to the real priorities of African people, I wonder how it could possibly be the same.[17]

This has to go beyond giving African computer scientists permission (and resources) to use the same algorithms and server farms that Facebook, Google, or Amazon use. Computer science research, including AI, could be asking different questions and setting different priorities. But at present, there is very little encouragement for computer scientists in Africa to do that. If an African scientist makes a proposal that contradicts any standard assumption of WEIRD computer science, it will generally not be popular with the WEIRD peer review community that manages all the conferences and journals. Sadly, the easiest way for a computer science researcher in Africa to have a successful career is to attend a WEIRD university, get employed by a WEIRD company, and work on the same problems that all the WEIRD people do.

I love learning how mathematical reasoning is done better in some ways by local communities with traditional indigenous knowledge in different parts of Africa and in other places around the world.[18] There should be ways to program that knowledge, bringing real human benefits of the kinds that I've already described in other chapters. But there is no reason to expect that these kinds of knowledge technology should work the same way as the

legacy technologies of colonialists and slavers. Indigenous ways of thinking will gain more power if they become the basis of indigenous programming languages that build on concepts of local culture rather than sexism
and racism. There is a wonderful international community of indigenous
researchers asking the same questions, although mostly among the First
Nations populations of WEIRD countries rather than in the Global South.

Nevertheless, they show that there is a future for computer science that
follows the agenda described by leading Māori academic Linda Tuhiwai
Smith. As she makes clear in her book *Decolonizing Methodologies*, these
would not be tools for WEIRD researchers to extract even more value from
the traditional knowledge systems of former colonies.[19] It would be genuinely exciting to have creative new ways to express algorithms, growing
from more diverse knowledge traditions, for example in the experimental programming language by Jon Corbett that draws on the language and
geometry of the Cree nation.[20] The vast number of different ways that programming *could* be done, the potential for languages in themselves to support new modes of expression, and the political implications of doing that
have all been explored by my friends Geoff Cox and Alex McLean in their
book for this same series at MIT Press, *Speaking Code*.[21] I hope we all see a
future when the liberating agenda of *Speaking Code* can be recognized in
computer science research programs arising from the Global South.

Although I am excited by the idea of indigenous programming languages (and perhaps even indigenous AI, though this has to address the
problem of how to simulate intelligence when the original definition of
intelligence comes from Western racism), and will do whatever I can to
support and advocate for Southern and Black leadership of that enterprise,
I will not suggest any prescriptions in this book of how it ought to be done.
I am proud to be associated with the work already being done by my collaborators from the South, to continue to learn from friends and mentors
whose work I have mentioned here, and to work with students from those
countries—but the most effective leadership and best ideas will come from
them, not from what I write here. I'm certainly excited by projects like the
work of Jon Corbett, and ideas developed by participants in the *Indigenous
Protocol* project convened by Jason Lewis in Hawai'i.[22] I hope that readers of
this book will find many other examples to draw on in the future.

14   Reimagining AI to Invent More Moral Codes

Friends who teach in English departments are amused when I explain that AI is a branch of literature, not science. It's true that a lot of AI research has been based out of computer science departments like my own, but there is an old academic joke that any discipline requiring the word "science" in its name is probably not a science.[1] We don't talk about "physics science," "chemistry science," or "biology science." Is there some doubt as to how "scientific" the subjects of "management science," "political science," or— yes—"computer science" really are?

The origins of the natural sciences were in looking objectively at the natural world, creating measurements, and developing theories from the evidence.[2] This is in contrast to research in the arts (whether literary, depictive, or mechanical), where the objects of study are things that humans make. In the arts, we try to make the world better—or make *something* in the world that is better—rather than just observing how things naturally are. We shouldn't be distracted by whether a discipline uses numerical measurements and mathematical calculations.[3] A researcher might work quantitatively by counting the number of different words used in James Joyce's *Ulysses*, but just because they are using math, this doesn't mean that they have suddenly become a physicist rather than a literary scholar.[4]

AI is a branch of literature because it is a work of human imagination. All AI research starts with some kind of human fantasy about what a computer *might* be able to do in the future. The daily work of an AI researcher, just like a novelist or playwright, involves typing on a computer keyboard to produce a text. If things go well, a successful AI program, like a successful novel or play, fills in enough convincing detail so that the initial concept becomes a fully realized imaginative world. Literary texts are evaluated when the results are presented or performed in front of an audience. In the case of a play, this might involve using stage machinery to present an illusion to the audience in a theatre. In the case of an AI program, the evaluation occurs when it is "performed" with computing machinery to present an illusion to the audience on a display screen.[5] The value and significance of literary works—whether poems, plays, novels, or AI programs—is decided by how the audience reacts, by what the critics say about it, and most importantly, whether people want to see more of this kind of stuff, perhaps after they have considered comments from the critics.

The idea of machines that behave like humans is not new in literature—there have been stories like this for many centuries, and artificial humans were a regular feature of plays, novels, and films long before the invention of the Turing Test or the first research meetings and funded projects in AI. But we are not obliged to *build* something just because it has been imagined. Thought experiments can simply be great literature. Franz Kafka's *Metamorphosis* explored the consequences of a man turning into an insect. We appreciate the implications without sponsoring research into human-insect studies or trying to create artificial insects by genetic manipulation. When killer robots from the future or artificial lovers appear in art, they are a metaphor for human anxieties and fantasies, effective even when they don't exist. Artificial general intelligence, an imaginative thought experiment in Alan Turing's Test, does not need to become a design objective, just as Kafka's creation can be appreciated without trying to design more human-like insects.

AI and the Entertainment Industry

It has been remarked that AI is the branch of computer science that tries to make computers work the way they do in the movies. This is a perfectly valid objective. If AI were recognized as a part of the entertainment industry, it could join the other sub-fields of computer science already devoted to entertainment. We enjoy digital effects in movies and explore imaginary worlds in virtual reality headsets. Sophisticated theatrical illusions and stage machinery have been a focus of innovation for humanity over centuries. AI fits comfortably alongside computer graphics and virtual reality within that entertainment tradition, and I will continue to enjoy them all. The necessary AI hardware is already installed at movie companies and in gaming consoles, because the deep neural networks used in AI research run on the same graphics processor units that power CGI animation and virtual reality games.

By this stage of the book, you probably won't be surprised that I consider AI to be a branch of the entertainment industry, best studied by academics trained in literature (perhaps with some mathematical tools from the digital humanities), rather than attempting to treat it as a natural science. However, I wouldn't want to suggest that entertainment and literature are unimportant. I think we should have more, and better. I also think academics should contribute to the entertainment industries among other branches of culture. One of the largest AI research centers in my own university right now is the Leverhulme Centre for the Future of Intelligence, which is based in the Philosophy department rather than Computer Science, and employs experts in science fiction criticism on its academic staff.

This might be a useful point to remind readers of the distinction I made at the start of the book between two kinds of machine learning "AI." One of them is purely an engineering technique for building better closed loop control systems that interact with the physical world. The other kind has to do with observing and simulating human behavior, although as I have explained at length, the simulation is really a kind of institutionalized plagiarism, in which actual behavior of real humans is simply recorded and rearranged as pastiche—neither original nor a copy.[6] Any appearance of surprising originality is simply random noise, which might sometimes be interesting when throwing dice for creative purposes, but only in the context of the right kind of game or artwork. This second kind of AI, the kind dedicated to the Turing Test, is a branch of the entertainment industry. The first kind, dedicated to measuring and acting in the physical world, is an engineering field reliant on understanding the relevant science.

Representations for Creative Engineering

This is not a book about engineering problems, although AI engineering certainly has its place (and I worked as an AI engineer myself for half a decade). Rather, it is a book about imagination, and imaginative tools. Many of the problems faced by humanity are problems of imagination, and not of natural science. Indeed, human wars, famine, pandemics, and the climate crisis all show us how engineering efforts, when lacking the right kind of imagination, have dreadful consequences. Perhaps the word "entertainment" is too glib, but there are many potential benefits from more creative opportunities for digital expression.

For that reason, I want to end this book by advocating for machine learning algorithms to be incorporated as an element of better creative tools, helping us make literature and art that *reimagines the world*. Sophisticated works of literature have always been reliant on sophisticated information representations, and the complexity of a large and thoughtful literary novel, stage performance, or movie is easily comparable to a large computer program. I have worked on many projects that studied the tools used by artists, to gain insights into how computers might support them and enable others to create great works.

For example, I spent a day with author Philip Pullman, when he visited Cambridge as a guest of Microsoft Research to talk about the tools that he used to write the *His Dark Materials* trilogy. Pullman explained a complex working process, involving walls full of sticky notes and color codes, voice dictation of a fluent narrative that would be typed out before being cut up and reorganized, and so on. It all sounded very much like the kinds of activities necessary to create a complicated computer program, which also involves revision and reorganizing, keeping all the various interconnections in mind as the named parts are moved around for structural clarity.

In planning the future relationship between programmable systems and machine learning systems, we must keep in mind what kinds of engineering tools we will need to organize our own thinking. Software tools have become an essential element in the design and operation of engineering products ranging from structural girders and field irrigation systems, to fabric stitching and heating boilers. It is important to understand that those kinds of *physical* engineering are quite different from technologies of *social* engineering, like wars and taxation systems, which are primarily works of imagination—the results of what people want from and do to each other, rather than mechanical actions in the physical world.

Nevertheless, in this century, all of these things (taxation as much as irrigation) rely critically on software. This means that there are programmers who work on them all. Machine learning algorithms are useful in all kinds of problems, including these, and programmers should use those algorithms when they are relevant.

Many of these problems, both physical and social, also offer opportunities for non-programmers to have more control over their surroundings, and to use computer technologies to reduce the extent to which we are dehumanized by systems that wastefully consume our attention rather than allow us to *attend to* the business of being human. As explained in earlier chapters, being in control of our own attention requires ways of telling computers what to do. We would all benefit from more diverse ways to achieve this, suited to the great diversity of situations in which computers can be helpful.

However, the considerations in designing tools for practical physical action are different from those that go into making creative tools that help produce works of literary imagination. Muddling the two kinds of systems together is unhelpful, both when critiquing AI and when designing more programmable and controllable software tools. A very current example of problematic muddling is the concept of the "autonomous vehicle," which has some design elements that are straightforward control systems (for example, keeping a certain distance from the edge of the road and travelling at a constant speed), and others that rely on social imagination (observing speed limits, knowing how to behave politely at an intersection, or the relative implications of an ambulance siren behind you versus a toddler chasing a ball at the curb). Some of these functions can be "objectively" explained in mathematical terms as being wholly determined by physical measurements, while others result from argument, negotiation, and attending to the cultural business of human intentions and social conventions.

How can we go about imagining new systems that allow users greater control, agency, accountability, transparency, and all the other positive features that are promised in human-centered AI initiatives?

Earlier chapters have shown how, if we are going to tell computers what we want them to do, we need *languages* through which to instruct them. In the early days of computing, these were described as programming languages. Computer scientists do still use the phrase "programming language," and it has become a routine feature of school education, skills initiatives for "learn to code," as well as a meme in geek culture events such as live-coding algoraves. However, the examples in this book have shown how many interactive abstractions deliver the power of code without looking like stereotypical programming languages anymore. They use the computer display to visualize algorithms and data, offering many different ways of instructing computers how to behave in the future. I've described the work of some innovators who integrate machine learning methods with programmable systems, offering mixed-initiative interaction in which the computer might offer to help, but the user remains in control of the machine and of their own attention.

These hugely diverse interactive displays, which offer different combinations of data, algorithm, inference, and control specification, can be understood as notational systems—what the screen shows, how that display is structured, and what the user must do to understand or modify the structure. In the least programmable forms of AI, such as pure voice interaction, the display might be completely invisible, or perhaps appear as a single colored light. In many other applications, an organization might be willing to provide information on a display screen, but be reluctant for users to modify what they see, or allow them to control algorithms in a way that would describe what the *user* (rather than the company) wants or needs.

If we think of user interfaces and computer displays as structured notations, in which the layout and design of the display help users to see how the structure might be modified, we have created a computer designed to be instructable rather than intelligent. Design for moral codes recognizes that everything we see on the screen of a computer is some kind of graphical, textual, numeric, diagrammatic, or pictorial code.

The systematic study of computer displays as notation systems originally came out of research into the usability of programming languages, but has since been supplemented with insights from research in graphic design, applied linguistics, cognitive science, and the history of engineering, among other disciplines. My PhD supervisor Thomas Green was one of the first researchers to see the need for a universal theory of notation combining insights from all of these disciplines and which could be applied to the design of all kinds of information systems. Green's *Cognitive Dimensions of Notations* framework has been adopted and extended in many ways, including in a proposed *Physics of Notations* that business school researcher Daniel Moody hoped might become a quantifiable science of engineering diagrams, and my own *Patterns of User eXperience*, which considers all the broader purposes and contexts for which interactive notational displays might be relevant.[7]

Design Patterns for Moral Codes

More detailed guidance for the designers of notational systems can be found in many other academic publications, but to give a flavor of the types of design properties that might feature in the future design of moral codes, I can present an overview of the design properties described in my Patterns of User eXperience (PUX) framework. PUX is directly inspired by the architectural pattern language of Christopher Alexander, which was adopted by the Smalltalk practitioners of chapter 7 as a way of describing how programmers might "live" within the abstract world of software tools. Unfortunately, their original ambition for a pattern language accessible to all users has since been reduced to a set of rather mundane software construction tricks, but my own approach returns to the more powerful idea of how to structure user experience.

Category 1: Reading Code.   The first category of user experience pattern relates to how we read code. Even people who prefer not to create coded information structures themselves benefit from being able to read the codes created by others (often called "explainability" or "transparency"). This is true whether the code was created by people (perhaps government policymakers defining new regulations in an algorithmic form), or automatically (perhaps when machine learning algorithms identify an opportunity to automate mundane actions or a language model recommends reusing a piece of code extracted from an online library). Particular kinds of experience occur repeatedly when reading a complex coded structure. These include searching for a particular piece of information, comparing one piece of information to another (possibly across different pages, parts of the system, or different applications), and even *sense-making*, in which the reader needs to gain an overall impression of what a complicated system is doing, or what its designers expect the reader to do.

For these user experiences of readership, there are notation properties that we know will be helpful. These include (obviously) making the relevant part of the code visible at all, but also presenting it in a way that is clear, concise, and visually draws your attention to the parts you need. This might involve viewing controls such that you can see detail within the relevant larger context (not always possible with simple zoom and scroll), or having paths marked out within the structure so that you can navigate from one place to another. We need to think about their linguistic properties: are the elements of the code meaningful because they look like what they describe, and is it possible to tell the difference between different things while also recognizing similarities among similar things? Clever diagrammatic notations allow the reader to recognize new patterns, even where the designer had not anticipated specific questions, by including structural correspondences between the graphical properties (such as linking, containment, color) and the structure of the problem domain.

Category 2: Creating Code. Beyond the ability to use a notational system to *read* information from an encoded information structure (already a desirable advance over current AI-based government and business systems), this book has emphasized the ambition not to surrender control to such systems, but to provide the ability for users to *write* code—telling the computer what they want to do. Giving instructions to a computer means writing a program of some kind, even if it is a very simple one. In a notational system, this means that the user changes the representation in some way, which is the second category of user experiences.

At the very simplest, a user might want to add a single instruction. This could be the first thing they are asking for (in which case a one-step program might be very simple). But before long, it could be useful to add another step, or add information to a structure originally created by someone else—perhaps a further item in an existing list, or to note an exception or special requirement. If all the necessary information is on hand, even a complex task might be a simple matter of copying things from one notation to another, one step at a time, like a well-organized person filling in their tax return after they have all the necessary documents on hand and in the right order.

It is more challenging to *modify a structure* that someone else has created, to adapt it to your own needs. In professional software engineering, this kind of "refactoring" is understood to be both challenging and risky; that insight led Thomas Green to identify the "sticky problem for HCI"—the cognitive dimension of viscosity. A notational system providing moral codes should consider the possibility of change. Even more ambitious, the most adventurous way to code is through *exploratory design*, working without knowing what structure you are hoping to create, as I did myself when building the

Palimpsest system described in chapter 8. Most creative and intellectual tasks are like this to some extent, and exploratory design can be a very satisfying activity. But it does introduce special constraints and requirements on the notation being used.

The most basic properties of a notational system for people to control their own information structures are access to the tools and a system that preserves what you have done. If making changes, it's important firstly to know what the function of each part is, then to be allowed to make changes fluidly when necessary, and ideally to be steered toward the specific actions you need. Those actions must somehow match your own idea of what you are trying to achieve, and if repetitive, may also need to be automated (an ideal opportunity for mixed-initiative machine learning).

Modifying the structure of a notation is where computer interaction starts to look like programming. For organizations that try to control what their customers and workers do within very limited parameters, these kinds of facilities will not be available at all. Standard user interfaces are very restricted in the amount of structural modification they allow, especially on mobile devices where modification might be limited to no more than "undo" (if you are lucky). The kinds of professional programming capability that *could* be extended to users with moral codes would allow users to change their mind, to be non-committal, and to try out partial products so that the implications of changes to a complex system can be investigated and evaluated (languages for creative learning, such as *Scratch* or *Sonic Pi*, often prioritize such capabilities). There may well be dependencies within the notation such that some things need to be done before others, in which case that order should correspond naturally to how people think about the problem. It may even be necessary for users to extend or modify the notation itself, including inventing new names. Very importantly, many people have things to say that do not fit within the formal model of the notation—programmers call these "comments" and they are a feature of every professional programming language. Some educational languages, and many other kinds of notation, don't provide any way to add useful information outside the formal structure, in the same way that you might add a penciled note on a page of this book.

Supporting creative activities through exploratory design requires a special kind of notational system, where the ability to change your mind is prioritized. The kinds of random surprise described in chapter 12 can be valuable tools for creators, as are notations that are less formal, ambiguous even, so that an artist might see different things each time they look at the screen. Some of those properties would be frustrating and unhelpful in technical and business contexts, meaning that notations designed for artistic creativity often look very different to engineering documents.

Interestingly, because computer science researchers spend so much time creatively exploring novel structures, computer science research languages like Haskell are also rather popular in creative arts contexts such as live coding.[8] At the same time, computer science research languages tend to be unpopular in practical and business applications—a fact sometimes puzzling to computer science researchers, but not so surprising in the light of the analysis I've provided here, where the trade-offs between these different priorities in the design of new moral codes should have become quite clear.[9]

Category 3: Code and Society.   Everything I have described so far is framed as though it is the experience of one person, attempting to achieve their own objectives (whatever those are) by expressing them in a coded formal notation. To some extent, that has been the tone of this whole book—the embattled individual versus the world, in which that person is beset by companies and governments conspiring to frustrate, oppress, and exploit them through software. That single-user perspective is indeed quite conventional in the field of human–computer interaction, which originally emerged from human-factors engineering, where the operator's control panel was often described as a "man-machine interface" in military and industrial settings. Nevertheless, I do understand (and take a strong interest in) the way that people do not use software systems in isolation, but often deal with problems in consultation with their friends and family, or interact with organizations through direct contact with human employees rather than software surrogates of those employees.

This is the third category of user experiences that we need to support. When the code of a notational structure is shared among a group of people, or becomes part of a social activity, the formal visual structure of the notated data and algorithms needs to be integrated into those social structures. Social situations are structured in ways that all of us have experienced since childhood, where visual material might illustrate a story, focus a discussion, persuade an audience, or simply collect and organize information. In these situations, notational codes should support social structures rather than disrupt or replace them. Many of the features already described are valuable in these situations, including the ability to escape the formality of the system and support diverse interactions between people. But there are also specific dynamics within the structure of particular social conventions, such as when contrasting alternative ideas for dramatic effect or persuasive purpose. A notation that supports comparison, on a display that can focus or draw attention to different things, becomes a resource for particular kinds of social action, for example when students in a lecture theatre use a WhatsApp group to exchange commentary on the slides they see.

This section has summarized findings from many years of work, and I hope that themes raised in earlier chapters can be recognized—especially the lesson that different notations are good for different purposes, that a mix of formal and informal is important, and that there are trade-offs between design decisions that will make a certain notation better for one purpose but not another. For designers who would like to dig into this topic more deeply, designing their own new notations, or identifying ways that existing interfaces can be made more controllable, I have published many academic papers with further examples and case studies. Building on original insights from Thomas Green and his collaborators, including Marian Petre, Rachel Bellamy, and Luke Church, the above principles have been only a brief summary of the ways that I apply Patterns of User Experience.[10] I have provided an online appendix to this book, with suggestions for further reading.[11]

Much of the early history of programming language design made the assumption that there would be one optimal way to program a computer, just like there is a standard mathematical notation for numeric digits or for algebra. Even today, there are programming language researchers who argue for one specific feature (usually their personal favorite) that must be included in every new language. Such researchers sometimes complain about unconventional languages, such as the graphical ones used by children, or perhaps refuse to recognize that some kinds of code (like the GUI or the spreadsheet) are really programming languages at all.

A comparative and human-centered approach to programming language design and critique allows us to recognize many more opportunities. In particular, recognizing that a programming language is how we tell a computer what to do raises the possibility that we might tell computers to do different kinds of things, and do so in different ways, some resembling literature more than engineering. Understanding the way in which each user interface is also a kind of programming language, including all the design potential discussed in this section, helps us see the opportunities for new moral codes.

This can also be a very different way of thinking about AI. For a typical AI researcher, the programming language is a thing *they* (the researcher) use, not something their customers or end-users should ever expect to see. AI research languages are often designed to support creative exploration by the AI researcher, but absolutely not creative exploration by the citizen or customer of the organization deploying an AI product.

This is the reason why the design options for creating new formal notations are an essential ingredient for turning intelligent user interfaces into moral codes. Many companies superficially promise their customers a degree of control over what the computer will do. But if the display doesn't look like a programming language or diagram, we should ask which aspects have been designed to support control. If an AI company offers only natural language interaction, we need to ask ourselves whether this product will allow us to tell the computer what to do, or whether the goal is for the computer to tell *us* what to do.

15 Conclusion

So, how do we design software that will let us spend the hours of our lives more meaningfully, attentively conscious and creative moral agents, rather than being condemned to bullshit jobs while the machines pretend to be human? My simple answer is that we need better programming languages and less AI. Other commentators on AI have emphasized the need for new legal policies, removal of bias, transparency of algorithms, improved data rights and sovereignty, explanation of algorithmic decisions, and so on. All of those would be helpful, and excellent books and articles on those topics have been published, but improved access to programming can support them all.

In this project, I have tried to emphasize lessons of history, especially principles of human-centric design that have remained important across generations of technical approaches and different kinds of representational code. However, people often tell me that the latest AI technologies are so different from anything we have ever seen before, that the lessons of history are not relevant. They say AI is now so different that lawyers and policy-makers have no idea what the implications might be, and that government regulation will either be too late, or else too early, so that it impedes progress. Perhaps it is true that AI has suddenly become fundamentally different in 2023, but after four decades in the field, I feel that many things have stayed the same, just as they did during previous AI booms when colleagues told me that fundamental changes had finally arrived. Although people might be right that history and policy are no longer relevant to their work, it's also possible that those arguments look more attractive to someone who is simply not inclined to read history, and who doesn't want to follow the rules (or who asks for "industry regulation"—new rules just for them, that legalize exploitative profits while minimizing investment risk).

People who think about AI ethics from the perspective of imagined future problems, rather than the historical practicalities of technical development, sometimes talk about the "alignment problem" for artificial general intelligence (AGI). The problem of alignment is supposedly that the AGI will have its own ideas about what might be useful or ethical, and that those ideas could be different from what human users want to achieve. In the introduction to the book, I've explained why I am not persuaded that AGI will ever be a useful ambition, especially not the more-human-than-human notion of superintelligence. However, even with the kinds of stochastic parrots we have today, we can see how the alignment problem might work out in practice. To some extent, concerns about the alignment problem return to the themes of old science fiction novels, such as Isaac Asimov's famous *Three Laws of Robotics*. In Asimov's work, the robots are not like the machines in factories, but metal-bodied *people*—like those in Star Wars, or like the androids and Vulcans in Star Trek, having more or less the same capabilities as human characters but with distinctive personal strengths and weaknesses in order to serve as plot points. The Three Laws are used as plot devices, where the plot turns on the need to circumvent or comply with one or another of the Laws.

In currently deployed large language model products, any "alignment" with the user's values comes either from text off the internet, guardrails added by the company, or the prompt supplied by the users themselves. I've discussed in chapter 5 whether the needs of any single user can really be "aligned" with the values of the internet as a whole. Users of the internet have a pretty good idea of what kinds of things are out there, and we also know that any illusion of alignment between a single reader and the whole internet is achieved mainly through filter bubbles, hiding the parts that you don't want to see because they aren't "aligned" with your personal values. When an LLM-based chatbot presents the content of the internet via a fictional first-person conversation, the illusion that the whole internet might have a single point of view, consistent with your own, is especially pernicious. The filter mechanisms become invisible, can't be explicitly controlled, and depend on contextual factors that you can only imagine. The ideal of alignment could only ever occur if the code was openly visible and controllable. The best way for a computer to understand your goals is not through mysterious "value alignment," but for you to tell it what you want through programming.

The title of this book refers to programming in the broadest sense, going beyond old-fashioned views of "code" as green text on terminal screen. I originally used the phrase "moral code" to point out that the way we design programming languages carries moral commitments, because attending to abstraction offers ways for people to control and construct their conscious lives. The phrase has also offered a convenient acronym, reminding us that moral codes do not need to look like the programming languages of 50 years ago. MORAL CODE is an agenda for the design of programmable computers that offer More Open Representations, Access to Learning, and Control Over Digital Expression. These aspirations empower us to attend to our own needs as creative moral agents and authors of our own lives, and to recognize the situations where social media technologies are designed to prevent this.

I've explained that many recent demonstrations of AI involve little more than scraping, re-arranging, and re-selling the intelligent online work of other humans, whose contributions are hidden inside a kind of computational fancy dress. The results can be an entertaining pastiche, but fundamentally achieve their intelligence in the same way as von Kempelen's chess-playing "Turk" from the eighteenth century—through the humans hidden inside. We have always found it entertaining when machines behave in human-like ways, even when these are magic tricks. In the same way, the magic tricks of AI demonstrations continue to entertain us today. We don't always want to spoil the illusion by drawing attention to the man behind the curtain.

However, there are some dangers associated with taking these entertaining technologies at face value. The less serious danger is that many AI experts downplay the difference between the two kinds of AI: objective mechanical tools and entertaining imitations of human subjectivity. This fallacy encourages magical thinking, in which future AI systems are imagined as being able to do everything a human can do and more, but it has little practical impact today, other than that important decisions being made by investors and policymakers might be misguided.

A more serious problem is that real people are doing the intelligent work behind the scenes, often with exploitative working arrangements, or even working for free, while huge profits are being made by people who are not doing the basic labor. Real hours of conscious attention are dedicated to training the machine, turning original thoughts and words into aggregated components. Perhaps the world has always been this way, and it would be overly idealistic to argue for anything else. But the dangerous fiction of AI is that the machine is doing this work all by itself, that no humans are involved, and thus that nobody deserves to be recognized and more fairly compensated, or to receive any share of the profits being made.

If we were to replace the search for better AI with a search for better programming languages, it would restore an earlier ambition of computer science—getting computers to do useful things. Everybody has their own personal goals and priorities, and what is useful to one person will not be useful to every other. For computers to be more generally useful, each person should be able to describe what they want, telling a potentially helpful computer how they want it to behave differently in the future.

It might perhaps have been possible that the language of instruction could just be our natural human language. Indeed, many current products are being developed with the assumption that natural language *will* be the best programming language. However, past evidence and recent experiments all suggest that a more nuanced approach is required.[1] The most successful "languages" for instructing computers have often involved visualizations, creating new kinds of abstract notation that are suited to different kinds of information processing and design tasks. Human language is not optimized for such things, and relying on speech as a technical notation is clearly unhelpful in many ways. We need to think more flexibly about every user interface as a kind of programming language, asking what kind of notation it offers, what we can use this notation for, and in what ways this would allow us to define and control future behavior of the machine.

Sadly, this technical manifesto promoting moral code requires some progress in an opposite direction from many research and business trends of today. In Shoshanna Zuboff's comprehensive explanation of *Surveillance Capitalism*, businesses grow by capturing the "data exhaust" of human attention and intelligence. That human data is repackaged and resold, with the objective of capturing even more human attention and delivering it to advertisers, who in turn use that data to influence the habits and decisions of human customers. Similarly, Rebecca Giblin and Cory Doctorow document how the creative industries have fallen prey to *Chokepoint Capitalism*, where a single company becomes the only conduit between artists and their audience, able to devalue creative work through algorithmic repackaging while minimizing the compensation to human creators.

Profitable surveillance and chokepoint businesses do not offer control to their customers and do not benefit from customers who are free to redirect their attention. Those business models are the exact mirror image of moral codes, the opposite of a better world where people would have the opportunity to instruct the computer and be able to make their own decisions on whether to invest attention in programming or not.

Accounting for attention—or rather the limited number of conscious hours in a human life—is perhaps the largest moral problem of all. At a purely physical level, consciousness could be measured as information processing—when I am awake (and sober), I have a fairly low limit on the number of things I can attend to. There is certainly a finite limit to the hours of my life that I can spend being attentive. Many of the experiences that fulfil me as a person, whether the comforting familiarity of a song I love, the playful creativity of optimal flow, or simply time spent in the same space with my family or colleagues, are valuable precisely because I am devoting attention to them.

We are also famously living in the era of the attention economy, where the largest and most profitable businesses in the world are those that *consume* my attention. The advertising industry is literally dedicated to capturing the conscious hours of my life and selling them to someone else. It might seem magical that so many exciting and useful software systems are available to use for free, but it is now conventional wisdom that if you can't see who is paying for something that appears to be free, then the real product being sold is *you*.[2] Our creative engagement with other people is mediated by AI-based recommendation systems that are designed to trap our attention through the process that Nick Seaver calls *captology*, keeping us attending to work sold by one company rather than another, replacing the freedom of personal exploration with algorithm-generated playlists or even algorithm-generated art.[3]

Every aspect of the alternative moral codes agenda might potentially be measured in terms of attention costs and benefits using information theory: More Open Representations allow information to be exchanged, Access to Learning allows it to be acquired, and Control Over Digital Expression allows it to be expressed. If computer users have access to appropriate notations—moral codes—they would also be able to use simple automation to spend the conscious hours of their lives in ways that are less mechanical, rather than more. If computer interfaces are designed as notational spaces, they offer freedom and negotiation and even forms of social organization, complex assemblies of intelligent decision making and deliberation that respect the humans creating them, rather than pretend humans were not involved.

This book has argued for an alternative technical agenda in which machine learning algorithms could be offered in service of coded instructions, rather than overriding human control. This is only a technical agenda, and much research remains to be done, but it does represent a clear alternative. Instead of pursuing AI that consumes, packages, and re-sells our precious hours of conscious life as documented by Nick Couldry and Ulises Mejias, we deserve greater control over our own attention, including the ability to instruct computers to carry out mechanical tasks on our behalf, to recognize how they work, and to use them for our own creative purposes.[4]

All these things can be better achieved with codes that are designed for doing so, not by building machines that pretend to be human. The less time we spend attending to machines, the more we can grow as people, building richer cultures and societies—not worrying about whether machines can be conscious, but being conscious ourselves, and *being human*. Forget hypothetical robot futures. Let's focus on moral codes that let us live better lives today.

Notes

Chapter 1

1. Mike Monteiro, *Ruined by Design: How Designers Destroyed the World, and What We Can Do to Fix It* (San Francisco, CA: Mule Design, 2019).

2. David Graeber, *Bullshit Jobs: A Theory* (London: Penguin Books, 2019); David Graeber, *The Utopia of Rules: On Technology, Stupidity, and the Secret Joys of Bureaucracy* (London: Melville House, 2015).

3. Geoffrey Bowker, foreword to *The Constitution of Algorithms: Ground-Truthing, Programming, Formulating*, by Florian Jaton (Cambridge: MIT Press, 2021), ix.

4. Kate Crawford, *Atlas of AI* (New Haven: Yale University Press, 2021), 7.

5. Alan M. Turing, "Computing Machinery and Intelligence," *Mind* 70, no. 236 (October 1950): 433–460, https://doi.org/10.1093/mind/LIX.236.433.

6. Despite Turing's view that an opinion poll would be an absurd way to approach this research question, there have since been many serious attempts to gain insight through opinion polls—albeit polls of AI experts rather than the general population. A considered review of notable examples alongside results from a further poll is provided by Vincent C. Müller and Nick Bostrom, "Future Progress in Artificial Intelligence: A Survey of Expert Opinion," in *Fundamental Issues of Artificial Intelligence*, ed. Vincent C. Müller (Berlin: Springer, 2016), 553–571; see also Andrew Hodges, *Alan Turing: The Enigma* (New York: Vintage Books, 1983).

7. Jessica Riskin, "The Defecating Duck, or, the Ambiguous Origins of Artificial Life," *Critical Inquiry* 29, no. 4 (2003): 599–633.

8. Shoshana Zuboff, *The Age of Surveillance Capitalism: The Fight for a Human Future at the New Frontier of Power* (London: Profile Books, 2019); Nick Couldry and Ulises A. Mejias, *The Costs of Connection: How Data is Colonizing Human Life and Appropriating it for Capitalism* (Redwood City, CA: Stanford University Press, 2020).

9. Glenn Zorpette, "Just Calm Down About GPT-4 Already," *IEEE Spectrum*, May 17, 2023, https://spectrum.ieee.org/gpt-4-calm-down.

10. Murray Shanahan, *Talking About Large Language Models* (2022), arXiv preprint arXiv:2212.03551.

11. Harry Collins, *Artifictional Intelligence: Against Humanity's Surrender to Computers* (Cambridge, UK: Polity Press, 2018); Jaron Lanier, *You Are Not a Gadget* (New York: Vintage, 2010).

12. I am writing this at a time when prominent researchers and founders of AI companies are, almost weekly, issuing new warnings and demands for international regulation. Commentators from outside the technology business are rightly skeptical about the motivations involved, and I will discuss some of the key dynamics later in this chapter. Nick Couldry suggests that investment in understanding these models is urgently needed by the technology companies themselves, and that their request for regulation is simply asking for public subsidy, with taxpayers funding what the company was going to do anyway. Nick Couldry and Ulises Mejias, *Data Grab: The New Data Colonialism and How to Resist It* (London: Allen Lane, forthcoming 2024).

13. Lawrence Lessig, *Code and Other Laws of Cyberspace* (New York: Basic Books, 1999).

14. Per-Olof H. Wikström, "Explaining Crime as Moral Actions," in *Handbook of the Sociology of Morality*, ed. Steven Hitlin and Stephen Vaisey (Berlin/Heidelberg: Springer Science & Business Media, 2010), 211–239.

15. Brian Christian, *The Alignment Problem: How Can Machines Learn Human Values?* (London: Atlantic Books, 2021).

16. A tool can't be unethical, but some tools are dangerous, and it makes sense to reduce dangers to the general population by regulating who gets access to poison, explosives, earthmoving machines, or firearms. This may be worth considering for social media in the future, especially if content becomes dominated by extremely large quantities of chatbot output.

17. Geoff Cox and Winnie Soon, *Aesthetic Programming: A Handbook of Software Studies* (London: Open Humanities Press, 2020), 30, http://aesthetic-programming .net.

18. Shannon Vallor, *Technology and the Virtues: A Philosophical Guide to a Future Worth Wanting* (Oxford: Oxford University Press, 2016); Ibo van de Poel, "Embedding Values in Artificial Intelligence (AI) Systems," *Minds and Machines* 30 no. 3 (2020): 385–409, https://doi.org/10.1007/s11023-020-09537-4.

19. For a spiritual perspective on the values and meanings that are inherent in consciousness, see Peter D. Hershock, *Buddhism and Intelligent Technology: Toward a More Humane Future* (London: Bloomsbury, 2021).

20. See Couldry and Mejias, *The Costs of Connection*, Chapter 5: "Data and the Threat to Human Autonomy."

21. Herbert A. Simon, "Designing Organizations for an Information-Rich World," in *Computers, Communications, and the Public Interest*, ed. Martin Greenberger (Baltimore: Johns Hopkins University Press, 1971), 38–52.

22. Per-Olof H. Wikström, Dietrich Oberwittler, Kyle Treiber, and Beth Hardie, *Breaking Rules: The Social and Situational Dynamics of Young People's Urban Crime* (Oxford: Oxford University Press, 2012).

23. Andreas Bandak and Paul Anderson, "Urgency and Imminence," *Social Anthropology/Anthropologie Sociale* 30, no. 4 (2022), 1–17, https://doi.org/10.3167/saas.2022 .300402. Bandak and Anderson point out that business leadership texts have even advocated the intentional use of urgency as a strategic asset, for example John P. Kotter, *A Sense of Urgency* (Boston: Harvard Business Press, 2009).

24. Novelist Susanna Clarke offered an impressively clear vision of what the world might have been like if the kind of promises now made by AI researchers to secure government funding had previously been used to realize the potential applications of magic. Susanna Clarke, *Jonathan Strange and Mr. Norrell* (New York: Bloomsbury, 2004).

25. Geoffrey Hinton, "Two Paths to Intelligence." Public lecture in the University of Cambridge Engineering Department, May 25, 2023, https://www.youtube.com /watch?v=rGgGOccMEiY.

26. Kate Devlin and Olivia Belton, "The Measure of a Woman: Fembots, Fact and Fiction" in *AI Narratives*, ed. Stephen Cave, Kanta Dihal, and Sarah Dillon (Oxford: Oxford University Press, 2020).

27. Stephen Cave, "The Problem with Intelligence: Its Value-Laden History and the Future of AI." In *Proceedings of the AAAI/ACM Conference on AI, Ethics, and Society* (2020), 29–35.

28. Stuart Russell, *Human Compatible: Artificial Intelligence and the Problem of Control* (London: Penguin, 2019).

29. Charles P. Snow, *The Two Cultures and the Scientific Revolution* (Cambridge: Cambridge University Press, 1959). Many facets of the history and legacy of Snow's provocative claims are discussed in a special issue of Interdisciplinary Science Reviews: Frank A.J.L. James, "Introduction: Some Significances of the Two Cultures Debate," *Interdisciplinary Science Reviews* 41, nos. 2–3 (2016): 107–117.

30. Simon J. Lock, "Cultures of Incomprehension?: The Legacy of the Two Cultures Debate at the End of the Twentieth Century," *Interdisciplinary Science Reviews* 41, nos. 2–3 (2016):148–166.

31. Philip E. Agre, "Toward a Critical Technical Practice," in *Bridging the Great Divide: Social Science, Technical Systems, and Cooperative Work*, ed. Geoffrey Bowker, Les Gasser, Susan Leigh Star, and Bill Turner (Mahwah, NJ: Lawrence Erlbaum, 1997), 131–158.

32. In the open review version available via the PubPub platform: https://moralcodes
.pubpub.org

Chapter 2

1. Graeber, *Bullshit Jobs*.

2. Eric Bergman, Arnold Lund, Hugh Dubberly, Bruce Tognazzini, and Stephen
Intille, "Video Visions of the Future: A Critical Review," in *CHI'04 Extended Abstracts
on Human Factors in Computing Systems* (2004), 1584–1585.

3. Andrew J Ko, Robin Abraham, Laura Beckwith, Alan Blackwell, Margaret Burnett,
Martin Erwig, Joseph Lawrence, Henry Lieberman, Brad Myers, Mary-Beth Rosson,
Gregg Rothermel, Chris Scaffidi, Mary Shaw, and Susan Wiedenbeck, "The State of
the Art in End-User Software Engineering," *ACM Computing Surveys (CSUR)* 43, no. 3
(2011): 1–44.

4. Eric Horvitz, "Principles of Mixed-Initiative User Interfaces," in *Proceedings of the
SIGCHI Conference on Human Factors in Computing Systems* (1999), 159–166.

5. Diana Forsythe, *Studying Those Who Study Us: An Anthropologist in the World of
Artificial Intelligence* (Redwood City, CA: Stanford University Press, 2001).

6. My student Tanya Morris demonstrated how the capabilities of a large language
model could help people struggling with special text formats like email addresses
by monitoring the attention needs of older users through their keystrokes, and
giving helpful advice at the time they need it most: Tanya Morris and Alan F.
Blackwell, "Prompt Programming for Large Language Models via Mixed Initiative
Interaction in a GUI," in *Proceedings of the Psychology of Programming Interest Group
(PPIG)* (2023).

7. Allen Cypher, ed. *Watch What I Do: Programming by Demonstration* (Cambridge:
MIT Press, 1993).

8. Joseph C. R. Licklider, "Man-Computer Symbiosis," *IRE Transactions on Human
Factors in Electronics*, HFE-1 (1960): 4–11. doi:10.1109/THFE2.1960.4503259.

9. Alan F. Blackwell, "First Steps in Programming: A Rationale for Attention Investment models," in *Proceedings of the IEEE Symposia on Human-Centric Computing Languages and Environments* (2002): 2–10; Alan F. Blackwell, Jennifer A. Rode, and Eleanor
F. Toye, "How Do We Program the Home? Gender, Attention Investment, and the
Psychology of Programming at Home," *International Journal of Human Computer Studies* 67 (2009): 324–341; Simon, "Designing Organizations for an Information-Rich
World."

10. Paul Dourish, "What We Talk About When We Talk About Context," *Personal
and Ubiquitous Computing* 8, no. 1 (2004): 19–30.

11. The consequences of getting this wrong often make reference to the classic scene in Disney's *Fantasia* where Sorcerer's Apprentice Mickey Mouse tries to automate a repetitive task, but gets his magic "programming" wrong.

12. A particular irony for me, as I have just spent most of my free time for the past two weeks mechanically converting the academic citations in these footnotes from the APA and ACM styles common in psychology and computing research, to the distinctive "Chicago" style mandated by MIT Press.

13. Lisanne Bainbridge, "Ironies of Automation," *Automatica* 19, no. 6 (1983): 775–779. It was my PhD supervisor Thomas Green who first drew my attention to how this related to programming: Thomas R.G. Green and Alan F. Blackwell, "Ironies of Abstraction," in *Proceedings 3rd International Conference on Thinking*, British Psychological Society, 1996.

14. John M. Carroll and Mary Beth Rosson, "Paradox of the Active User," in *Interfacing Thought: Cognitive Aspects of Human–Computer Interaction*, ed. John M. Carroll (Cambridge: MIT Press, 1987), 80–111.

15. Do *not* try these commands out on your own computer! They are intended for use when deleting large amounts of data.

16. For one of the first comprehensive investigations of this topic, see Bonnie A. Nardi, *A Small Matter of Programming: Perspectives on End User Computing* (Cambridge: MIT Press, 1993). A pioneering example introducing the concept was Allan MacLean, Kathleen Carter, Lennart Lövstrand, and Thomas Moran, "User-Tailorable Systems: Pressing the Issues with Buttons," in *Proceedings of the SIGCHI Conference on Human Factors in Computing Systems* (1990), 175–182.

17. In a rare breach of academic publishing protocol, the journal publisher did apologize for its automated error, retracting and modifying the online digital version of that paper so that the electronic archive differs from the supposedly authoritative paper one. If your library has a printed paper copy of Volume 13, Issue 4 of ACM Transactions on CHI from 2006, you can still find "Seymour Articlet" immortalized in print. A few seconds of automation by one person has resulted in years of corrective aftermath—including the time I have wasted writing this footnote, and the time you have wasted reading it!

18. An example from September 2022, when I write this note, was the first official action of the UK Conservative government led by Prime Minister Liz Truss. Before this date, the EU Capital Requirements Directive made it illegal for staff in the UK banking industry to receive bonuses more than 200 percent of their nominal salary. The Truss government simply removed the regulation, making any further calculation of this amount unnecessary.

19. See James Noble and Robert Biddle's Notes on Postmodern Programming, which I discuss again later in this book. James Noble and Robert Biddle, "Notes on Postmodern

Programming," in *Proceedings of the Onward Track at OOPSLA 02, the ACM conference on Object-Oriented Programming, Systems, Languages and Applications*, ed. Richard Gabriel, Seattle, Washington, 2002, (2002), 49–71, http://www.dreamsongs.org/.

20. Daniel Kahneman, *Thinking, Fast and Slow* (New York: Farrar, Straus and Giroux, 2011).

21. Albert Bandura, *Self-Efficacy: The Exercise of Control* (New York: W.H. Freeman, 1997).

22. Laura Beckwith, Cory Kissinger, Margaret Burnett, Susan Wiedenbeck, Joseph Lawrance, Alan Blackwell, and Curtis Cook, "Tinkering and Gender in End-User Programmers' Debugging," in *Proceedings of the SIGCHI Conference on Human Factors in Computing Systems* (2006), 231–240.

23. Green and Blackwell, "Ironies of Abstraction."

24. The question of whether language is itself a notation enters tricky philosophical grounds. Anthropologist Tim Ingold argues convincingly that written text evolved like music notation, originally designed to support spoken performance rather than 'speaking' by itself, in Tim Ingold, Lines: A Brief History (Abingdon, UK: Routledge, 2016). Spoken language, being transient, might not look like a notation. But a voice recording can be used in many of the same ways as written text—it's just a lot less convenient to look forward and back, make changes, and so on. I discuss these user experiences of notation in chapter 14. Even more speculatively, perhaps all language is encoded in the listener's brain as a neural recording than can itself be "replayed," "edited," and so. If our brain contains language symbols, perhaps thinking is an internal kind of "reading" and "writing"? This is much the same intuitive principle of operation as Turing's *other* famous thought experiment—the "Turing Machine."

Chapter 3

1. Alan F. Blackwell, "The Age of ImageNet's Discovery," in *A Cat, a Dog, a Microwave . . . Cultural Practices and Politics of Image Datasets*, ed. Nicolas Malevé and Ioanna Zouli (London: The Photographers' Gallery, 2023). See also Couldry and Mejias, *The Costs of Connection*.

2. Gareth James, Daniela Witten, Trevor Hastie, and Robert Tibshirani. *An Introduction to Statistical Learning.* (New York: Springer, 2013).

3. Adrian Mackenzie, *Machine Learners: Archaeology of a Data Practice* (Cambridge: MIT Press, 2017).

4. These are actual lines of code from the textbook used in my first AI class: Eugene Charniak and Drew McDermott, *Introduction to Artificial Intelligence* (Reading, MA: Addison Wesley, 1986), 16–20.

Chapter 4

1. Jo L. Walton, "A Brief Backward History of Automated Eloquence," in *Ghosts, Robots, Automatic Writing: An AI Level Study Guide*, ed. Anne Alexander, Caroline Bassett, Alan Blackwell, and Jo Walton (Cambridge, UK: Cambridge Digital Humanities, PREA, 2050/2021), 2–11.

2. David J. Ward, Alan F. Blackwell, and David J.C. MacKay. "Dasher—A Data Entry Interface Using Continuous Gestures and Language Models," in *Proceedings of UIST 2000: 13th Annual ACM Symposium on User Interface Software and Technology*, San Diego, CA, (2000), 129–137.

3. Malcolm Longair and Michael Cates, "Sir David John Cameron MacKay FRS. 22 April 1967—14 April 2016," in *Biographical Memoirs of Fellows of the Royal Society* 63 (2017): 443–465, https://doi.org/10.1098/rsbm.2017.0013.

4. Textual descriptions of Dasher are very hard to imagine if you have not seen this unusual system operating. A demonstration by David MacKay, excerpted from a Google TechTalk, is available online (YouTube video, created 26 Oct 2007) https://youtu.be/0d6yIquOKQ0.

5. Anne Alexander, Caroline Bassett, Alan Blackwell, and Jo Walton, *Ghosts, Robots, Automatic Writing: an AI Level Study Guide* (Cambridge UK: Cambridge Digital Humanities/PREA, 2050/2021).

6. Anne Alexander, Caroline Bassett, Alan Blackwell, and Jo Walton, "Embracing the Plagiarised Future," Panel presentation at *Critical Borders: Radical (Re)visions of AI, Jesus College Cambridge*, 18–21 October 2021.

7. From Jo and Thomas Green's Christmas circular of 2022: "At a recent conference someone started his paper with a long piece written by an AI machine imitating his style. It sounded just like all his other papers. Far be it from anyone in this house to conjecture that maybe the others were written by AI too."

8. Diana E. Forsythe, "Engineering Knowledge: The Construction of Knowledge in Artificial Intelligence," *Social Studies of Science* 23 no. 3 (1993): 445–477.

9. Kevin Schaul, Szu Yu Chen, and Nitasha Tiku, "Inside the Secret List of Websites that Make AI like ChatGPT Sound Smart," *Washington Post*, April 19, 2023.

10. Emily M. Bender, Timnit Gebru, Angelina McMillan-Major, and Shmargaret Shmitchell, "On the Dangers of Stochastic Parrots: Can Language Models Be Too Big? 🦜," in *Proceedings of the 2021 ACM conference on fairness, accountability, and transparency* (March 2021), 610–623.

11. Max Planck, as cited in Thomas S. Kuhn, *The Structure of Scientific Revolutions* (Chicago: University of Chicago Press, 1970), 151. Planck's hypothesis has been studied empirically: Pierre Azoulay, Christian Fons-Rosen, and Joshua S. Graff Zivin,

"Does Science Advance One Funeral at a Time?" *American Economic Review* 109, no. 8 (2019): 2889–2920. doi: 10.1257/aer.20161574.

12. Claude E. Shannon, "A Mathematical Theory of Communication," *Bell System Technical Journal* 27 no. 3 (1948): 379–423; See also Claude E. Shannon and Warren Weaver, *The Mathematical Theory of Communication* (Champaign, IL: University of Illinois Press, 1949).

13. This exclamation point, like the excessive use of italics throughout the paragraph, was not really very surprising, or indeed very creative—this is another example of redundancy, and might easily have been suggested by an especially clichéd predictive text editing program, in which case I would not need to take responsibility for it.

14. Shannon and Weaver, *The Mathematical Theory of Communication*.

15. Daniel C. Dennett, "Intentional Systems," *The Journal of Philosophy* 68, no. 4 (February 1971): 87–106; Daniel C. Dennett, *The Intentional Stance* (Cambridge: MIT Press, 1987).

16. "Umbrage of Parrots," *The Times* (London), June 16, 1949, p. 5. Thanks to Willard McCarty for drawing my attention to this piece.

17. Simon Schaffer, "Enlightened Automata," in *The Sciences in Enlightened Europe*, ed. William Clark, Jan Golinski, and Simon Schaffer (Chicago: University of Chicago Press, 1999), 126–166.

18. Jia Deng, Wei Dong, Richard Socher, Li-Jia Li, Kai Li, and Li Fei-Fei. "Imagenet: A Large-Scale Hierarchical Image Database," in *Proceedings of CVPR 2009 IEEE conference on computer vision and pattern recognition* (2009), 248–255.

19. George A. Miller, Richard Beckwith, Christiane Fellbaum, Derek Gross, and Katherine J. Miller, "Introduction to WordNet: An on-line lexical database," *International Journal of Lexicography* 3, no. 4 (1990): 235–244.

20. Couldry and Mejias, *The Costs of Connection*.

21. Yvonne Rogers, Helen Sharp, and Jennifer Preece, *Interaction Design: Beyond Human–Computer Interaction* (Hoboken, NJ: John Wiley & Sons, 2023); Gerald M. Weinberg, *The Psychology of Computer Programming* (New York: Van Nostrand Reinhold, 1971); Stuart K. Card, Allen Newell, and Thomas P. Moran, *The Psychology of Human–Computer Interaction* (Hillsdale, NJ: Lawrence Erlbaum Associates, 1983).

22. Louis L. Bucciarelli, *Designing Engineers* (Cambridge: MIT Press, 1994).

23. Devlin and Belton, "The Measure of a Woman: Fembots, Fact and Fiction."

24. Forsythe, *Studying Those Who Study Us*.

25. Alison Adam, *Artificial Knowing: Gender and the Thinking Machine* (Abingdon, UK: Routledge, 2006)

26. Yorick Wilks, ed., *Language, Cohesion and Form: Margaret Masterman (1910–1986)* (Cambridge UK: Cambridge University Press, 2005). Another British A.I. Pioneer, Margaret Boden, describes her studies with the maverick Masterman in the preface to Margaret A. Boden, *Mind as Machine: A History of Cognitive Science* (Oxford: Oxford University Press, 2008); Karen Spärck Jones, *Language Modelling's Generative Model: Is it Rational?* (Unpublished manuscript, 2004). https://www.cl.cam.ac.uk/archive /ksj21/langmodnote4.pdf (accessed 13 May 2023).

27. Shanahan, *Talking About Large Language Models.*

28. Simon, "Designing Organizations for an Information-Rich World."

Chapter 5

1. Clarisse Sieckenius De Souza, *The Semiotic Engineering of Human–Computer Interaction* (Cambridge: MIT Press, 2005).

2. Most text on the internet is written by people, at least for now. In the future, there may be large amounts of text on the internet that has been generated by LLMs. But training LLMs on their own output will not achieve the goal of imitating human intelligence. On the contrary, widespread pollution of the internet by publishing automatically generated text from LLMs would be like urinating in one's own drinking water.

3. Couldry and Mejias, *The Costs of Connection.*

4. Nikhil Vyas, Sham Kakade, and Boaz Barak, "Provable Copyright Protection for Generative Models," arXiv preprint (2023), arXiv:2302.10870.

5. Dan Milmo, "Italy's Privacy Watchdog Bans ChatGPT Over Data Breach Concerns," *The Guardian*, April 1, 2023.

6. In my own experiments in March 2023 asking various LLMs to answer a 20-year-old exam question on the usability inspection method of Heuristic Evaluation, output included plausible-looking references to works by the relevant author (Jakob Nielsen), but suggesting an apparently arbitrary range of pages in an unrelated book. Many people expect to see rapid degradation in the quality of scientific citation through reporting of superficially plausible but fabricated data. Another LLM nearly led me to report a completely fabricated quote from Donna Haraway in this book, after a typing error in someone else's presentation inadvertently replaced Haraway's characteristic phrase "mortal critters" with the words "moral critters." When I used an LLM search engine to locate the original quote, the chatbot obligingly fabricated verbatim text, supposedly by Haraway, that appeared to endorse my own ideas about a transhumanist perspective on moral codes.

7. Shanahan, *Talking About Large Language Models.*

8. Nick Seaver, *Computing Taste: Algorithms and the Makers of Music Recommendation* (Chicago: University of Chicago Press, 2022).

9. Bonnie E. John, "Information Processing and Skilled Behavior," in *HCI Models, Theories, and Frameworks: Toward a Multidisciplinary Science*, ed. John Carroll (San Francisco, CA: Morgan Kaufmann, 2003), 55–101.

10. See, e.g. Hershock, *Buddhism and Intelligent Technology*.

11. Collins, *Artifictional Intelligence*.

12. Nick Bostrom's thought experiment of an autonomous "paperclip factory" that destroys the world because it has been programmed to make more paperclips no matter what, demonstrates how dystopian stories about the dangers of AI rely on the machine being given goals that are even less likely than evil lairs and white cats.

Chapter 6

1. Graeber, *The Utopia of Rules*.

2. Horst W.J. Rittel and Melvin M. Webber, "Dilemmas in a General Theory of Planning" *Policy Sciences* 4, no. 2 (1973): 155–169.

3. Ian Arawjo, "To Write Code: The Cultural Fabrication of Programming Notation and Practice," in *Proceedings of the 2020 CHI Conference on Human Factors in Computing Systems* (2020).

4. Ole-Johan Dahl and Kristen Nygaard, "SIMULA: an ALGOL-based simulation language," *Communications of the ACM* 9, no. 9 (1966): 671–678.

5. Ivan E. Sutherland, *Sketchpad, A Man-Machine Graphical Communication System*, 1963. Facsimile of the original PhD thesis, with an introduction by Alan F. Blackwell and Kerry Rodden. Technical Report 574. Cambridge University Computer Laboratory, 2003, http://www.cl.cam.ac.uk/TechReports/UCAM-CL-TR-574.pdf.

6. Sutherland, *Sketchpad*.

7. In contrast to Sutherland's (rather simplistic) drawing of bridge loads corresponding to visible mechanical components, it might be argued that the notorious Tacoma Narrows Bridge disaster of 1940 occurred in part because the wind forces that caused it to collapse had not been sufficiently "visible" in the representations used by engineers during the design process.

8. Abigail J. Sellen and Richard H.R. Harper, *The Myth of the Paperless Office* (Cambridge: MIT Press, 2003).

9. Crawford, *Atlas of AI*.

10. Ken Garland, *Mr. Beck's Underground Map: A History* (Capital Transport Publishing, 1994).

11. Douglas T. Ross, "A Generalized Technique for Symbol Manipulation and Numerical Calculation," *Communications of the ACM* 4, no. 3 (1961): 147–150.

12. See the editors' introduction to the online facsimile of Sutherland's *Sketchpad*.

13. Alan C. Kay, "The Early History of Smalltalk," *ACM SIGPLAN Notices* 28, no. 3 (1993): 69–95. Reprinted in *History of Programming Languages II* ed. Thomas J. Bergin Jr and Richard G. Gibson Jr, (Reading, MA: Addison-Wesley, 1996), 511–578.

14. Alan C. Kay, "A Personal Computer for Children of All Ages." In *Proceedings of the ACM annual conference* (1972).

15. David C. Smith, *Pygmalion: A Computer Program to Model and Stimulate Creative Thought* (Basel, Stuttgart: Birkhauser, 1977).

16. Jeff Johnson, Teresa L. Roberts, William Verplank, David Canfield Smith, Charles H. Irby, Marian Beard, and Kevin Mackey, "The Xerox Star: A Retrospective," *Computer* 22, no. 9 (1989): 11–26.

17. Douglas K. Smith and Robert C. Alexander, *Fumbling the Future: How Xerox Invented, Then Ignored, the First Personal Computer* (New York: William Morrow, 1999).

Chapter 7

1. Thomas R.G. Green, "The Cognitive Dimension of Viscosity: A Sticky Problem for HCI," in *Proceedings of the IFIP TC13 Third International Conference on Human–Computer Interaction* (1990), 79–86.

2. Ben Shneiderman, "Direct Manipulation: A Step Beyond Programming Languages," *Computer* 16, no. 8, (Aug. 1983): 57–69.

3. Alan F. Blackwell, "Metacognitive Theories of Visual Programming: What Do We Think We Are Doing?" in *Proceedings IEEE Symposium on Visual Languages* (1996), 240–246.

4. Wolfgang Mieder, "'A Picture is Worth a Thousand Words': From Advertising Slogan to American Proverb," *Southern Folklore* 47, no. 3 (1990): 207.

5. Keith Stenning and Jon Oberlander, "A Cognitive Theory of Graphical and Linguistic Reasoning: Logic and Implementation." *Cognitive Science* 19, no. 1 (1995): 97–140.

6. Mitchel Resnick, John Maloney, Andrés Monroy-Hernández, Natalie Rusk, Evelyn Eastmond, Karen Brennan, Amon Millner, Eric Rosenbaum, Jay Silver, Brian Silverman, and Yasmin Kafai, "Scratch: Programming for All," *Communications of the ACM* 52, no. 11 (November 2009): 60–67.

7. Kent Beck, *Extreme Programming Explained: Embrace Change* (Reading, MA: Addison Wesley, 2000); Ken Schwaber, *Agile Project Management with Scrum* (Redmond, WA: Microsoft Press, 2004).

8. Although beyond the scope of this book, philosopher Brian Cantwell Smith offers a deep critique of the ways of thinking that might be considered to underpin

both the concept of any encyclopedia (including Wikipedia), and the epistemological foundations of object-oriented programming. See Brian Cantwell Smith, *On the Origin of Objects* (Cambridge: MIT Press, 1996), and also the development of these ideas in relation to AI: Brian Cantwell Smith, *The Promise of Artificial Intelligence: Reckoning and Judgment* (Cambridge: MIT Press, 2019).

9. Kent Beck and Ward Cunningham, "Using Pattern Languages for Object-Oriented Programs," Tektronix, Inc. Technical Report No. CR-87–43 (September 17, 1987), presented at OOPSLA-87 workshop on Specification and Design for Object-Oriented Programming. Available online at http://c2.com/doc/oopsla87.html/.

10. Alan Blackwell and Sally Fincher, "PUX: Patterns of User Experience," *Interactions* 17, no. 2 (2010): 27–31.

11. Christopher Alexander's keynote delivered to the 1996 OOPSLA conference observed: "I think that insofar as patterns have become useful tools in the design of software, it helps the task of programming in that way. It is a nice, neat format and that is fine. However, that is not all that pattern languages are supposed to do. The pattern language that we began creating in the 1970s had other essential features. First, it has a moral component. Second, it has the aim of creating coherence, morphological coherence in the things which are made with it. And third, it is generative: it allows people to create coherence, morally sound objects, and encourages and enables this process because of its emphasis on the coherence of the created whole." Transcript of live recording made in San Jose, California, October 1996, at the 1996 ACM Conference on Object-Oriented Programs, Systems, Languages and Applications (OOPSLA). Available online at http://www.patternlanguage .com/archive/ieee.html (retrieved 12 August 2022).

Chapter 8

1. This term refers to a product innovation within a company that has not been explicitly approved by senior management. Many case studies document how critical these can be to the long-term success of leading manufacturers. Perhaps the most famous example in the computer industry is documented in Tracy Kidder's Pulitzer Prize-winning book, *The Soul of a New Machine* (Boston, MA: Little Brown, 1981).

2. As a result, the deployed product pushed the state-of-the-art in program synthesis in two ways: (a) introducing efficiency in the synthesis process via goal-directed top-down synthesis based on symbolic backpropagation, and (b) dealing with ambiguous specifications by incorporating program-ranking techniques.

3. Details of that program can be found at https://aka.ms/prose-research-fellowship.

4. Maria I. Gorinova, Advait Sarkar, Alan F. Blackwell, and Karl Prince, "Transforming Spreadsheets with Data Noodles," in *Proc. 2016 IEEE Symposium on Visual Languages and Human-Centric Computing (VL/HCC).* (2016), 236–237.

5. Brad A. Myers, "Demonstrational Interfaces: A Step Beyond Direct Manipulation," *Computer* 25, no. 8 (1992): 61–73.

6. Ben Shneiderman, "Direct Manipulation: A Step Beyond Programming Languages," *Computer* 16, no. 8, (Aug. 1983): 57–69.

7. Of course, even with the help of a powerful language, a complex problem may remain fundamentally complex.

8. Zuboff, *The Age of Surveillance Capitalism.*

9. Seaver, *Computing Taste.*

10. Christopher Scaffidi, Mary Shaw, and Brad Myers, "Estimating the Numbers of End Users and End User Programmers," in *Proceedings of the 2005 IEEE Symposium on Visual Languages and Human-Centric Computing (VL/HCC '05)*, 207–214.

11. Raymond R. Panko, "What We Know About Spreadsheet Errors," *Journal of Organizational and End User Computing (JOEUC)* 10, no. 2 (1998): 15–21.

12. Diana Robinson, Luke Church, Alan F. Blackwell, Alain Vuylsteke, Kenton O'Hara, and Martin Besser, "Investigating Uncertainty in Postoperative Bleeding Management: Design Principles for Decision Support," in *Proceedings of the British HCI Conference* (2022); Alan F. Blackwell, Nicola J. Bidwell, Helen L. Arnold, Charlie Nqeisji, Kun Kunta, and Martin Mabeifam Ujakpa, "Visualising Bayesian Probability in the Kalahari," in *Proceedings of the 32nd Annual Workshop of the Psychology of Programming Interest Group (PPIG 2021)*; Samuel Aaron and Alan F. Blackwell, "From Sonic Pi to Overtone: Creative Musical Experiences with Domain-Specific and Functional Languages," in *Proceedings of the first ACM SIGPLAN Workshop on Functional Art, Music, Modeling & Design* (2013), 35–46. See also Alan F. Blackwell, Emma Cocker, Geoff Cox, Alex McLean, and Thor Magnusson, *Live Coding: A User's Manual* (Cambridge: MIT Press, 2022).

13. Mariana Mărășoiu, Alan F. Blackwell, Advait Sarkar, and Martin Spott. "Clarifying Hypotheses by Sketching Data," in *Proceedings of the Eurographics/IEEE VGTC Conference on Visualization (2016)*, 125–129.

14. Mariana Mărășoiu, Detlef Nauck, and Alan F. Blackwell, "Cuscus: An End User Programming Tool for Data Visualisation," in *Proceedings of End-User Development: 7th International Symposium, IS-EUD 2019*, Hatfield, UK, July 10–12, 2019, 115–131.

15. William Playfair, *Commercial and Political Atlas* (London: Corry, 1786). See also James R. Beniger and Dorothy L. Robyn, "Quantitative Graphics in Statistics: A Brief History," *The American Statistician* 32, no. 1 (1978): 1–11. https://doi.org/10.2307/2683467. Accessed 9 Aug. 2022.

16. Otto Neurath, *Isotype: International Picture Language* (London: Kegan Paul, 1936). See also James McElvenny, *Otto Neurath's Isotype and His Philosophy of Language*, 2013,

https://hiphilangsci.net/2013/08/21/otto-neuraths-isotype-and-his-philosophy-of
-language/.

17. e.g. Edward R. Tufte, *The Visual Display of Quantitative Information* (Cheshire, CT: Graphics Press, 1983).

18. Mike Bostock, "D3: Data-Driven Documents" (2001), https://github.com/d3/d3 /wiki accessed 9 Aug. 2022.

19. Richard C. Lupton and Julian M. Allwood, "Hybrid Sankey Diagrams: Visual Analysis of Multidimensional Data for Understanding Resource Use," *Resources, Conservation and Recycling* 124 (2017): 141–151.

20. Jacques Bertin, *Semiology of Graphics.* (Madison, WI: University of Wisconsin Press, 1983).

21. Casey Reas and Ben Fry, "Processing: Programming for the Media Arts," *AI & Society* 20 no. 4 (2006): 526–538.

22. Alan F. Blackwell, "Palimpsest: A Layered Language for Exploratory Image Processing," *Journal of Visual Languages and Computing* 25 no. 5 (2014): 545–571.

23. For professional artists who can't afford the license costs of Photoshop, including me, the powerful open-source package GIMP is a valuable alternative that has been created by a volunteer community.

24. Advait Sarkar, Mateja Jamnik, Alan F. Blackwell, and Martin Spott, "Interactive Visual Machine Learning in Spreadsheets," in *Proceedings of the 2015 IEEE Symposium on Visual Languages and Human-Centric Computing (VL/HCC)* (2015), 159–163.

Chapter 9

1. Apple Computer, Inc., *Macintosh Human Interface Guidelines* (Reading, MA: Addison Wesley, 1992); Microsoft Corporation, *The Windows Interface Guidelines for Software Design* (Redmond, WA: Microsoft Corporation, 1995); e.g. Stephen. A Hill, *Practical Introduction to the Human Computer Interface in a Semester* (London: DP Publications, 1995), 22; Susan Weinschenk, Pamela Jamar, and Sarah C. Yeo, *GUI Design Essentials: for Windows 95, Windows 3.1, World Wide Web* (New York: Wiley, 1997), 60; Wilbert O. Galitz, *The Essential Guide to User Interface Design: An Introduction to GUI Design Principles and Techniques* (New York: Wiley, 2007), 84; Theo Mandel, *The Elements of User Interface Design* (New York: Wiley, 1997), 69; Alan Dix, Janet Finlay, Gregory D. Abowd, and Russell Beale, *Human Computer Interaction, 2nd ed.* (Hemel Hempstead, UK: Prentice Hall, 1998), 149; Christine Faulkner, *The Essence of Human–Computer Interaction* (Hemel Hempstead, UK: Prentice Hall, 1998), 89.

2. Ted H. Nelson, "The Right Way to Think About Software Design," in *The Art of Human–Computer Interface Design*, ed. Brenda Laurel (Reading, MA: Addison Wesley, 1990), 235–243.

3. Alan F. Blackwell, "Chasing the Intuition of an Industry: Can Pictures Really Help Us Think?" in *Proceedings of the first Psychology of Programming Interest Group Postgraduate Student Workshop*, (1996), 13–24.

4. Alan F. Blackwell, *Metaphor in Diagrams*, unpublished PhD Thesis, Cambridge University, 1998; Alan F. Blackwell and Thomas R.G. Green, "Does Metaphor Increase Visual Language Usability?" in *Proceedings 1999 IEEE Symposium on Visual Languages VL'99* (1999), 246–253.

5. Alan F. Blackwell, "The Reification of Metaphor as a Design Tool," *ACM Transactions on Computer-Human Interaction (TOCHI)* 13, no. 4 (2006): 490–530.

6. George Basalla, *The Evolution of Technology* (Cambridge, UK: Cambridge University Press, 1988).

7. Alan C. Kay, "User Interface: A Personal View," in *The Art of Human–Computer Interface Design*, ed. Brenda Laurel (Reading, MA: Addison Wesley, 1990), 191–207.

8. Henry Lieberman, "An Example Based Environment for Beginning Programmers," *Instructional Science* 14 no. 3 (1986): 277–292; Henry Lieberman, "Integrating User Interface Agents with Conventional Applications," *Knowledge-Based Systems* 11, no. 1 (1998): 15–23; Henry Lieberman, Bonnie A. Nardi, and David Wright, "Training Agents to Recognize Text by Example," in *Proceedings of the Third Annual Conference on Autonomous Agents* (April 1999), 116–122; *Your Wish Is My Command: Programming by Example*, ed. Henry Lieberman, (San Francisco, CA: Morgan Kaufmann, 2001).

9. Bruce Tognazzini, *Tog on Interface* (Reading, MA: Addison-Wesley, 1992).

Chapter 10

1. Geoff Cox and Alex McLean, *Speaking Code: Coding as Aesthetic and Political Expression* (Cambridge: MIT Press, 2012).

2. Frank DeRemer and Hans H. Kron, "Programming-in-the-Large Versus Programming-in-the-Small," *IEEE Transactions on Software Engineering* 2 (1976): 80–86.

3. Resnick, Maloney, et al., "Scratch: Programming for All."

4. Tony Hoare, "The Verifying Compiler: A Grand Challenge for Computing Research," *Journal of the ACM (JACM)* 50, no. 1 (2003): 63–69.

5. Donald MacKenzie, *Mechanizing proof: computing, risk, and trust* (Cambridge, MA: MIT Press, 2004).

6. Peter J. Denning, "Remaining Trouble Spots with Computational Thinking," *Communications of the ACM (CACM)* 60, no. 6 (June 2017): 33–39, https://doi.org/10.1145/2998438.

7. Steve McConnell, *Code Complete: A Practical Handbook of Software Construction* (Redmond, WA: Microsoft Press, 1993).

8. Malcolm McCullough, *Abstracting Craft: The Practiced Digital Hand* (Cambridge: MIT Press, 1998); Rikard Lindell, "Crafting Interaction: The Epistemology of Modern Programming," *Personal and Ubiquitous Computing* 18, no. 3 (2014): 613–624; Shad Gross, Jeffrey Bardzell, and Shaowen Bardzell, "Structures, Forms, and Stuff: The Materiality and Medium of Interaction," *Personal and Ubiquitous Computing* 18, no. 3 (2014): 637–649.

9. Donald Schön and John Bennett, "Reflective Conversation with Materials," in *Bringing Design to Software*, ed. Terry Winograd (Reading, MA: Addison-Wesley, 1996), 171–189, https://hci.stanford.edu/publications/bds/9-schon.html; Richard Sennett, *The Craftsman* (New Haven, CT: Yale University Press, 2008); Andrew Pickering, *The Mangle of Practice: Time, Agency, and Science* (Chicago: University of Chicago Press, 1995).

10. See also J. B. Rainsberger, "A Model for Improving Names," *The Code Whisperer*, June 15, 2011 (updated January 14, 2019), https://blog.thecodewhisperer.com/permalink/a-model-for-improving-names.

11. It's important to note here that I am describing the typical uses of these tools, not the potential for them to be used in other ways. The whole field of End-User Software Engineering is dedicated to helping regular users gain access to more of the capabilities enjoyed by professional programmers. Where commercial products such as Microsoft's Excel span the boundary between casual, informal use on one hand, and large-scale business-critical applications on the other, they must support software engineering processes to some extent. I have worked for many years with teams at Microsoft Research whose goal is to enhance Excel in these ways, including my former student and colleague Advait Sarkar at Microsoft Research Cambridge, who has offered many insightful comments on earlier drafts of this book. See A. Ko et al. "The state of the art in end-user software engineering;" Simon Peyton Jones, Alan F. Blackwell, and Margaret Burnett, "A User-Centred Approach to Functions in Excel," in *Proceedings of the Eighth ACM SIGPLAN International Conference on Functional Programming* (2003), 165–176; Advait Sarkar, Andrew D. Gordon, Simon Peyton Jones, and Neil Toronto, "Calculation View: Multiple-Representation Editing in Spreadsheets," in *Proceedings of the 2018 IEEE Symposium on Visual Languages and Human-Centric Computing (VL/HCC)* (2018), 85–93.

12. Gregg Rothermel, Lixin Li, Christopher DuPuis, and Margaret Burnett, "What You See Is What You Test: A Methodology for Testing Form-Based Visual Programs," in *Proceedings of the 20th International Conference on Software Engineering* (1998), 198–207.

13. Aaron Wilson, Margaret Burnett, Laura Beckwith, Orion Granatir, Ledah Casburn, Curtis Cook, Mike Durham, and Gregg Rothermel, "Harnessing Curiosity to

Increase Correctness in End-User Programming," in *Proceedings of the SIGCHI Conference on Human Factors in Computing Systems* (2003), 305–312.

14. Advait Sarkar, Sruti Srinivasa Ragavan, Jack Williams, and Andrew D. Gordon, "End-User Encounters with Lambda Abstraction in Spreadsheets: Apollo's Bow or Achilles' Heel?," in *Proceedings of the IEEE Symposium on Visual Languages and Human-Centric Computing (VL/HCC)* (2022), 1–11.

Chapter 11

1. In a chapter 5 endnote, I described some of my own recent experiences with the "formal" aspects of academic writing, including details like precise page numbers and exact quotes, which are cheerfully ignored by LLMs. In programming languages, precise numbers and exact words are absolutely critical, even more so than in the formal practices of scientific citation.

2. Noble and Biddle, "Notes on Postmodern Programming."

3. Ben Shneiderman, *Human-Centered AI* (Oxford University Press, 2022).

4. Jacob Austin, Augustus Odena, Maxwell Nye, Maarten Bosma, Henryk Michalewski, David Dohan, Ellen Jiang, Carrie Cai, Michael Terry, Quoc Le, and Charles Sutton, "Program Synthesis with Large Language Models," *arXiv preprint* (2021), arXiv:2108.07732.

5. Although it is worth noting that, in my own experiments, these models have also produced source code in other languages that completely misinterprets the syntax of that language, replacing it with alternative punctuation that the LLM seems to have acquired from Python or C++, but is invalid in the programming language I have asked for.

6. William Byrd and Greg Rosenblatt, *Barliman smart editor prototype* (GitHub repository), https://github.com/webyrd/Barliman.

7. Mar Hicks reproduces an advertisement for an office computer called *Susie* (Stock Updating and Sales Invoicing Electronically), with text claiming that it could be "programmed in plain language from tape or by the typist." See Mar Hicks, *Programmed Inequality: How Britain Discarded Women Technologists and Lost its Edge in Computing* (Cambridge: MIT Press, 2017), 124–125.

8. Hicks, *Programmed Inequality*, 233–238.

9. A fact obscured in the historical record by the greater secrecy of the British code-breaking projects, as noted by Hicks, *Programmed Inequality*, 34

10. A more detailed and authoritative account of this period can be found in Martin Campbell-Kelly, "The Development of Computer Programming in Britain (1945 to 1955)," *Annals of the History of Computing* 4, no. 2 (1982): 121–139.

11. Thanks to Anica Alvarez Nishio for suggesting this explanation.

12. Steven L. Tanimoto, "VIVA: A Visual Language for Image Processing," *Journal of Visual Languages and Computing* 1, no. 2 (1990): 127–139. See also Blackwell, Cocker et al., *Live Coding: A User's Manual.*

13. Steven L. Tanimoto, "A Perspective on the Evolution of Live Programming," in *Proceedings of the First International Workshop on Live Programming (LIVE)* (2013), 31–34.

14. Advait Sarkar, Andrew D. Gordon, Carina Negreanu, Christian Poelitz, Sruti Srinivasa Ragavan, and Ben Zorn, "What Is It Like To Program With Artificial Intelligence?" in *Proceedings of the 33rd Annual Conference of the Psychology of Programming Interest Group (PPIG)* (2022).

15. Sarkar et al., "What is it Like to Program with Artificial Intelligence?"

16. Alan F. Blackwell, "SWYN: A Visual Representation for Regular Expressions," in *Your Wish is My Command: Giving Users the Power to Instruct Their Software*, ed. Henry Lieberman (San Francisco, CA: Morgan Kauffman, 2001), 245–270.

17. We could imagine that someone might accidentally create source code for a piece of auto-destructive software art, such as Alex McLean's Forkbomb.pl, winner of the Transmediale software art award in 2001. The original program, with notes by Alex McLean on its invention, can be found at https://slab.org/2016/07/04 /forkbomb-pl/. The text of the book you are reading now also includes a dangerous and destructive piece of code, flagged with an endnote warning readers not to try it. I have just confirmed that the same piece of code can be generated by an LLM (Google Bard v1.0.0, last updated: 2023-06-18 01:27:26 PST), which does helpfully follow it with the advice "WARNING: This command is destructive and will delete all files below the root directory, so be sure to use it with caution."

18. Nardi, *A Small Matter of Programming.*

Chapter 12

1. Margaret A. Boden, *Creativity and Art: Three Roads to Surprise.* (Oxford: Oxford University Press, 2010). See also Margaret A. Boden, "Creativity and Artificial Intelligence," *Artificial Intelligence* 103, no. 1–2 (1998): 347–356.

2. Margaret A. Boden, *The Creative Mind: Myths and Mechanisms (2nd Ed.)* (Abingdon, UK: Routledge, 2004).

3. Boden's comment comes from her gloss on the remark of Lady Ada Lovelace that "[Babbage's] Analytical Engine has no pretensions whatever to originate any- thing. It can do [only] whatever we know how to order it to perform." Boden

acknowledges as correct and important the emphasis on programming, which this book shares, but goes on to identify four further "Lovelace-questions": 1. Can computers help us understand human creativity? 2. Could computers appear to be creative? 3. Could a computer appear to recognize creativity? 4. Could a computer be really creative independent of the programmer? (Boden, *The Creative Mind*, 16–17).

4. Nathaniel Ming Curran, Jingyi Sun, and Joo-Wha Hong, "Anthropomorphizing AlphaGo: A Content Analysis of the Framing of Google DeepMind's AlphaGo in the Chinese and American Press," *AI and Society* 35, no. 3 (2020): 727–735. doi: https://doi.org/10.1007/s00146-019-00908-9.

5. Shannon, "A Mathematical Theory of Communication"; Shannon and Weaver, *The Mathematical Theory of Communication*.

6. Myron Tribus, *Thermodynamics and Thermostatics: An Introduction to Energy, Information and States of Matter, With Engineering Applications* (Princeton, NJ: D. Van Nostrand, 1961), 64.

7. When first drafting this chapter, my 2022 playlist shuffles mysteriously often to repeat the chorus "What we fi do? We're stuck in a loop," from the album *Gbagada Express* by Nigerian artist BOJ. ("In a Loop," featuring Molly and Mellissa, lyrics by Molly Ama Montgomery, Mobolaji Odojukan, Melissa Adjua Montgomery).

8. The central role of comfort and similarity in pop music, through which success-ful pop songs sound much the same as older songs, is a constant factor in the pop industry, reflected in the saying that "where there's a hit, there's a writ," as reported by globally successful singer-songwriter Ed Sheeran after winning yet another court case alleging copyright infringement. Ramon Antonio Vargas, "Defending copyright suits 'comes with the territory', says Sheeran," *The Guardian*, May 8, 2023. https://www.theguardian.com/music/2023/may/07/ed-sheeran-copyright-lawsuit. For an authoritative overview of this topic from a legal perspective, see Hayleigh Bosher, Copyright in the Music Industry: A Practical Guide to Exploiting and Enforcing Rights (Cheltenham, UK: Edward Elgar Publishing, 2021).

9. Not a real death metal band.

10. There are many aesthetically pleasing mathematical functions that are easy to define, but hard to predict, like the digits of π. Margaret Boden devotes chapter 9 of *The Creative Mind* to these topics of "Chance, Chaos, Randomness and Predict-ability." This fascinating intersection of mathematical and artistic research is too large for me to discuss further, but as an example (suggested by Alex McLean), pro-grammer Martin Kleppe tweeted a beautiful fractal image resulting from this simple formula: "(x ^ y) % 9" that can be rendered in a web browser by putting the follow-ing text in a .html file:

```
<canvas id="c" width="1024" height="1024">
<script>
  const context=c.getContext('2d');
  for (let x=0; x<256; x++) {
    for (let y=0; y<256; y++) {
      if ((x ^ y) % 9) {

        context.fillRect(x*4, y*4, 4, 4);

      }
    }
  }
</script>
```

Martin Kleppe on (eX)Twitter: "I'm fascinated by this simple formula to create bit fields that look like alien art: (x ^ y) % 9 https://t.co/jZL15xzEDL" / @aemkei, 2 April 2021).

11. Alex McLean, *Manjunath B C—Vocal patterns in Konnakol*. Recorded video interview, streamed live on June 14, 2022. https://algorithmicpattern.org/events /manjunath-b-c/.The extract containing this quote can be found at the time code: https://youtu.be/6kYwZ8S-qBQ?t=1762.

12. Tuck Wah Leong, Frank Vetere, and Steve Howard, "Randomness as a Resource for Design," in *Proceedings of the 6th ACM Conference on Designing Interactive Systems (DIS)* (2006), 132–139.

13. Brian Eno and Peter Schmidt, *Oblique Strategies: Over One Hundred Worthwhile Dilemmas* (Limited edition, boxed set of cards) (London: printed by the authors, 1975); See also Kingsley Marshall and Rupert Loydell, "Control and Surrender: Eno Remixed—Collaboration and Oblique Strategies," in *Brian Eno: Oblique Music*, ed. Sean Albiez and David Pattie (London: Bloomsbury Academic, 2016), 175–192.

14. The Japanese aesthetic of *Wabi-Sabi* is another example of material imperfection that might be used as a counter to computational predictability. Vasiliki Tsaknaki and Ylva Fernaeus, "Expanding on Wabi-Sabi as a Design Resource in HCI," in *Proceedings of the 2016 ACM CHI Conference on Human Factors in Computing Systems* (2016), 5970–5983.

15. Dennett, "Intentional Systems" and *The Intentional Stance.*

16. In another completely unsurprising footnote, I am unwilling to reveal which of the sentences in this book demonstrate either one, or the other, of those two approaches.

17. This word was generated by the GPT-3 model text-davinci-002, temperature setting 0.7, in response to the prompt "Please give me a random word" on 12

September 2022. Accessed on that date via https://beta.openai.com/playground (site no longer supported).

18. Walter G. Vincenti, *What Engineers Know and How They Know It* (Baltimore: Johns Hopkins University Press, 1990).

19. Claudia Fritz, Alan F. Blackwell, Ian Cross, Jim Woodhouse, and Brian C.J. Moore, "Exploring Violin Sound Quality: Investigating English Timbre Descriptors and Correlating Resynthesized Acoustical Modifications with Perceptual Properties," *The Journal of the Acoustical Society of America* 131, no. 1 (2012): 783–794.

20. Robin was actually moving the position of the sound post. For a technical reflection on my own experience as a bass player, see Alan F. Blackwell, "Too Cool to Boogie: Craft, Culture and Critique in Computing," in *Sound Work: Composition as Critical Technical Practice*, ed. Jonathan Impett (Leuven: Leuven University Press / Orpheus Institute, 2022), 15–33.

21. Nick Collins, Alex McLean, Julian Rohrhuber, and Adrian Ward, "Live Coding in Laptop Performance," *Organised Sound* 8, no. 3 (2003): 321–330; Alan F. Blackwell and Nick Collins, "The Programming Language as a Musical Instrument," in *Proceedings of the Psychology of Programming Interest Group (PPIG)* (2005), 120–130; Alan F. Blackwell, Alex McLean, James Noble, and Julian Rohrhuber, edited in cooperation with Jochen Arne Otto, "Collaboration and Learning Through Live Coding (Dagstuhl Seminar 13382)," *Dagstuhl Reports* 3, no. 9 (2014), 130–168; Blackwell, Cocker et al., *Live Coding: A User's Manual*.

22. Nick Collins and Alex McLean, "Algorave: Live Performance of Algorithmic Electronic Dance Music," in *Proceedings of the International Conference on New Interfaces for Musical Expression (NIME)* (2014), 355–358.

23. Aaron and Blackwell, "From Sonic Pi to Overtone"; Samuel Aaron, Alan F. Blackwell, and Pamela Burnard, "The Development of Sonic Pi and its Use in Educational Partnerships: Co-Creating Pedagogies for Learning Computer Programming," *Journal of Music, Technology and Education* 9, no. 1 (2016): 75–94.

24. Ingeborg Hoesterey, *Pastiche: Cultural Memory in Art, Film, Literature* (Bloomington and Indianapolis: Indiana University Press, 2001).

25. Attributed to Roger de Piles, apparently in a treatise originally dated 1677, although with a complex history of citation and attribution as discussed by Hoesterey, *Pastiche*, 4–6.

26. Jackson Arn, "How Jony Ive Remade Visual Culture in Apple's Image," Artsy .net, Jul 11, 2019, https://www.artsy.net/article/artsy-editorial-jony-remade-visual -culture-apples-image.

27. Abigail Cain, "What Steve Jobs Learned from the Bauhaus," Artsy.net, Oct 10, 2017 https://www.artsy.net/article/artsy-editorial-steve-jobs-learned-bauhaus.

28. Jamie Grierson, "Photographer admits prize-winning image was AI-generated," *The Guardian*, April 17, 2023.

29. Alexander Mordvintsev, Christopher Olah, and Mike Tyka, *Deepdream—a code example for visualizing neural networks* (2015), https://ai. googleblog. com/2015/07 /deepdream-code-example-for-visualizing. html.

30. Schön and Bennett, "Reflective Conversation with Materials."

31. Mihaly Csikszentmihalyi, *Flow: The Psychology of Happiness* (New York: Random House, 2013).

32. Chris Nash and Alan F. Blackwell, "Flow of Creative Interaction with Digital Music Notations," in *The Oxford Handbook of Interactive Audio*, ed. Karen Collins, Bill Kapralos, and Holly Tessler (Oxford University Press, 2014), 387–404; Chris Nash and Alan F. Blackwell, "Liveness and Flow in Notation Use," in *Proceedings of the International Conference on New Interfaces for Musical Expression (NIME)* (2012), 76–81.

33. Chris Nash and Alan F. Blackwell, "Tracking Virtuosity and Flow in Computer Music," in *Proceedings of the International Computer Music Conference (ICMC)* (2011), 575–582.

34. Notation and visualization enthusiasts are intrigued by the distinctive tracker representation, which represents time flowing down the screen and different instruments arranged in columns across it. The result can be thought of as an orchestra score turned on its side, with the time direction changed from horizontal to vertical, and the musical staves for each instrument changed from lines to columns.

35. Ilias Bergström and Alan F. Blackwell, "The Practices of Programming," in *Proceedings of the 2016 IEEE Symposium on Visual Languages and Human-Centric Computing (VL/HCC) (2016)*, 190–198; Saeed Aghaee, Alan F. Blackwell, David Stillwell, and Michal Kosinski, "Personality and Intrinsic Motivational Factors in End-User Programming," in *Proceedings of the 2015 IEEE Symposium on Visual Languages and Human-Centric Computing (VL/HCC)* (2015), 29–36; Alan F. Blackwell, "End-User Developers—What Are They Like?" in *New Perspectives in End-User Development*, ed. Fabio Paternò and Volker Wulf (Berlin: Springer, 2017), 121–135.

36. Rebecca Giblin and Cory Doctorow, *Chokepoint Capitalism: How Big Tech and Big Content Captured Creative Labor Markets and How We'll Win Them Back* (Boston: Beacon Press, 2022).

37. *CODE: Collaborative Ownership and the Digital Economy*, ed. Rishab Ghosh (Cambridge: MIT Press, 2006).

38. Kevin Holm-Hudson, "Quotation and Context: Sampling and John Oswald's Plunderphonics," *Leonardo Music Journal* 7 (1997): 17–25, https://doi.org/10.2307/1513241.

39. Hoesterey, *Pastiche*, 9

40. Mark Blythe, "Pastiche Scenarios," *Interactions* 11, no. 5 (2004): 51–53.

41. Blackwell, "The Age of ImageNet's Discovery"; Couldry and Mejias, *The Costs of Connection*.

42. Creative Commons Announced, May 16 2002, https://creativecommons.org/2002/05/16/creativecommonsannounced-2/.

43. A newspaper report led with "German artist Boris Eldagsen says entry to Sony world photography awards was designed to provoke debate." Jamie Grierson, "Photographer admits prize-winning image was AI-generated," *The Guardian*, April 17, 2023, https://www.theguardian.com/technology/2023/apr/17/photographer-admits-prize-winning-image-was-ai-generated.

44. Mark Brown, "New Rembrandt to be Unveiled in Amsterdam," *The Guardian*, April 5, 2016, https://www.theguardian.com/artanddesign/2016/apr/05/new-rembrandt-to-be-unveiled-in-amsterdam; Rich Pelley, "'We got bored waiting for Oasis to re-form': AIsis, the band fronted by an AI Liam Gallagher," *The Guardian*, April 18, 2023; https://www.theguardian.com/music/2023/apr/18/oasis-aisis-band-fronted-by-an-ai-liam-gallagher; Joseph Grasser and Susie Ruiz-Lichter, "Ghostwriter in the Machine: Copyright Implications for AI-Generated Imitations," *Global IP & Technology Law Blog*, May 15, 2023, https://www.iptechblog.com/2023/05/ghostwriter-in-the-machine-copyright-implications-for-ai-generated-imitations/.

45. Giblin and Doctorow, *Chokepoint Capitalism*.

46. Seaver, *Computing Taste*.

47. Barry Barclay, *Mana Tuturu: Maori Treasures and Intellectual Property Rights* (Auckland: Auckland University Press, 2005).

Chapter 13

1. Joseph Henrich, Steven J. Heine, and Ara Norenzayan, "The Weirdest People in the World?" *Behavioral and Brain Sciences* 33, no. 2–3 (2010): 61–83.

2. For a survey of the reasons we might doubt this assumption, see Geoffrey Lloyd, *Cognitive Variations: Reflections on the Unity and Diversity of the Human Mind* (Oxford, UK: Clarendon Press, 2007).

3. Sebastian Linxen, Christian Sturm, Florian Brühlmann, Vincent Cassau, Klaus Opwis, and Katharina Reinecke, "How Weird is CHI?" in *Proceedings of the 2021 ACM CHI Conference on Human Factors in Computing Systems* (2021), 1–14. See also recent work by Advait Sarkar and colleagues, at Microsoft Research, and "End-User Programming is WEIRD: How, Why and What to Do About It."

4. Karl Marx, "The Chapter on Capital (Fragment on Machines)," *Grundrisse*, trans. Martin Nicolaus (London: Penguin, 1973), 690–695, 699–711.

5. Keith Breckenridge, *Biometric State*, (Cambridge, UK: Cambridge University Press, 2014).

6. Michael J.G. Cattermole and Arthur F. Wolfe, *Horace Darwin's Shop, A History of the Cambridge Scientific Instrument Company 1878–1968* (Bristol, UK: Adam Hilger, 1987).

7. Francis Galton, "Regression Towards Mediocrity in Hereditary Stature," *The Journal of the Anthropological Institute of Great Britain and Ireland* 15 (1886): 246–263. For a more extended discussion of statistical terminology see Alan F. Blackwell, "Objective Functions: (In)humanity and Inequity in Artificial Intelligence," *HAU: Journal of Ethnographic Theory* 9, no. 1 (2019): 137–146.

8. Cave, "The Problem with Intelligence"

9. Ruha Benjamin, *Race After Technology: Abolitionist Tools for the New Jim Code*, (Cambridge, UK: Polity Press, 2019).

10. Angela Saini, *Superior: The Return of Race Science* (London: 4th Estate, 2019).

11. Jane Margolis and Allan Fisher, *Unlocking the Clubhouse: Women in Computing* (Cambridge, MA: MIT Press, 2002).

12. Crawford, *Atlas of AI*.

13. Nicola J. Bidwell, "Moving the Centre to Design Social Media in Rural Africa," *AI and Society* 31 (2016): 51–77; Heike Winschiers-Theophilus and Nicola J. Bidwell, "Toward an Afro-Centric Indigenous HCI paradigm," *International Journal of Human–Computer Interaction* 29, no. 4 (2013): 243–255; Nicola J. Bidwell, Tigist Sherwaga Hussan, Satinder Gill, Kagonya Awori, and Silvia Lindtner, "Decolonising Technology Design," in *Proceedings of the First African Conference on Human Computer Interaction (AfriCHI'16)* (2016), 256–259, https://doi.org/10.1145/2998581.2998616.

14. Margaret Burnett, Simone Stumpf, Jamie Macbeth, Stephann Makri, Laura Beckwith, Irwin Kwan, Anicia Peters, and William Jernigan, "GenderMag: A Method for Evaluating Software's Gender Inclusiveness," *Interacting with Computers* 28, no. 6 (2016): 760–787.

15. Rachel Adams, "Can Artificial Intelligence be Decolonized?" *Interdisciplinary Science Reviews* 46, no. 1–2 (2021): 176–197; Rachel Adams, "Helen A'Loy and Other Tales of Female Automata: A Gendered Reading of the Narratives of Hopes and Fears of Intelligent Machines and Artificial Intelligence," *AI and Society* 35, no. 3 (2020): 569–579; Abeba Birhane, "Algorithmic Injustice: a Relational Ethics Approach," *Patterns* 2, no. 2 (2021): 100205; Abeba Birhane, Elayne Ruane, Thomas Laurent, Matthew S. Brown, Johnathan Flowers, Anthony Ventresque, and Christopher L. Dancy, "The Forgotten Margins of AI Ethics," in *Proceedings of the 2022 ACM Conference on Fairness, Accountability, and Transparency (FAccT)* (2022), 948–958; Shaowen Bardzell, "Feminist HCI: Taking Stock and Outlining an Agenda for Design," in *Proceedings of the SIGCHI Conference on Human Factors in Computing Systems* (2010), 1301–1310.

16. https://www.dair-institute.org

17. Alan F. Blackwell, Addisu Damena, and Tesfa Tegegne, "Inventing Artificial Intelligence in Ethiopia," *Interdisciplinary Science Reviews* 46, no. 3 (2021): 363–385.

18. e.g. Helen Verran, *Science and an African Logic* (Chicago, IL: University of Chicago Press, 2001).

19. Linda Tuhiwai Smith, *Decolonizing Methodologies: Research and Indigenous Peoples* (London: Bloomsbury, 2021).

20. Jon M. R. Corbett, "Indigenizing Computer Programming for Cultural Maintenance," in *Conference Companion of the 2nd International Conference on Art, Science, and Engineering of Programming* (2018), 243–244, https://doi.org/10.1145/3191697 .3213802.

21. Cox and McLean, *Speaking Code.*

22. *Indigenous Protocol and Artificial Intelligence Position Paper*, ed. Jason Edward Lewis, *Honolulu, Hawai'i: The Initiative for Indigenous Futures and the Canadian Institute for Advanced Research (CIFAR)* (2020), https://doi.org/10.11573/spectrum .library.concordia.ca.00986506. See also Jason Edward Lewis, Noelani Arista, Archer Pechawis, and Suzanne Kite, "Making Kin with the Machines," *Journal of Design and Science* 3, no. 5 (2018), https://doi.org/10.21428/bfafd97b.

Chapter 14

1. The QuoteInvestigator site suggests that this remark was first attributed to Frank Harary in Gerald M. Weinberg, *An Introduction to General Systems Thinking* (New York: Wiley, 1975), 24–25.

2. I am not a historian of science, but gained some insight into the development of the "natural sciences," as they are called in Cambridge, through my time serving on the Council of the Cambridge Philosophical Society. See Susannah Gibson, *The Spirit of Inquiry: How One Extraordinary Society Shaped Modern Science* (Oxford University Press, 2019).

3. Alan F. Blackwell, "Wonders Without Number: The Information Economy of Data and its Subjects," *AI and Society* (2022), https://doi.org/10.1007/s00146-021-01324-8.

4. This specific example alludes to the work of Max Bense, as reported by Bronač Ferran, *Auto-Poetics: Hansjörg Mayer's Titles of the Nineteen-Sixties*, unpublished PhD thesis (Birkbeck College, 2023), 166, https://eprints.bbk.ac.uk/id/eprint/51176/.

5. Brenda Laurel, *Computers as Theatre* (Reading, MA: Addison-Wesley, 2013).

6. Hoesterey, *Pastiche.*

7. See Daniel Moody, "The 'physics' of notations: Toward a Scientific Basis for Constructing Visual Notations in Software Engineering," *IEEE Transactions on Software*

Engineering 35, no. 6 (2009): 756–779; and for an assessment of how effective this approach has been, Dirk Van Der Linden and Irit Hadar, "A Systematic Literature Review of Applications of the Physics of Notations," *IEEE Transactions on Software Engineering* 45, no. 8 (2018): 736–759; Blackwell and Fincher, "PUX: Patterns of User Experience"; and Alan F. Blackwell, "A Pattern Language for the Design of Diagrams," to appear in *Elements of Diagramming: Design Theories, Analyses and Methods*, ed. Clive Richards (Abingdon UK: Routledge, forthcoming); Thomas R. G. Green, "Cognitive Dimensions of Notations," in *People and Computers V: Proceedings of the Fifth Conference of the British Computer Society*, ed. Alistair Sutcliffe and Linda Macaulay (Cambridge: Cambridge University Press, 1989), 443–460; Thomas R. G. Green and Marian Petre, "Usability Analysis of Visual Programming Environments: A 'Cognitive Dimensions' Framework," *Journal of Visual Languages and Computing* 7, no. 2 (1996): 131–174.

8. Alex McLean, "Making Programming Languages to Dance to: Live Coding with Tidal," in *Proceedings of the 2nd ACM SIGPLAN International Workshop on Functional Art, Music, Modeling and Design* (2014), 63–70.

9. For further consideration of alternative design trade-offs between the priorities of business users and of computer scientists, see George Chalhoub and Advait Sarkar, "'It's Freedom to Put Things Where My Mind Wants': Understanding and Improving the User Experience of Structuring Data in Spreadsheets," in *Proceedings of the 2022 ACM CHI Conference on Human Factors in Computing Systems* (2022), 1–24.

10. Blackwell, "A Pattern Language for the Design of Diagrams."

11. See the "Appendix: Further Reading" chapter of *Moral Codes* at https://moralcodes .pubpub.org.

Chapter 15

1. Michael Xieyang Liu, Advait Sarkar, Carina Negreanu, Benjamin Zorn, Jack Williams, Neil Toronto, and Andrew D. Gordon, "'What It Wants Me To Say': Bridging the Abstraction Gap Between End-User Programmers and Code-Generating Large Language Models," in *Proceedings of the 2023 ACM CHI Conference on Human Factors in Computing Systems* (2023), 1–31.

2. Attributed by the QuoteInvestigator site to Richard Serra and Carlota Fay Schoolman "Television Delivers People" (1973), https://quoteinvestigator.com/2017/07/16 /product/.

3. Seaver, *Computing Taste*.

4. Couldry and Mejias, *The Costs of Connection*.

Index

Aaron, Sam, 157–158
Abstract data type, 84
Abstraction
  as the basis of names, 131–132
  as cognitive challenge, 90–91
  to control the future, 123, 191
  in diagrams and notations, 34–35, 81
  and specification, 24, 74, 79
  in symbolic learning, 41–42
Academic publication, 165
Adams, Rachel, 173
Addiction, 71–72
Africa, 170, 174
Agents, intelligent, 122
Agile development, 92–94, 96
Agre, Philip, 17–18
Aleatoric composition, 153–154, 161
Alexander, Christopher, 97, 98, 183
Algorave, 157, 181
Alignment problem, 9, 10, 16, 135, 190
AlphaGo, 150
Amazon, 59
Ambiguity, 186
Anthropology, 169
Anthropometrics, 170
Artificial general intelligence (AGI), 7, 9, 13, 15, 57, 190
Arts vs. sciences, 177
Asimov, 9, 190

Attention
  consumed by AI products, 28, 63, 76
  controlled for autonomy, 181, 191
  as economic commodity, 11–12, 27, 191, 193
  as gift and exchange, 11, 71
Attention investment
  and flow experience, 161
  to justify automation, 31–34
  in social exchanges, 71–72
  in software engineering, 132–134
  prioritizing convenience, 123
  theory, 27–28
  trade-off in power of tools, 96, 100
Autonomous vehicles, 5, 181
Auto-Tune, 161

Babbage, Charles, 169
Bardzell, Shaowen, 173
Bauhaus, 159–160
Beck, Kent, 93, 96
Bertin, Jacques, 110
Bidwell, Nicola, 173
Birhane, Abebe, 173
Black Mirror, 75
Board games, 74, 78
Bob (Microsoft software), 119
Boden, Margaret, 149
Booth, Kathleen, 142
BrainCel prototype, 113–114

Bullshit, 2, 21, 26, 76, 189
Burnett, Margaret, 132–133, 173

Capitalism
  and commodification of attention,
    12, 71
  and compensation of authors, 67
  and creative industries, 165
  and exploitation of ghost labor,
    191–192
  and regulation of AI businesses,
    68–69, 189
  and surveillance, 7
Captivation, 103, 165, 192–193
Chaos theory, 152
Chatbots, 63–67, 124
Chokepoint Capitalism (Giblin and
    Doctorow), 165, 192
Clippy (Microsoft software), 28, 100
Cloud computing, 83
COBOL, 142–143, 147
Code completion, 136–138
Code comprehension, 145
Code reuse, 134, 138, 146, 183
Cognitive dimensions of notations,
    182
Cognitive science, 23
Colonialism, 170–171
Comfort, 154, 157–160, 193
Command line, 24, 30, 35, 102, 104
Comments, 185
Computational thinking, 129
Computer science education, 37, 139,
    181
Consciousness, 11, 57, 76, 77, 193
Control systems, 5–6, 179, 181
CoPilot (software), 137, 138, 140
Copyright, 139, 163, 165–166
Crafting code, 130–131
CRC cards, 97
Creative commons, 163
Creativity, 53, 149–153
Critical technical practice, 17

Cunningham, Ward, 93, 95, 96
Cuscus prototype, 110–111
Cybernetics, 5
Cypher, Allen, 23–26, 101, 122

Dahl, Ole-Johan, 80, 83, 92
Darwin, Horace, 170
Dasher (text entry software), 47–48
Data protection, 67
Data science, 38, 100, 109, 114, 115
Data structures, 79, 83
Data wrangling, 100, 101
Decolonizing computing, 173–175
Designer's deputy, 66
Design patterns, 97–98, 183
Desktop metaphor, 85, 117, 123
Desktop publishing, 164
Diagrams, 81–83, 87, 90, 117, 184
Digital arts, 156–157, 162, 163, 185
Digital humanities, 179
Direct manipulation, 35, 90–91, 102
Diversity, 174
Do Anything Now (DAN), 69
D3.js visualization library, 110

Eager (Apple prototype), 25–26
Embodiment, 15, 55, 62
Enclosure of the commons, 163
End-user programming
  offering empowerment, 86–87
  in Excel, 100–101
  for product automation, 29–31
  versus professional programming, 26
  as a research field, 23
  and self-efficacy, 33
  with visual formalisms, 147
End-user software engineering, 132
Entertainment, AI as, 178–179
Excel (Microsoft software)
  FlashFill feature, 99–100
  with functional programming,
    210n11
  and testing, 133

user diversity, 169
and visualization, 106, 110–113
Existential risk, 13
Experimental programming, 129
Expert systems, 24, 25, 43–45
Explanation, 102–103, 105, 183

Facebook, 167
Female programming innovators,
    141–143
Fiction, 13, 14, 190
Filter bubbles, 190
Fine-tuning (of language models),
    49–50
FlashFill, 26, 99–100, 105
Flat design, 119, 134
Flow experience, 161, 164, 193
Formal verification, 128–129
FORTRAN, 79
Fortune telling, 154

Galton, Francis, 170
Gamification, 74
Gapminder visualization, 111
Gebru, Timnit, 173
Gender
    in constructing male norms, 15, 62
    in female-led programming advances,
        142–143
    and male encoding of expertise,
        62–63
    and misogyny in online discourse, 67
    and self-efficacy, 33–34
    and structural injustice, 9
    and women in computing, 172–173
General Magic. See Magic Cap (General
    Magic software)
Generative prompt
    as basis for value alignment, 190
    as creative tool, 160–162
    for jailbreaking LLMs, 69
    as programming language, 143, 147
    as source of LLM message, 154, 160

Genre, 152
GitHub, 95, 134, 138, 139
Goals, 72–76, 190, 192
Goldberg, Adele, 143
Goldstine, Adele, 142
Graeber, David, 2, 21
Graphical User Interface (GUI)
    constraining the user, 123
    focused on user tasks, 102
    origins, 80
    as a programming language, 104
    providing cognitive benefits, 91
    in the Smalltalk environment, 84–85
Green, Thomas, 89, 168, 182, 184,
    187
Guardrails, 63, 68–69, 139, 190
Gulwani, Sumit, 99–101, 103

Hallucinations, 69, 137
Haskell (programming language),
    186
Have I Been Trained? (website), 165
Hip-hop, 163
Hopper, Grace, 142
Horvitz, Eric, 23, 28
Human–computer interaction (HCI)
    as an academic field, 18, 61
    and the adoption of anthropology,
        168–169
    from individual versus social
        perspective, 186
    as a theory of user behavior, 72–73, 77
Hybrid system design, 26

Icon, 85
IDE (integrated development
    environment), 115
Illusion, 178, 191
Illustration work, 164
Image generation, 164
ImageNet, 58
Indigenous knowledge, 174–175,
Information, 11, 193

Information structures
  as a basis for design patterns, 182–188
  in creative work, 180
  for explanation and control, 105–107
  as a working environment, 97
  as world models, 79–84, 87
Information theory, 52–54, 150–153
Instability, 156
Intelligence, 171
Intention, 154, 160, 163
Intuitive, 117–121, 168
Isotype, 110

Kay, Alan, 84–85, 89, 92, 122

Labeling, 114
Lagado, philosophers of, 90, 101
Language model, 48–50, 54, 63
Lieberman, Henry, 122
Literature, AI as, 4, 6, 13, 177–179, 181, 188
Live coding, 152, 157–158, 161, 186
Liveness, 144–145
Live programming, 144
London Underground diagram, 83
Love letters, 28

Machine learning, 6, 38–40
Macintosh (computer), 35, 85, 118
MacKay, David, 47
Macro programming, 29–30, 74
Magic
  allowing self-definition of AI, 13, 135
  as an allegory of science and technology, 197n24
  as an ambition for user interaction, 122
  as a basis of fantasy, 18
  as a claim of unlimited power, 14
  and the illusion of control, 123
  as stage entertainment, 191

Magic Cap (General Magic software), 119–120, 124
MagicLink (Sony software). See Magic Cap (General Magic software)
"Man–machine interface," 186
Māori spiritual guardianship (Mana Tuturu), 166
Mărășoiu, Mariana, 108–110
Marx, Karl, 169
Masterman, Margaret, 63
Materiality of code, 130
McConnell, Steve, 129–130
McLean, Alex, 152
Mechanical Turk, 57–58
Metamorphosis (Kafka), 178
Metaphor, 117–119, 123
Metaverse. See Virtual reality
Misogyny. See Gender
Mixed-initiative interaction
  and attention investment, 28–29
  automated with machine learning, 72–73, 185
  in end-user programming, 182
  for hybrid system design, 26
  as originally defined, 23
  and spreadsheet testing, 133
Mnemonics, 118
Monopsony, 165
MORAL CODE (acronym), 17, 83, 191
Movies, as definition of AI, 4, 13, 15, 45, 178
Music, 151–153, 157, 161–162
Musk, Elon, 5
Myers, Brad, 101

Naming, 131–134, 185
Nardi, Bonnie, 147
Nash, Chris, 161–162
Neural networks, 40
Neurath, Otto, 110
Nicholas Nickleby, 60
No-code/low-code, 101
Noise. See Randomness

Notation
  as alternative to natural language, 192
  as basis for abstraction, 34–35
  for design documentation, 95
  design principles, 182–188
  as explanation, 106
  as moral codes, 193
  as the representation of structure, 87
  as user interface, 123
Nygaard, Kristen, 80, 83, 92

Object orientation, 84, 92, 97
ObjectReuser, 138
Open source, 92
Oswald, John, 163

Palimpsest (prototype), 112–113
Parrots, 55, 60, 70
Pastiche, 159–163, 179, 191
Pattern language, 97–98, 183
Patterns of user experience (PUX), 183–188
Photoshop, 112–113, 164
Physics of notations, 182
Piano keyboard, 151, 158, 162
Plagiarism
  in authorship of Internet content, 67
  in code replication, 101
  institutionalized via Mechanical Turk, 59–60
  in replaying stored content, 161, 179
  when misappropriating cultural property, 166
Play, 162, 163
Playfair, William, 110
Policy. See Regulation of AI
Postmodernism, 159–160
Postmodern programming, 138–140
Practice exercises, 139–140, 145
Predictive text
  automating textual labor, 60
  developed over forty years, 47–48

of individual writing style, 50
  and least surprise, 54
  and meaningful communication, 70
  for writing source code, 136–138
Privilege, 66
Processing (programming language), 111
Programming by example, 21, 24–25, 99, 147
Programming in the large, 127, 129, 134
Programming languages
  as abstract specification, 35
  as alternative to AI, 125
  by comparison to spreadsheets, 104
  design approaches, 187
  designed by women, 141–143
  for encoding knowledge, 44–45
  using graphical syntax, 107
  optimized for instruction, 22, 181
  providing agency and control, 10
  for speaking to computers, 16, 61
Program synthesis, 99, 101
Prompt. See Generative prompt
Psychology, 168–169
Pullman, Philip, 180
Puppets, 57–59, 191
Putin, Vladimir, 15
Pygmalion (programming language), 85

Quantification, 177, 182

Racism
  in AI norms of whiteness, 62
  as a basis for structure, 9, 12
  encoded via machine learning, 15
  in expectations of coding, 33–34
  in the origins of AI, 170–172
  as reflected in the Internet, 67
Randomness, 53–57, 152–153, 156–157
Recommendation algorithm, 165
Refactoring, 131, 144, 184
Regression, 171
Regulation of AI, 7, 68, 189, 191

Remixing, 163
Repetition
  and automation, 21–35, 126, 185
  as the basis of familiarity, 151
  in contrast to creativity, 77, 79
  lacking meaning, 135
  revealing goals, 72
  for skilled practice, 139
Reuse. *See* Code reuse
Ross, Doug, 84
Round trip updates, 144

Sammet, Jean, 142
Sarkar, Advait, 113
Secondary notation. *See* Comments
Science, 177
Science fiction, 14, 179, 190
Scratch (programming language), 91, 127, 185
Scripting languages, 30
Security threats in code generation, 146
Self-efficacy, 33
Self-Raising Data (Mărăşoiu), 109
Sense-making, 183
Serialism (music), 151
Servants, 22
Shannon, Claude, 52
Signal and noise. *See* Information theory
SIMULA, 80
Sketchpad, 80–85
Skeuomorphism
  in chatbots, 68, 124
  in user interface design, 118–121
  in voice interaction, 122
Smalltalk, 84, 89–94, 143
Social engineering, 180
Social media, 11, 191
Social situations, 186–187
Software
  engineering, 22, 38, 128–129
  maintenance, 143–144
  reuse (*see* Code reuse)

rot, 144
  quality, 145
Sonic Pi (programming language), 157–158, 185
Spiral development, 94
Spreadsheets
  as creative paradigm, 113
  defining a musical score, 162
  defining visualization, 110
  enabling business, 126
  extended for software engineering, 132–133
  illustrating structure, 107
  as model for software tools, 115
  providing access to data, 103–105
Stability. *See* Instability
Stack Overflow, 95, 134, 138, 139
Stereotyping, 73
Stochastic parrots, 51–54
Subjectivity, 7, 11
Superintelligence, 13, 135, 190
Supervised machine learning, 58, 59, 115
Surprisal, 150
Surprise, 53, 149, 154–157, 185
Surprise-Explain-Reward, 133
Surveillance, 25–26, 73, 103, 123, 192
Sutherland, Ivan, 80–83
Symbiosis. *See* Hybrid system design

Tableau (software), 115
Tanimoto, Steve, 144
Tarot cards, 56, 154
Technical debt, 145
Testing, 130–133
Thermostat, 5,6
Tools, 9, 10
Trade-offs, 68, 106–107, 168, 186–187
Transparency, 103, 113, 123, 183
Trump, Donald, 15, 48–49
Turing, Alan, 3–5, 13, 41
Turing Test, 1, 3–7, 12, 15, 62
12-bar blues, 151

Twitter (X), 8, 11
Two Cultures, 17

Undo, 185
User-centered design, 24, 26
User experience. *See* Patterns of user
    experience (PUX)
User interfaces
  versus code, 117–124
  as designer's deputy, 65
  determining potential actions, 73–74
  and multimodality, 101, 192
  as notations, 182
  as space for exploration, 78
  superior to speech, 188
User journey, 77–79, 86, 89

Value alignment. *See* Alignment
    problem
Victor, Bret, 92
Vile Pürveyors of Execration, 152
Violin acoustics, 157
Virtual reality, 121
Viscosity, 89, 91, 184
Visualization, 106, 109–110, 115, 192
Visual programming language, 85, 90,
    102, 107
Visual Studio (Microsoft software), 115,
    141
Voice interaction, 122, 182, 192

Waterfall development, 94–95
WEIRD (acronym), 167–168
Wicked problems, 78
Wikipedia, 68, 94–96
Word (Microsoft software), 28–30
World-building, 79